# The Right to Be Known

# The Right to Be Known

## *Epistemic Reparations and the Making of Rounder Stories*

JENNIFER LACKEY

OXFORD
UNIVERSITY PRESS

OXFORD
UNIVERSITY PRESS

Oxford University Press is a department of the University of Oxford. It furthers the University's objective of excellence in research, scholarship, and education by publishing worldwide. Oxford is a registered trade mark of Oxford University Press in the UK and in certain other countries.

Published in the United States of America by Oxford University Press
198 Madison Avenue, New York, NY 10016, United States of America.



CIP data is on file at the Library of Congress

ISBN 9780197833957

DOI: 10.1093/9780197833988.001.0001

Printed by Integrated Books International, United States of America

The manufacturer's authorized representative in the EU for product safety is Oxford University Press España S.A. of Parque Empresarial San Fernando de Henares, Avenida de Castilla, 2 – 28830 Madrid (www.oup.es/en or product.safety@oup.com). OUP España S.A. also acts as importer into Spain of products made by the manufacturer.

*To Baron*

# Contents

# Acknowledgments

In Chapter 3 of this book, I discuss the power of "coconstructed narratives"—narratives about our lives that emerge through a shared process of talking, listening, and learning, and that can be epistemically generative not only for those hearing them but also for those telling them. In many respects, the pages that follow feel like a coconstructed project. I have been thinking about what I now call "epistemic reparations" and the "right to be known" for nearly a decade, and any attempt to convey the depth of either the support I have received or my corresponding gratitude will be inadequate. But I say throughout this book that the mere fact that we may never be able to truly make up for the gross violations and injustices of the past and present does not mean we shouldn't roll up our sleeves right now and get to work trying to do so. In a similar spirit, I will do my best in these acknowledgments to highlight some of the remarkable people across the globe who have inspired, nurtured, and championed my work on this project even though my efforts will invariably fall short.

What first pulled me into this work wasn't a philosophical theory or argument, or even thinking about institutionalized epistemic reparations, such as a truth and reconciliation commission; rather, it was the experience of listening to deeply personal, individual stories in some of the darkest corners of prisons in the United States. In these one-on-one exchanges, I was struck by not only the violence and trauma of incarceration, but also by the profound epistemic wreckage left in its wake—the systematic unraveling of how people come to know themselves and the world and, just as devastatingly, how they are themselves known in and by the world. I am especially indebted to Demetrius Cunningham, William Peeples, and James Soto, whose own wrongful convictions made vivid to me the additional and distinctive epistemic wrongs inflicted on them by the false and vilifying narratives of their lives.

At the same time, I have also seen how the simple, radical act of bearing witness can bend the arc of a life, opening up ways for people to see themselves, their pasts, and their possibilities refracted anew through the power of being known. For refusing erasure, for their unrelenting insistence on the humanity of those who have been demonized, and for their unshakable courage in reclaiming and rewriting their own narratives, my heartfelt gratitude goes to the Northwestern Prison Education Program (NPEP) community: Shurese Bailey, Antony Bell, Michael Bradley-El, Stephanie Bonds, Robert Boyd, Michael Broadway, Ariel Bueno, Elbonie Burnside, Jeffery Campbell, Lester Carroll, Justin Cavazos, Orhan Cerimagic, Robert Cloutier, Pierre Cole, Patrick Comi, Vanecha Cooper, Oliver Crawford, Demetrice Crite, Demetrius Cunningham, Jacob Currey, Joel E. Davis, Yaphet Davis, Bryan Dean, Taurean Decatur, Margaret DeFrancisco, Regina DeFrancisco, Bonnie Diana, Mark Dixon, Christopher Douglas, Edmond Duffin, Anthony Ehlers, Jeanine A. Elam, Tiffany Fassler, Leon Fields, Paul Forbes, Justin Foster, Amanda Fredrickson, Nikolas Gacho, Miguelangel Garcia, Juan Garnica, Maria Garza, Katrina Giles, Thomas Gordon, Jason Gorham, Christopher Greathouse, Donnell Green, Lynn Green, Shawnette Green, Terrance Groves-El, Oscar Gutierrez, James Hale, Anthony Harris, Marquis Harrison, Craig Harvey, Darvin Henderson, Falanzo Hixson, Joshua Hoeniges, Broderick Hollins, Latosha Howard, Pierre James, Darryl Johnson, Jamal Jones, Michael Jorgensen, James Lenoir, Tevin Louis, Brian McClendon, Joyce McGee, Benard McKinley, Todd Mandoline, Michael Melichar, Flynard Miller, Scot Miller, Paul Modrowski, Ramon Montague, Dedric Moore, Abdul-Malik Muhammad, Darion Nance, Jabari Nicks, Hugo Ocon, Michael Ortega, Patricia Ouska, André Patterson, Taki Peacock, William Peeples, Brandon Perkins, Chelsea Raker, Erika Ray, James Ray, Giovanni Rios, De'Andre Robinson, De'Wayne Robinson, Leon Robinson, Irene Romaniuk, Stanley Russell, Mohammad Salahat, Diandra Samuels, Jason Samuels, Scott Sanders, Kevin Scott, Charles Serrano, Cindy Shepheard, Kobie Singleton, LeShun Smith, Blanca Solis, James Soto, Shawn Thigpen, Anthony Triplett, Ian Valencia, Melinda Warfel, Orlando Watkins, Dahnyah Williams, Will Williams, Romell Winters, and Brandon V. Wyatt.

Many thanks, also, to friends, students, and colleagues for providing thoughtful, incisive feedback on various ideas in this book, including Jason Kawall, two anonymous reviewers for Oxford University Press, and audience members at a 2020 COGITO conference (virtual); Union College; my 2021 Sontag Lecture at Pomona College; my 2022 Presidential Address at the Central Division of the American Philosophical Association in Chicago; the 2022 Syracuse University Graduate Conference; Colgate University; the European Epistemology Network in Glasgow, Scotland; Georgia State University; the University of Minnesota; the VII Brazilian Society for

Analytic Philosophy in Rio de Janeiro, Brazil; the Epistemic Wrongs and Epistemic Reparations Conference at the African Centre for Epistemology and Philosophy of Science in Johannesburg, South Africa; the University of Miami; the Group Epistemology Workshop at the University of Leeds; the University of Gothenburg; the Philosophy of Education Society of Great Britain at the University of Oxford; the University of Alberta (virtual); the ArgLab Research Colloquium in Lisbon, Portugal; the Horace Mann Medal Forum at Brown University; the Bled Conference on Applied Epistemology: Ignorance, Vice, and Bias; the Social Epistemology Network Conference on the Isle of Bute in Scotland; the Epistemic Blame and Epistemic Reparations Conference in Winnipeg, Canada; Penn Carey Law School; Wake Forest University; Emory University; Université Laval; the Society for Applied Philosophy at the University of Oxford; the Conversations with the Apartheid Past Conference in Johannesburg, South Africa; the Narrative Possibilities Workshop at Princeton University; the North American Society for Social Philosophy at Creighton University; the European Face of Political Epistemology Conference in Cres, Croatia; the International Seminar on Criminal Sciences in São Paulo, Brazil; the Applied Epistemology Workshop at the University of North Carolina, Chapel Hill; Bucknell University; the International Seminar on Evidence and Criminal Justice in Brasília, Brazil; the University of California, Berkeley School of Law; The Ohio State University; a Conference on Epistemic Injustice in Tokyo, Japan; Tulane University; the Ranch Metaphysics Workshop in Tucson, Arizona; the Analytic Philosophy Symposium at the University of Texas at Austin; Stanford University; the 2025 Central Division of the American Philosophical Association; the Sociedad Argentina de Análisis Filosófico in Buenos Aires; the University of Buenos Aires; the University of Amsterdam; and the University of Illinois at Urbana-Champaign.

A fellowship from the National Endowment for the Humanities gave me much-needed time during the 2023–2024 academic year to focus on the research for this book, and generous support from the Buffett Institute for Global Affairs enabled both the building of global collaborations and the chance to engage in the practice of epistemic reparations that dramatically expanded the reach of the project. My sincere thanks to everyone who made these opportunities and, therefore, this book, possible.

Micol Bez, the Graduate Fellow for the Buffett Institute's Epistemic Reparations Working Group, has been a tireless and inspiring force in countless ways, from her own illuminating research on understanding sexual violence through the lens of epistemic reparations to the extraordinarily diverse set of talents that she has devoted to this work—as photographer, artist, grant writer, event planner, instructor, "Right to Be Seen" facilitator, and connection maker. For taking on all of these roles, and so much more, I am truly grateful.

Over the past few years, I've had the joy and privilege of collaborating with Cameron Boult, Veli Mitova, and Sarah Wright on work connected to the right to be known and epistemic reparations. Together, we've dreamed about and planned events across the globe—from Chicago and Manitoba to Johannesburg and Mpumalanga—that have made philosophical work alive, urgent, and impactful in ways I never imagined possible when I first set out on this path. Along the way, they've provided feedback, asked questions, raised objections, and challenged me to think deeper and broader about nearly every issue in this book, all while keeping me grounded with laughter, love, and friendship. My warmest and deepest thanks to them.

I owe a special debt of gratitude to Lauren Leydon-Hardy, who began as my graduate student and has long since become one of my most valued colleagues and dearest friends. From the earliest moments of what would grow into the Northwestern Prison Education Program to the many years we've spent discussing the ideas in this book, she has brought an unflinching commitment to authenticity and a shared moral vision that have helped shape the contours of both this book and my own story.

Anthony Ehlers, who is not only an exceptionally gifted artist but also a journalist, an activist, a member of the first cohort of incarcerated students to graduate from a top ten university, and an NPEP Teaching Fellow, created the powerful image for the cover of this book. Anthony's painting vividly depicts one of the core theses developed in the arguments that follow: epistemic reparations require replacing unjust "flat" stories, which are agentially closed and portray subjects as static, one-dimensional, and psychologically simplistic, with "rounder" ones, which are agentially open and represent individuals as dynamic, multidimensional, and psychologically complex. Anthony himself knows firsthand how the American criminal legal system, in concert with the media, casts those with convictions into narratives that reduce their lives to shadows, stripping away all layers, texture, and nuance and locking up not just bodies but identities as well. Yet he also knows how to resist this with his pen and his paintbrush, creating work that insists on both depth and truth, and I am profoundly grateful to him for so generously sharing his vision and his talent with this project.

In June of 2024, the NPEP community suddenly and tragically lost a beloved graduate of our program, Michael Broadway, due to the conditions and lack of adequate healthcare at Stateville Correctional Center.[1] Michael was so much to us—friend, mentor, student, listener, teacher, author, peacemaker—and his death left our community shaken, devastated, and unmoored. In the immediate aftermath, those in nearby cells who witnessed Michael struggling to breath and calling for help recounted, relentlessly and at great risk to themselves, the events leading up to his final moments. And then, in the weeks and months that followed, stories and artwork and poems about Michael's life started emerging from every corner of the NPEP community: about how he never offered an unkind word about anyone, how he comforted people in their loneliest moments, how his hope was a lifeline, how his writing was an inspiration, how his smile lit up even the darkest spaces, and how his love radically expanded what seemed possible. After an experience that forever changed us, I witnessed the harnessing of our shared grief into what I now see as ensuring that Michael's right to be known is fulfilled. I am deeply grateful to the NPEP community for modeling how to engage in epistemic reparations—including through their "Write to Be Known" initiative—with such thoughtfulness, love, and an enduring commitment to justice.

Over the past two years, I've been reminded again and again that the weight of the most difficult, life-altering work—the kind that reshapes who we are—can only be carried through the collective strength of a community. I have been blessed beyond measure to do the work in NPEP alongside friends and colleagues Sheila Bedi, Annie Buth, Alex Kotlowitz, Mary Pattillo, Michelle Paulsen, and Terry Truax. When forces in life have threatened to take every good thing, their wisdom and courage, moral clarity and guidance, and unwavering care and support have been a sustaining refuge for me, providing both anchor and compass.

This work is the latest chapter in a story my mother began speaking into existence as a young woman. Some of my earliest memories as a child are of spending long hours playing with my sister in the courtyard of our local community college while my mom sat through classes and took exams, chasing a future she imagined not only for herself but for us as well. She was a single mother, working multiple jobs and raising three children entirely on her own, yet she filled our kitchen with conversations about the works of

[1] Paddock and Friedman (2024).

Freud and Piaget, Jane Austen and Thomas Hardy. I remember her walking me through *Tess of the d'Urbervilles*, chapter by chapter, as she read it in one of her literature classes, and I watched her give up sleep to obtain an associate's and then a bachelor's degree. As I witnessed her navigate a world ill-equipped for and often hostile to single mothers with ever increasing levels of wisdom and courage and strength, these early years burned into my mind a single fact about education—it is uniquely empowering. But as Toni Morrison so poignantly reminds us, "your real job is that if you are free, you need to free somebody else. If you have some power, then your job is to empower somebody else" (Houston 2003). When I reflect on the work created, nurtured, and sustained by NPEP, it is clear that this call to action is woven into the very fibers of our community. We have faculty members teaching students to write new policies and new stories of their lives and to understand their experiences with new concepts and new vision. We have on-campus students providing life-saving academic and wellness support when NPEP students have been in solitary confinement, or have suffered the loss of a mother or child and been unable to grieve while in prison, or have been on lockdown during a global pandemic and watched friends in their cells take their last breaths before their eyes. At the heart of it all, we have our beautiful and brilliant NPEP graduates and students, who relentlessly pour themselves into building a world that is better than the one they inherited. We thus have an entire community whose members channel their own freedom and power to free and empower others every day. And though my beloved mother, Janice Nora Lackey (1940–2012), did not live to see the creation of NPEP, there is no doubt in my mind that the roots of our collective labor of love trace back to her own devotion to education, and so I owe her a lifetime of gratitude—for the life she lived, for the fire she lit, and for the legacy that continues to grow in her light.

Chapter 4 of this book is about being known, and the one enduring truth I have known about myself—the single most powerful force shaping my life—is my commitment to being a mother. Yet, just as I explore throughout this book the vital importance of being able to reimagine and revise our stories, my bold and brilliant daughters, Isabella (Izzy) and Catherine (Cat) Reed, breathed real life into my conception of motherhood with their wholly unique, multidimensional characters and, in so doing, rewrote my own story. They didn't just make me a mother—they made me *their* mother. I am especially grateful to my brave and wondrous Izzy for teaching me every day to be open to and to nurture the greatest gifts each of us has to offer the world, and to my creative and fierce Cat for showing me the power of moving through the world with clarity and conviction.

This book is dedicated to my husband, Baron Reed. Growing up, marriage was never part of the story I envisioned for my future but I have since learned that this is because I didn't know it was possible for someone like Baron to exist—someone so utterly unearthly, so singular in character: the strongest person I know, but also the kindest; unfailingly loving while truthful to his core; the wisest counsel who can make me laugh harder than anyone on the planet; relentlessly committed to rationality and yet endlessly poetic; the most brilliant while also the humblest; someone who knows who you are, and who you can be, long before you know yourself. None of this—me, this work, this book, this life—would be what it is without Baron, my coconstructor in everything.

# Introduction

This book is about stories so I will start by telling you one.

About a year and a half ago, I found myself at Stateville Correctional Center, a maximum-security men's prison 40 miles southwest of Chicago, waiting to greet one of the recent graduates of the Northwestern Prison Education Program (NPEP). This fact alone was not unusual, as I had spent countless hours at Stateville over the past decade, teaching in and serving as the Director of NPEP. But what marked this moment as different from all of the others is that I was standing on the *other* side of the wall—the one that separates the unfree from the free—to welcome James Soto home after 42 years of imprisonment. James is the longest wrongfully incarcerated person in the history of the state of Illinois, having spent his twenties, thirties, forties, and fifties in some of the most unforgiving spaces in the United States for crimes he not only didn't commit, but also for which police coerced witnesses—through targeted arrests, interrogations that involved the deprivation of sleep and food, and threats of facing the death penalty—to point the finger at James.[1] Bearing witness to James in his first moments as a non-incarcerated person, in plain clothes and what has since become his signature fedora, and being able to hug him without the relentless surveillance and intervention of correctional officers, was extraordinary and unforgettable.

In the weeks and months that followed his release, however, James grappled not only with the challenges of a world utterly foreign to the one he left behind decades earlier at the age of 19, but also with conveying to others the weight of the injustices and violations that he suffered. In one interview, he said, "Just imagine, you know you're innocent, yet nobody's hearing you, nothing's being done,"[2] and in others he described the "horrendous conditions"[3] of prison: the aggression, violence,[4] deadly heat,[5] rodent

[1] Buckley (2025).
[2] Friedman (2024).
[3] Perlman and Feurer (2024).
[4] Ehlers (2024).
[5] Hope (2024).

*The Right to Be Known*. Jennifer Lackey, Oxford University Press. © Oxford University Press 2026.
DOI: 10.1093/9780197833988.003.0001

and cockroach infestations,[6] lack of clean drinking water,[7] and profound loss.[8] Yet despite all of this, the hardest part of incarceration, according to James, is something less tangible and in many respects deeper—it is being broken down into a "numerical existence,"[9] being robbed of one's true story, being seen as someone or something entirely at odds with who one is, being regarded as not a human or a person. As if speaking directly to those who subjected him to over four decades of this total erasure of his identity, James says "I am a human being. I am a person" (Buckley 2025).

My last book, *Criminal Testimonial Injustice*,[10] examined how stories can be stolen from people in a myriad of ways, especially by the criminal legal system in the United States. Backed into a corner, lied to about the evidence in question, threatened with the death penalty, more time in prison, or the loss of one's children, desperate, confused, and terrified, people will say just about anything. Not only will eyewitnesses confidently point to someone whom they know did not pull the trigger—as in James's case—but suspects will falsely confess to the most violent of actions, innocent defendants will plead guilty to unimaginable crimes, victims will recant reports of life-altering assaults and violations, and those who are convicted will express profound remorse for things they simply did not do. The resulting testimony then plays a massively oversized evidential role in the American criminal legal system, grounding convictions even in the face of powerful counterevidence, for instance, or serving as the central factor for the granting of parole.

I call the fundamental wrong inflicted in such cases *agential testimonial injustice*, where testimony is *extracted* from a victim in a way that bypasses, exploits, or subverts his epistemic agency[11] and is then afforded an unwarranted *excess* of credibility. Epistemic agency is commonly understood as grounded in a person's responsiveness to reasons or evidence. If you come to believe that the death penalty should be abolished because I present compelling arguments on behalf of this conclusion that you appreciate, then I have respected your epistemic agency in bringing about this result. In contrast, if I hack into your social media accounts and inundate your feeds with anti-death-penalty propaganda to elicit this belief, then I have bypassed or

[6] Raju (2024).
[7] Raju (2024).
[8] Hope (2024).
[9] Buckley (2025).
[10] Lackey (2023).
[11] The first appearance of the concept of "epistemic agency" in the philosophical literature is in Reed (2001).

subverted your epistemic agency. I am not engaging with you as a rational agent who can recognize and respond to the force of reasons, but rather, I am treating you as a puppet whose psychology can be shaped and molded according to my aims.

While talk of epistemic agency in relation to beliefs is not new, what I show in *Criminal Testimonial Injustice* is that similar considerations can be extended to speech, especially to testimony offered in the criminal legal system. In particular, epistemic agency is exercised with respect to a person's *testimony* when it is responsive to reasons or evidence. If you admit guilt for harming a person because I present reasons that you find persuasive about the power of restorative justice, then I have appealed to your epistemic agency to elicit this speech. In contrast, if I get you to admit guilt for such a harm through coercive threats of life in prison or deceptive promises of leniency, then I have exploited or undermined your epistemic agency. I am regarding you as a mere epistemic means to my desired end rather than as an epistemic end in yourself. I want you to say certain words, perhaps to acquire evidence to press charges or to affirm a conviction at a parole hearing, and you're not regarded as a knower whose autonomy and dignity deserve to be respected, but only as a source of epistemic outputs that I can exploit and use.

Within the American criminal legal system specifically, I show that agential testimonial injustice is the result of brute State power[12] that targets the epistemic agency of its citizens. It is found from start to finish in the process, with ignorance and malice, aimed similarly at defendants, witnesses, and victims, through small acts of influence and will-crushing threats, engulfing the innocent as well as the guilty. Whether a suspect is being interrogated or a victim is reporting a sexual assault, an eyewitness is making an identification or a defendant is seeking parole, testimony is extracted from individuals

[12] This is a critical difference between my notion of agential testimonial injustice and the traditional conception of testimonial injustice originally developed in Miranda Fricker's (2007). Crucially, the most fundamental level of explanation on Fricker's view is *prejudice*. Imagine, for instance, that we could root out and eradicate all prejudice from our society. For Fricker, this would thereby result in the elimination of testimonial injustice. Sure, speakers may still suffer deficits of credibility for a host of non-prejudicial reasons, but they wouldn't amount to instances of testimonial injustice. On my view of agential testimonial injustice, in contrast, the most fundamental layer of explanation is *power*—within the criminal legal system, it is the way the State wields its power and turns its citizens into puppets to be shaped and molded to meet its desired ends. Of course, prejudice plays a role in the way State power operates, as has been clearly demonstrated by numerous scholars, resulting in the radically disproportionate percentage of Black people incarcerated in the United States. And the eradication of all prejudice from society would likely result in the State flexing its power in a more evenhanded way. But within my framework, this would not thereby eliminate agential testimonial injustice, as the State would continue to wield its power to undermine the epistemic agency of its citizens.

through processes that compromise their epistemic agency and is then unreasonably regarded as representing the testifiers' truest or most reliable selves. In this way, the State treats its citizens as instruments to be used and exploited to meet its desires and goals, constructing narratives that are often life-shattering for their characters, and rendering the testifiers in question complicit in the resulting undoing.

Importantly, however, narratives inflict distinctively epistemic wrongs themselves, ones that go beyond the extraction of the testimony and the excess of credibility it is then afforded. Focusing on false confessions in particular, NPEP student Scot Miller poignantly conveys this when he writes, "[a]n extracted false confession creates a false narrative of that person's life. In other words, the extracted confession turns a person's life into a lie. That lie is then believed over the truth of that person's life, victimizing him over and over again. This seems to be the ultimate crime—stealing the essence of someone's life while they yet breathe" (personal correspondence). Scot is here drawing our attention to the distinctive power that the story about his life has, which is not only false but also renders him unknown in deep and lasting ways, thereby involving additional violations that cry out for understanding. This is especially crucial to recognize in a case like James's, where the person who is the direct subject of the agential testimonial injustice is the eyewitness compelled to give false testimony, and yet James is the person who is most injured by the false narrative and the wrongful conviction that it grounds.

The immense power of stories is one of the starting points of the current project. Consider, for instance, some of the different ways in which wrongful convictions such as James's create and promote stories that block the main character from being known. There are stories that render who he truly is invisible—perhaps denying his innocence, ignoring his honest and trustworthy character, or marginalizing his loving relationships. There are stories that demonize or distort him—perhaps as being a liar, a murderer, irredeemable, or monstrous. There are stories that are extracted from him—perhaps of guilt, responsibility, and remorse. There are stories that he is prevented from telling due to his vilification and isolation—perhaps about who he is today or who he plans to be tomorrow. There are stories that attempt to justify how he is treated—perhaps as deserving of the brutal and inhumane conditions of his incarceration. There are stories that are taken from him—perhaps of what he could have accomplished or who he could have been had he not been wrongfully convicted. In each case, the epistemic agency of the subject of the stories is compromised in violating and unjust ways. While *Criminal Testimonial Injustice* provides an analysis of some of the distinctive epistemic wrongs involved in creating these sorts of stories in the criminal legal system, the present book focuses on how to understand the epistemically reparative work called for in response.

Of course, even if there are dimensions of these epistemic wrongs that are unique to the American criminal legal system, being unknown in these ways is not. Across historical periods and global spaces, entire peoples, cultures, and communities, as well as the individuals within them, have been robbed of their stories—have been erased, silenced, vilified, and distorted. The effects of colonialism, for instance, epistemically devastate not only existing and possible stories, but also storytellers, bodies of knowledge, traditions, practices, languages, and so much more. Generally, then, one of the questions at the heart of this book is this: If stories are being stolen in widespread and pernicious ways, aren't we obligated to help give them back? If epistemic agency is systematically bypassed, exploited, or subverted, don't we have duties to cultivate, repair, or restore it? If people are unknown in deep and unjust ways, shouldn't we come to know them?

While this is the background for the current project, I begin Chapter 1 not with recounting these epistemic wrongs but, rather, with survivors offering accounts of the reparative power of being known. The aim is to set the stage for looking forward—for understanding the normative force of the call to give victims their stories back.[13] In the pages that follow, I argue that those who suffer gross violations and injustices that result in or constitute not being known due to invisibility, vilification, or systematic distortion[14] are wronged in distinctively epistemic ways and have the *right to be known* as *epistemic reparations*.

I develop the right to be known by drawing from a framework provided by the United Nations Commission on Human Rights that outlines the rights of victims of gross violations and injustices, one of which is what they call the *right to know*. In particular, they hold that victims and their families have the right to "know the truth about the circumstances in which violations took place and, in the event of death or disappearance, the victims' fate"

[13] Because some prefer being referred to as "survivors" and others prefer "victims," I will, for the most part, use these interchangeably when discussing those who have been subject to gross violations and injustices except when it comes to those who are deceased, where I will use only "victims."

[14] Of course, this "or" is not exclusive, as not being known can involve invisibility, vilification, and systematic distortion. I also leave open the possibility that this list is not exhaustive and that there are other epistemic wrongs that call for being known as a form of epistemic reparations.

(United Nations 2005). I argue in Chapter 1 that this framework from the UN is illuminating not only for what it includes, but also for what it leaves out. Importantly, it highlights that there can be a right to a distinctively epistemic good, such as knowledge, and that it is one that is generated by a gross violation or injustice. For instance, members of an ethnic group victimized by genocide—unlike those who were not targets—have the right to know whether there was state involvement in the violence, whether their loved ones were murdered, where their bodies are located, and so on. At the same time, the UN's framework fails to include what I argue is an equally critical dimension—what I call the *right to be known*. These same members of an ethnic group have the right to have their stories of violation and injustice be given proper uptake, not only so that others bear witness to their suffering and restore their status in the community, but also so that there is an accurate and complete public or historical record. If victims have the right to know about an atrocity, but no victims themselves contribute to the record of the atrocity, then it is virtually impossible that the information conveyed and documented will be reliably produced. A historical record of genocide told only by perpetrators, for instance, will almost certainly be distorted, biased, and incomplete. In addition to the right to know, then, the UN's framework crucially needs to be expanded to also include the right to be known.[15] Both rights, I maintain, can be captured by an account of what I call *epistemic reparations*,[16] which I characterize as intentionally reparative actions or processes that aim to restore, coproduce, or create epistemic goods for those who have been epistemically wronged by parties who acknowledge these wrongs and whose reparative actions are intended to redress them.

Before saying more about what I will do in the following chapters, let me highlight what I will *not* be doing. Despite the fact that the title of this book is *The Right to Be Known*, I will not be saying much at all about how to understand rights in general. This is because I will be taking as my normative

[15] Since many instances of not being known discussed in this book can be traced, to various degrees, to the impact of colonialism, it is worth highlighting that much decolonial work stresses the importance of the general point here—that the colonized should be producers of knowledge, rather than merely consumers (Chatterjee 1997), that they should be centered when it comes to knowledge generation relevant to their geographical and socio-political location (Ndlovu-Gatsheni 2018), that they should be regarded as epistemic authorities in these areas (Mitova 2025a), and so on. Given this, we might understand some of these claims in terms of the colonized having the right to be known as acts of epistemic reparations.

[16] The first instance of the term "epistemic reparations" can be found in Lackey (2021a) and is further developed in Lackey (2022). There are related, but importantly different epistemic concepts in the literature, which I will discuss in Chapter 5, such as "epistemic amelioration" (Almassi 2018), "epistemic amends" (Song 2020), and "epistemic redress" (Hull 2022).

starting point the framework found in the UN's report from the Commission on Human Rights. Given that victims of gross violations and injustices have the right to know, my view is that they also have the right to be known. Otherwise put, my account holds that the right to be known is grounded in considerations similar to those that ground the right to know and, thus, the right to be known rests on a case equally strong to that supporting the right to know. This approach has at least two advantages. First, much of the most original work in this book centers around the introduction and development of the "right to be known" and "epistemic reparations" and so it makes sense to devote attention to understanding these phenomena rather than rights in general, which have already been discussed broadly and extensively for centuries. Second, the goal of this project is not merely or even primarily to formulate abstract academic theories but, rather, to develop a framework for real change in the world. To this end, the UN is said to be the "one, universal organization in the world . . . that can set globally accepted standards and norms of behavior" (Sills 2002, p. 1). Since the UN sets as a global standard that victims of gross violations and injustices have the right to know, my aim here is to make clear that this standard should also include the right to be known.

In what follows, I will make the case for epistemic reparations, which I understand as being politically and legally weighty in the same way that other kinds of reparations are. Just as we would not use the term "reparations" to describe what is needed to make up for the moral wrong we inflicted on a friend for breaking a promise to take her shopping so, too, I think that we should not use the term "epistemic reparations" to make up for ordinary, everyday epistemic wrongs, such as not giving a coworker the amount of credibility she deserves in her area of expertise, or failing to properly attribute an idea to a community member. To be sure, these sorts of wrongs may normatively demand reparative work—some moral, some epistemic, and some both. But it would be odd for your friend or coworker to ask for "reparations" precisely because they have political and/or legal heft, with paradigmatic cases involving governments or institutions being required or expected to engage in them, including through various forms of legislation and policies that target deep, pernicious systemic injustices. While I will argue that there is also normative pressure for each of us to engage in epistemic reparations even when we are not ourselves perpetrators or complicit in the infliction of the epistemic wrongs in question, this is still to be distinguished from the broader category of "epistemic repair" or "epistemic redress." The latter may be helpful or necessary in striving for a world that is more epistemically just and may be crucial for interpersonal relations at the collective and individual levels, but they are nonetheless importantly different from what is at issue in this book.[17]

Since the focus in this book is on epistemic reparations that have the same sort of political and legal weight as, say, material reparations, I will largely focus on gross violations and injustices that are systemic and perpetrated by groups or other collectives, such as the epistemic wrongs inflicted through the criminal legal system in the United States, colonialism and apartheid in South Africa, and the Residential School System in Canada. This, of course, does not preclude individual actors who played powerful roles in these violations from bearing direct responsibility for engaging in epistemic reparations as well. In addition to the State, for instance, a specific prosecutor who deliberately concealed evidence favorable to the defense may be culpable for epistemically repairing some of the harm suffered by the defendant who ends up wrongfully convicted and incarcerated because of this, or a particular apartheid officer may also bear responsibility for epistemic reparations to victims of violence that he inflicted while working for the South African government. But in both cases, they are part of a much larger system of injustice targeting specific groups of people.

At the same time, what originally brought me to this project was sitting in hallways and classrooms of prisons in America listening to stories of the trauma, violence, heartbreak, and horrors inflicted by the carceral system, along with the epistemic devastation that comes in their wake. While similar themes often emerged, most of these conversations were one-on-one with particular incarcerated individuals, many of them students I have been in community with for over a decade—people I have come to know, love, and admire. I often saw unfold before my very eyes the power of bearing witness to their stories: the shifts and transformations of the lenses through which they view themselves, others, their pasts, their possibilities, their futures, their legacies. And so while just about everything I say in the pages that follow about the right to be known and epistemic reparations applies just as much at the level of groups, many of the stories will be about specific

[17] For ease of expression, I may use terms like "epistemically reparative" or "epistemic repair" but unless otherwise noted, I will be discussing epistemic reparations only in the sense of what is owed in cases of epistemic wrongs that result from or constitute gross violations and injustices. I should also note that although I will be developing an account of epistemic reparations, many features of the framework could be extended to a broader view of epistemic repair.

individuals, both because this is how I found my way to this work and because of the power and insight they convey.

Relatedly, one of the dimensions of the framework developed in this book that is worth highlighting is its combined theoretical and practical power. It provides the resources for not only understanding the distinctively epistemic rights of survivors of gross epistemic wrongs and the obligations we all have to be a part of the corresponding reparative work, but also for grasping the concrete steps that can be taken to fulfill them right now. In academic work, it is a constant temptation—even when it takes up urgent issues involving real and ongoing suffering—to conduct inquiry in a way that is overly abstract and disconnected from the actual experiences of the people whose lives are being considered. But this project is connected with survivors of the injustices at issue in deep, multifaceted, and essential ways. It has, for instance, both guided and been shaped by intentionally practicing the cocreation of epistemic goods as epistemic reparations in a variety of spaces. In 2023, I received a grant from the Buffett Institute for Global Affairs to develop the right to be known and epistemic reparations in both theory and practice from a global perspective. Partnering with a group of local and international collaborators, we have engaged in work and hosted events in South Africa on the right to be known in the context of apartheid-era violence, at the Canadian Museum of Human Rights on the right to be known in Indigenous communities, especially for Residential School survivors, and in Illinois on carceral injustice and epistemic reparations. In each location, bearing witness to the stories and experiences of survivors was centered; new academic work on relevant issues was presented; the events were hosted in epistemically reparative spaces; and efforts were made to document, publish, or otherwise promote the knowledge being generated. So, the framework of this book has already been implemented into successful models of how to simultaneously theorize about and practice epistemic reparations across geographical locations, disciplines, and groups.

At the same time, the views developed in this project have been engaged with for years by an enormously diverse group of readers and audiences. In addition to the stories of survivors being featured in their own words throughout the chapters that follow, the questions, challenges, and suggestions I have received from quite literally across the globe—including from victims of the very violations that are centered in this work—have shaped my thinking in ways that have added invaluable breadth, depth, and texture. Moreover, throughout the book, there will be concrete examples, including in the conclusion with corresponding links, to ways of taking up the work of knowing the unjustly unknown at this very moment in time. My hope is that this will inspire more rigorous academic research that takes place in community, collaboration, and practice with people from a radically broad range of perspectives and walks of life.

It is tempting to regard epistemic reparations as involving a simple "one-and-done" transaction. If I let my friend use my car and she unlawfully sells it, then seeking restitution in a civil case may ask the court, in part, to restore me to where I was before my car was sold. Being paid the fair market value of the car when it was borrowed is a straightforward one-time transaction that aims to make me whole. But in the central cases at issue in this book, there is no "one-and-done" transaction that sufficiently provides epistemic reparations. There is no single act that would restore victims and survivors to where they were or would have been epistemically in the absence of colonialism, racism, or an unjust criminal legal system. As Naomi Roht-Arriaza asks in the case of reparations more broadly, "[w]hat could replace lost health and serenity, the loss of a loved one or of a whole extended family, a generation of friends, the destruction of culture of an entire community" (2004, p. 122)? In the epistemic case, what single act could possibly make up for the effects of, say, deep, widespread, and pernicious intergenerational invisibility; the distortion of an entire group of people—along with their language, culture, and practices; or even decades of the vilification of a single person, such as James Soto?

And yet, despite this, this book is not one of despairing about what is not possible. Instead, it is about building a theoretical framework for engaging in the *ongoing process* of providing epistemic reparations. It is about developing the tools for holding governments and institutions responsible for the distinctively epistemic wrongs inflicted by their actions and inactions. It is about recognizing that focusing on only the ideal of total epistemic reparations, or on only the deficiencies of each particular act, can lead to retreating, inertia, or complacency. It is about seeing that it is not only perpetrators—whether collectives or individuals—who need to engage in the business of making up for the epistemic wrongs of the past, but each one of us as well. It is about the urgent need to roll up our sleeves every day and make whatever contributions we can, however small, to bearing witness to, and restoring the status of, victims of gross violations and injustices. It is about exploring concrete ways to engage in the process of providing epistemic reparations by federal, state, and local governments and other institutions—including, among many others, working with survivors to facilitate truth and reconciliation commissions, community dialogues, restorative justice circles, venues for recording stories, memorials, storytelling workshops, and educational materials—and by individuals—including, again among many others, working with survivors to support the creation of their narratives across a range of mediums, listening and learning from them, providing platforms, sharing their stories, and amplifying their voices.

But how, it may be asked, do I reconcile the inability to truly make up for the scale and depth of many of the epistemic wrongs at issue in this book with the demand to nonetheless engage in the work of repairing them? Is this a call to take up work that is destined to be futile? By way of response, notice, first, that epistemic wrongs that result from or constitute gross violations and injustices typically involve ongoing harm. The vilification of Black men in the American criminal legal system, for instance, is often traced to the history of slavery and Jim Crow, revealing the deep and ongoing intergenerational epistemic effects that gross violations and injustices often bring in their wake.[18] But rather than simply exacerbating the tension at issue, this further supports the need for viewing the demand of epistemic reparations as similarly ongoing. More precisely, moving away from a strictly *act-based account* of reparations, where there are discrete acts on each side of the wrong and repair, to a *process-based account*, where there are ongoing processes on each side of the wrong and repair, alters expectations in ways that can be motivating rather than deflating. The work of epistemic reparations does not fit into a "one-and-done" transactional model precisely because the wrongs themselves often don't fit into such a model. And so shifting over to seeing our engagement in this epistemic work as an ongoing process may similarly shift our expectations about what each single act needs to accomplish.

This brings us to a second feature of the framework developed in this book that helps with the tension between the magnitude of the wrongs at issue and the call to immediate action: while the duties to engage in epistemic reparations fall on each of us, there is often *discretion* in how we fulfill many of them. As I develop in Chapter 5, the relevant duties are on a spectrum, with perfect epistemic duties lying at one end, which those who bear responsibility for the epistemic wrongs in question, such as perpetrators, must fulfill. At the other end lie imperfect epistemic duties, which we all need to fulfill regardless of whether we are responsible for the relevant epistemic wrongs,

[18] See, for instance, Alexander (2012) and Forman Jr. (2017).

but for which there is latitude in how we do so. And in between lie duties that have normative force of greater specificity than standard imperfect epistemic duties but less so than their perfect counterparts, such as those involving complicity and special relationships. Given this, although we cannot look at the epistemic wrongs that arise from or constitute gross violations and injustices as distant problems of others, we also need not shoulder the burden of addressing every single one on our own. Just as the imperfect duty of charity in the moral realm requires that we ought to engage in some charitable giving as a member of the moral community, with discretion permitted in how we do so specifically, the imperfect epistemic duty here requires that we know some relevant survivors of gross violations and injustices, with latitude in how we do so specifically. This is crucial, as there are countless victims who should be known as acts of epistemic reparations, and yet it is simply not possible for each of us to do all of this epistemic work on our own.

Finally, and related to the previous two points, if engaging in epistemic reparations is an ongoing process and we each have at least an imperfect epistemic duty to do something, then it is obvious that a single act of epistemic reparations will almost certainly be only *partial*, leading to a greater appreciation of the need for *collective action*. Recognizing that one group or person may not be responsible for righting all of the wrongs of, say, the vilification of Black men in the American criminal legal system but that we nonetheless can and should play our part in doing so makes clear that each act will be only a step in the reparative process. In this way, doing nothing because it won't be enough or because it is someone else's problem should be replaced with doing something, even if it is a small gesture, because it will be part of an ongoing collective process that we all have at least the imperfect duty to participate in. Indeed, it is only through collective action that we will be able to make substantive progress on the deep, pernicious epistemic wrongs at issue in this book.

While this book is devoted to reparations that are epistemic in nature and, even more specifically, to the right to be known, I should emphasize at the outset that this framework is fully compatible with the necessity of other kinds of reparations. Making the case for the importance of knowing survivors of gross violations and injustices does not in any way diminish the need to also provide material reparations, such as monetary compensation or the return of land; political reparations, such as the restoration of citizenship or voting rights; psychological reparations, such as relieving suffering, anger, or a sense of violation; moral reparations, such as recognizing and restoring the dignity of victims and reaffirming or reestablishing the moral order of a community; and so on. Sometimes we see, say, the material without the epistemic: a check is handed to a survivor of police violence with no one bearing witness to who he is or the suffering he endured, and other times we see the epistemic without the material: a truth and reconciliation commission is held for stories of violations to be shared without any monetary compensation for the intergenerational economic devastation suffered by the survivors. But just as many gross violations and injustices inflict harms that reverberate across communities, generations, and every dimension of individual persons, so, too, do reparations need to be communal, intergenerational, and multidimensional. At the same time, I focus my attention on the epistemic side here not only because it has been virtually entirely absent from both academic and nonacademic discussions of reparations, but also because it is frequently highlighted by survivors as vital for repairing gross violations and injustices. In this way, my goal is to provide a framework for understanding the distinctive features of epistemic reparations, especially the right to be known, and to add to our grasp of the ongoing wrongs and corresponding reparative work that needs to be undertaken.

As noted earlier, I defend the view that those who suffer gross violations and injustices that result in or constitute not being known due to invisibility, vilification, or systematic distortion are wronged in distinctively epistemic ways and have the right to be known as epistemic reparations. I will be relying on paradigmatic cases of gross violations and injustices rather than providing anything like an analysis of them. In other words, rather than spending page after page asking whether this is really a gross violation or injustice, I will for the most part simply begin with examples that clearly are. Not only is this in keeping with what is found within the framework of the UN itself,[19] it also avoids devoting an excessive and what I regard as an unhelpful amount of attention to the gray or borderline cases, leaving the real work of this project to the forward-looking goal of understanding epistemic reparations.

Moreover, because I focus almost entirely on actual rather than fictionalized cases in this book, just about all of them will have multiple

[19] As the United Nations Human Rights Council Complaint Procedure notes, "[r]esolutions or decisions of the General Assembly, the Human Rights Council and the Economic and Social Council do not contain any clear definition of . . . 'gross violation.'" The Council goes on to provide the following rough characterization: "'gross violations', refer to violations of civil and political and economic, social and cultural rights, occurring in any part of the world and under any circumstances . . . ." (United Nations Human Rights Council n.d.).

kinds of normativity at play. Consider, for instance, a group or individual who is vilified by the criminal legal system in America or suffers the systematic distortions of apartheid in South Africa. Does the wrongdoing involve the moral dimensions of the criminal legal system and apartheid, the epistemic dimensions of vilification and systematic distortion, or both? The answer here, as well as elsewhere throughout the forthcoming chapters, is both. This is because the actual cases involving real people that breathe life into this project are fused with the moral and the epistemic.

But, it may be further asked, should we describe, say, a wrongful conviction as a moral gross violation that results in the epistemic wrong of vilification or does being falsely demonized as a murderer itself constitute an independent gross violation? I do not find it particularly useful to settle this question, as the account holds that epistemic reparations are owed whether a gross violation or injustice *results in* or *constitutes* not being known due to one of the epistemic wrongs identified. So, either way, the wrongfully convicted survivor has the right to be known. Given this, splitting hairs to separate what is entirely moral from what is entirely epistemic, or creating artificial thought experiments to ask whether there are pure moral wrongs or pure epistemic wrongs that fall within the framework, will make little difference to the central aims of this project.

At the same time, the book is on the right to be known, and so my primary focus is on the distinctively epistemic features of the phenomena at issue, especially those that are often connected with gross violations and injustices. After developing the central dimensions of the epistemic reparations framework in Chapter 1, I turn, in Chapter 2, to the power that stories have to both epistemically wrong and to serve as the corresponding epistemic reparations called for in response. As we saw earlier in the quote from Scot Miller, for instance, a false narrative that fuels a wrongful conviction inflicts an additional epistemic wrong on victims, one that shapes who he is taken to be and ultimately who he is able to become. He may not be recognized as a reliable narrator of his life, or even as a storyteller at all, and so his epistemic agency may be denied. He may have a vilifying story extracted from him through manipulation or deception, and so his epistemic agency may be bypassed or erased. He may be coerced into providing a distorting story that serves the needs of the State, and so his epistemic agency may be exploited or coopted. Fulfilling his right to be known involves promoting an epistemically reparative counterstory, one that is not only truthful but also cultivates the centering or restoring of his epistemic agency.

Importantly, however, I show that it is not only false stories that can rise to the level of inflicting a gross violation and injustice demanding of epistemic reparations. I support this through the introduction of the concept of "misknowing," which applies when only a narrow, one-dimensional set of facts are centered about a person or persons, often focusing on those that are most injurious. I show further that misknowing is often caused, fueled, and exacerbated by what I call "flat stories," which are agentially closed and depict the subject in static, one-dimensional, and psychologically simplistic terms.[20] I illustrate this through the role that narratives play in the United States criminal legal system, which I take to be a paradigmatic case of misknowing that is driven by flat stories. For example, even for someone who is guilty of murder, the public narrative of him is often that he is essentially a murderer, only a murderer, and always a murderer. This is because defendants—whether innocent or guilty—are vilified and distorted by the media, relegated to isolated carceral settings that are under nearly constant surveillance, and afforded very few avenues for communication with the outside world. This results in demonizing images, labels, and narratives, developed and promoted by the criminal legal system and the media, socially locking defendants into these stories, sometimes for life. Consider, for instance, Donald Trump's post on his Truth Social site from May 4, 2025, in which he writes that he is "directing the Bureau of Prisons, together with the Department of Justice, FBI, and Homeland Security, to reopen a substantially enlarged and rebuilt ALCATRAZ" (2025). The goal, according to Trump, is to "lock up" those he calls "the dregs of society, who will never contribute anything other than Misery and Suffering" (2025). A day after the post, Stephen Miller, White House Deputy Chief of Staff, was defending Trump's plans to Fox News's Laura Ingraham, saying:

> There are people in this country, as President Trump has said, who will do nothing with their lives but rape, maim, and murder. They cannot be rehabilitated, they cannot be saved, they cannot be coached into some better way of living. They are always going to hurt. They are always going to steal. They are always going to attack. We need a place in this country where we can send people to visually demonstrate the total separation from society—the fact that they are not going to live among us and will never live among us. (Sanders 2025)

[20] Of course, both individuals and groups or collectives can be misknown.

These sorts of comments promote flat stories about many people with criminal convictions in the United States, especially those involving so-called violent offenses. They are depicted as one-dimensional: they do "nothing" with their lives but rape, maim, and murder; psychologically simplistic: "they cannot be rehabilitated, they cannot be saved, they cannot be coached into some better way of living," claims that are often defended with the view that at least certain people with criminal convictions are *essentially* violent or "deviant"; and static and agentially closed: they "will never contribute anything other than Misery and Suffering" because "They are always going to hurt. They are always going to steal. They are always going to attack." These flat stories are themselves often fueled by "recidivism stories and statistics"[21] that cultivate "fearmongering" about protecting the public from "dangerous people."[22] However, while the Bureau of Justice Statistics reports very high recidivism rates—over 75% of those released from prison are rearrested within the first six years[23]—data show that people convicted of "violent offenses are . . . among the least likely to be rearrested for any crime, convicted of any crime, or incarcerated for any crime" (Staudt 2025). Indeed, "people with rape and sexual assault convictions have the lowest overall . . . re-arrest rate of any offense group" (Staudt 2025). In New York, for instance, only about 2% of people were reincarcerated for sex-related crimes within three years of release. Moreover, arrests are often driven by race, neighborhood, and economic status rather than by level of criminal activity. Given all of this, it is reasonable to conclude that while the sorts of flat stories found in the comments by Trump and Miller contribute to laws and policies that inflict catastrophic amounts of harm on people, they are largely unwarranted. When such stories rise to the level of constituting gross violations and injustices, my view maintains that epistemic reparations require "rounder stories," which are agentially open and portray a person or persons in dynamic, multidimensional, and psychologically complex terms.

In Chapter 3, I explore how the process of talking, listening, and learning provides a model of a particularly powerful form of epistemic reparations. While there are many different ways to come to know someone, I show that there can be epistemic disadvantages to *perspective taking*, which involves

[21] Recidivism rates can also be highly misleading, as they often also include "technical violations" of probation or parole. The Council of State Governments, for instance, estimated that in 2021, 29% of prison admissions nationwide were for such technical violations. See Saunders (2024).

[22] Staudt (2025).

[23] Alper et al. (2018).

imaginatively occupying the perspectives and experiences of others, and epistemic advantages to *perspective sharing*, which involves others sharing their firsthand perspectives and experiences with others either directly or indirectly. Talking, listening, and learning is a form of perspective sharing and the interactive nature of this process can make it epistemically generative for both those who are telling their stories and those who are appropriate listeners, leading in many cases to "coconstructed" narratives. An appropriate listener response of, say, compassion or outrage may facilitate a survivor's own account of what happened shifting from self-blame to the centering of systemic injustices, thereby resulting in a narrative that is coconstructed by both speaker and listener. This, in turn, can lead to the repairing of epistemic wrongs, the creation of new narratives and new identities, and, ultimately, the development of new selves.

Crucially, however, the primary focus of this book is on *knowing* survivors of gross violations and injustices. In many paradigmatic cases, knowing involves some sort of listening and leads to a deeper understanding of the person in question. But knowing is distinct from both listening and understanding. I can listen with no uptake at all—no shifts in my beliefs, attitudes, or perceptions. I can listen to someone wrongfully vilified and continue to believe with the same degree of conviction and hatred in my heart that he is a monster. Even if the person does not pick up on this and so feels that the wrong has been partially repaired, this might be an instance of psychological reparations, but it would not be epistemic reparations. Epistemic reparations *need some reparative shift in epistemic states* and listening, by itself, does not necessarily do this.[24] At the same time, understanding[25] as the minimum needed for epistemic reparations is too demanding. For instance, understanding is said to involve knowledge of causes[26] or modal relationships,[27] a grasp of how various pieces of information relate to one another,[28] or a certain set of abilities.[29] But I can know a survivor of carceral injustice as an act of epistemic reparations through his story of emotional trauma without, say, knowing the corresponding causes or modal relationships and without having a set of abilities for grasping how all of the dimensions of his narrative

[24] This is why the title of Chapter 3 is Talking, Listening, and *Learning*, where the "learning" involves the talking and listening leading to the conveying or creating of knowledge.

[25] I will not here wade into the discussion of whether understanding is just a species of knowledge.

[26] Lipton (2004).

[27] Grimm (2014, 2017).

[28] Zagzebski (2001) and Kvanvig (2003).

[29] Hills (2009).

relate to one another. Especially when it is clear that individual acts are steps in an ongoing process of epistemic reparations, it should be similarly apparent that each act does not require anything as specific or demanding as understanding. And since the scale and depth of wrongdoing in the cases at issue here make the question of completing the process distant or idealized, it is not necessary to answer whether understanding is needed for complete epistemic reparations in general.

There is another reason to prefer knowledge to either listening or understanding in the account here. Given that the normative starting point of the framework developed in this book is the one found in the UN's Commission on Human Rights outlining the rights of victims of gross violations and injustices, the right to be known parallels the existing right to know. The UN argues that victims have the right to know, for instance, what happened to their loved ones during a genocide or whether there was state involvement in their murders. While it would clearly be too weak to say that survivors merely have the right to listen in such cases, as knowledge crucially also involves truth and evidence, it would also be too specific or demanding to say that they have the right to understand, as it may in fact never be possible to grasp how all of the pieces of a political and social situation led to mass atrocity. Knowledge fills the space between these two ends of the epistemic spectrum. But if victims have the right to know, then they should also have the right to be known—to be recognized as epistemic agents themselves rather than as mere receptacles of knowledge that has already been produced. Their stories should be given proper uptake, their voices should be amplified, their status in the community should be restored, and they should be contributors to the historical record of the violations or injustices in question.

In Chapter 4, I specifically explore how to understand what it means to know someone as an act of epistemic reparations, and I characterize two different ways of doing so: *bearing witness* and *restoring status*. While knowing someone in a bearing witness sense minimally requires giving proper uptake to a victim's story, which needs to be appropriately anchored in reality, knowing someone in a restoring status sense instead focuses on the perception of a victim and his relations within his relevant communities, involving, for instance, his name being "cleared," his reputation being repaired, or his appropriate status being cultivated or restored. Crucially, however, knowing persons in either sense will be radically heterogenous in form, content, and elements. It may involve everything from one-on-one conversations and truth and reconciliation commissions to memorials and museums;

from updating beliefs and attitudes to coconstructing rounder narratives; from sharing posts on TikTok and Instagram to listening to an album; from written testimony and documentaries to artwork and poetry. Given this, although I briefly connect the framework developed here with a traditional account of testimonial knowledge, what will be the most original in this book is not identifying the lowest common denominator that all epistemic reparations share but, rather, exploring some of the paradigmatic ways fulfilling a victim's right to be known might be done. Moreover, as noted earlier, Chapter 5 is devoted to developing a framework for understanding the corresponding duties to know such victims of gross violations and injustices, one that carves out space for both perfect and imperfect duties and that applies to both perpetrators and non-perpetrators. The ultimate goal of both chapters, then, is to shed light on the normative demands that epistemic reparations generate, as well as the concrete steps that can be taken to fulfill them, so that each of us might get to work right now in the ongoing process of addressing the epistemic wrongs of those who have been relegated to the margins of the unknown.

In a recent interview, James Soto asks, "What really is the measure of justice for someone who has [wrongfully] spent 42 years in prison?" and then quickly responds, "I don't know if we can actually put a metric to that" (Perlman and Feurer 2024). It is both this sort of question and response that inspire, fuel, and guide the pages that follow. There are wrongs so violating and unjust in magnitude, depth, and impact that they seem to entirely defy repair. Even focusing on only James and the epistemic dimensions of what he endured, how do we comprehend or calculate the damage to him of 42 years of being regarded as a murderer, a monster, a number, a criminal, a nonperson? 42 years of having his epistemic agency erased while a false and vilifying narrative of his life is curated, extracted, and promoted by the State? 42 years of the contours of his life being shaped and distorted by a story that is utterly foreign to who he is and what he values? Yet just as James raises the seemingly impossible question of what justice might look like in his case, so, too, we need to collectively ask this question every single day with respect to every gross violation and injustice, even when the weight of the violence and cruelty in the world threatens to crush us individually. Perhaps even more importantly, we need to listen to and learn from survivors themselves—across time periods, geographical locations, and circumstances—about how to bear witness and contribute to the restoration of their status. For it is only through each of us doing our part as members of both local and global collectives, and coming to know those victims most impacted by injustice, that we will begin to truly grasp what epistemic reparations demand and, in so doing, to reimagine what is possible.

As James studies for the LSAT with the hope of attending law school so that he can focus on exonerating other people with wrongful convictions, it is fitting to bring this introduction to a close with a call to action in his own words about what fulfilling his right to be known might involve: "I want to change the paradigm of this horrible experience to make it a positive thing.... I want to be known as someone who helped" (Buckley 2025).

# 1
# Epistemic Reparations and the Right to Be Known

The South African Truth and Reconciliation Commission (TRC) was established in 1995 to investigate human rights violations that took place under apartheid. The mandate of the Commission was to investigate and record gross abuses of human rights during 1960 and 1994, to offer reparation and rehabilitation to victims, and, when appropriate, to grant amnesty to perpetrators.[1] While being interviewed by the TRC, one victim, Lucas Baba Sikwepere, recounted having been shot multiple times by an apartheid-era police officer, which led to multiple bullets being lodged in his neck and face, causing blindness and severe headaches. When the commissioner asked, "How do you feel, Baba, about coming here to tell your story?" Sikwepere responded, "I feel what has been making me sick all the time is the fact that I couldn't tell my story. But now I—it feels like I got my sight back by coming here and telling you the story" (Daye 2011, p. 126).

Of course, Sikwepere did not literally regain his sight by testifying to the TRC. Instead, he is communicating that something powerful or transformative occurred through the act of telling his story. But notice that "telling" is distinctively interpersonal here; it is clear that Sikwepere would not have had the experience he had if he told his story with no listener or if the audience members ignored him. He didn't want to just utter words into the void—he needed to be *listened to* and *heard* by other people. Otherwise put, Sikwepere needed *to be known* in order to feel "like [he] got [his] sight back."

We see a similar desire to be known in Zora Neale Hurston's *Barracoon: The Story of the Last "Black Cargo,"* which is a first-person narrative of Cudjo Lewis, also known as Oluale Kossola, who was the last known survivor of the middle passage. In the story, Kossola recounts his life in a West African village, his abduction by slave traders, and the profound trauma and grief he experienced at the loss of his home and family. When Hurston says to Kossola,

[1] Department of Justice, South Africa (n.d.).

*The Right to Be Known*. Jennifer Lackey, Oxford University Press. © Oxford University Press 2026.
DOI: 10.1093/9780197833988.003.0002

"I want to know who you are," he cries out, "Thankee Jesus! Somebody come ast about Cudjo! I want to tellee somebody who I is, so maybe dey go in de Affickey soil some day and callee my name and somebody dere say, 'Yeah, I know Kossula'" (2018, p. 18). In his review of *Barracoon*, Ismail Muhammad writes:

> Kossola's narrative is marked by a deep familiarity with violence and an irreversible sense of loneliness and loss . . . . We sense the monumental contours of his grief not only at the deaths of his wife and children but also at the gaping wound that resulted from being torn from a home to which he will never return. His utmost desire is to be *known* again. (2018)

Kossola's desire to be known here is connected not only with his own personal violations and identity but also with his beloved community and homeland of Africa, from which he was violently abducted.

This is not an uncommon experience. The act of telling and being heard, especially after suffering gross violations and injustices, reflects a deep human desire for many. In describing his reflections as a commissioner for the United Nations Truth Commission for El Salvador, for instance, Thomas Buergenthal writes:

> Many of the people who came to the Commission to tell what happened to them or to their relatives and friends had not done so before. For some, ten years or more had gone by in silence and pent-up anger. Finally, someone listened to them, and there would be a record of what they had endured. They came by the thousands, still afraid and not a little skeptical, and they talked, many for the first time. One could not listen to them without recognizing that the mere act of telling what had happened was a healing emotional release, and that they were more interested in recounting their story and being heard than in retribution. (1995, p. 321)

Again, "telling" here is crucially being understood as involving uptake by other people. Indeed, what is clearly the aim in all of these cases is being heard or known by others, not the mere reporting of words. But there is another dimension to highlight: being listened to is an end itself rather than one that is purely instrumental. To be sure, reporting gross violations and injustices is often a means to the end of preventing these same abuses from happening to others in the future, or educating the public about atrocities, and so on.

In the above passages, however, the victims in question are highlighting the need or wish to be known as independent from these other aims.

This is not unique to paradigmatic cases of human rights violations. Lewis "Jim" Fogle served 34 years for the 1976 murder and rape of a 15-year-old girl in Pennsylvania, Deann Katherine Long. The conviction was based largely on the testimony of a jailhouse informant and, in 2014, DNA testing done by the Pennsylvania Innocence Project excluded Fogle as the contributor of the male DNA found at the scene. Despite the fact that Fogle was both released from prison and exonerated in 2015, there is something else that he wants: "I want people to know the truth about my case" (Innocence Project in Print 2015, p. 16). Knowing the truth about his case is to know the truth about *him*—that he did not take the life of Long and is thus not a murderer and rapist. In other words, even after the external injustices of incarceration and wrongful conviction have been reversed, there is a further desire that Fogle has—*to be known.*

Moreover, the desire to be known is not restricted to the first-person case. The deaths of George Floyd, Breonna Taylor, and other Black Americans at the hands of police violence ignited a global reckoning with the systemic racism of America's criminal legal system. "Say Their Names" is a common cry among those protesting America's pernicious investment in policing, criminalization, and incarceration.[2] This call to say the names of the victims, however, is not a call to simply utter words or to shout a refrain. It is, rather, to do something epistemic—to remember the victims and to bear witness to them.[3] It matters not just that we know that there are victims of police violence, but that we *know them.* Being known, then, is important at both the first-person and third-person levels.

In what follows, I provide the first discussion in the philosophical literature of the epistemic significance of the phenomenon of "being known" and the relationship it has to reparations that are distinctively epistemic. Drawing on a framework provided by the United Nations Commission on Human Rights, I argue that victims of gross violations and injustices not only have the *right to know* what happened, as the UN maintains, but they also have a right that is altogether absent from these discussions—the *right to be known.* I then make the case for expanding the standard conception of reparations

[2] See, for instance, The New Yorker (2020).

[3] In Chapter 4, I develop two different senses of knowing a survivor—"bearing witness" and "restoring status"—as acts of epistemic reparations. But for the purposes of developing the general framework here, I will largely gloss over this distinction.

to include actions intended to redress distinctively epistemic wrongs and I provide an account of how to best understand these *epistemic reparations* that captures both the right to know and the right to be known possessed by survivors of gross violations and injustices.

## 1. The Right to Know and the Right to Be Known

In 1997, the United Nations Commission on Human Rights issued a report addressing the protection and promotion of human rights through actions that combat the impunity of perpetrators of civil and political human rights violations. In particular, the report sets forth three rights that victims of gross violations and injustices have, one of which is the "right to know"[4] and is characterized as follows:[5]

> This is not simply the right of any individual victim or his nearest and dearest to know what happened, a right to the truth. The right to know is also a collective right, drawing upon history to prevent violations from recurring in the future. (United Nations 1997)

The knowledge in question in this report involves the occurrence, causes, circumstances, and perpetrators of gross human rights violations and breaches of international humanitarian law. The right to know these facts is both individual and collective, and the bearers of these rights are victims, their families, communities, "society," or "a people."

As an example, roughly 150,000 Indigenous children were removed and separated from their families and communities to attend Residential Schools in Canada, and the Indian Residential Schools (IRS) Settlement Agreement, which "represents the consensus reached between legal counsel for former students, legal counsel for the Churches, the Assembly of First Nations, other Indigenous organizations and the Government of Canada," included the establishment of a TRC of Canada.[6] Many of the goals of the TRC of Canada clearly reflect the right to know as found in the UN's report, such as:

[4] Lani Watson also provides an excellent discussion of the right to know in her (2022).
[5] The other two are the "right to justice" and the "right to reparation."
[6] Government of Canada, *Indian Residential Schools Settlement Agreement.*

- Promote awareness and public education of Canadians about the IRS system and its impacts;
- Identify sources and create as complete an historical record as possible of the IRS system and legacy. The record shall be preserved and made accessible to the public for future study and use;
- Produce and submit to the Parties of the Agreement a report including recommendations to the Government of Canada concerning the IRS system and experience including: the history, purpose, operation, and supervision of the IRS system, the effect and consequences of IRS (including systemic harms, intergenerational consequences and the impact on human dignity) and the ongoing legacy of the residential schools.[7]

The TRC of Canada thus emphasizes making known to former students, their families, their communities, and all Canadians the occurrence, causes, circumstances, and perpetrators of the IRS system. In particular, the TRC requires promoting awareness and public education of the IRS system, creating, preserving, and making accessible to the public a historical record of the system, and producing and submitting a report that provides a detailed account of the IRS system.

While the UN's focus is on states and governments fulfilling the right to know, individuals, especially perpetrators, can do so as well. Consider, for instance, the case of Laurencia Mukalemera, whose husband was murdered by Hutu Tasian Nkundiye during the Rwandan genocide.[8] Nkundiye acknowledges that "what we did was horrible," and remains haunted by memories of the victims of violence at his own hands. After he returned from prison, he reached out to Mukalemera, who says, "I didn't know that it was Nkundiye who killed my husband. He came and told me he did it and showed me where my husband's body was buried. When he confessed and apologized, I forgave him" (Associated Press 2019a). This is a paradigmatic example of fulfilling a victim's right to know. Mukalemera suffered many wrongs as a result of her husband's murder, including some that are distinctively epistemic in nature, such as not knowing what precisely happened to him, who was responsible, and where his remains are. Nkundiye sought to redress some of these wrongs by conveying to Mukalemera knowledge of

[7] Government of Canada, *Schedule N: Mandate of the Truth and Reconciliation Commission of Canada*.

[8] Associated Press (2019a).

who the perpetrator was of her husband's murder—Nkundiye himself—as well as by sharing with her the location of her husband's body, taking responsibility for the horror he inflicted on her and her family, and apologizing.

In 2005, the UN released an update[9] to the principles to combat impunity in which the right to know was fleshed out in greater detail, along with the corresponding duties on the part of states or governments. According to this report, victims and their families have the "imprescriptible right to know the truth about the circumstances in which violations took place and, in the event of death or disappearance, the victims' fate" (United Nations 2005). In addition, the report holds that it is an "inalienable" right of "every people" to know about the perpetration and circumstances surrounding heinous crimes. These two aspects of the report concern rights-bearers and the nature of the rights, but there are also corresponding duties of the states or governments in question. In particular, there is the "duty to preserve memory," which involves the preservation of archives and other evidence concerning violations of human rights and humanitarian law, as well as the facilitation of knowledge of these violations, including protecting the collective memory from extinction and guarding against the development of revisionist and negationist views. Finally, there is the duty "to give effect to the right to know," which includes ensuring an independent and effective operation of the judiciary along with access to the archives regarding human rights violations.

There are at least four features that emerge from this UN report that are instructive. First, possessing certain kinds of knowledge is a *right* that belongs to individuals and communities. This is significant, as the more common rights we hear about are moral or political in nature. Second, and related, there can be a right to something distinctively *epistemic*. It is quite rare for discourse on rights to focus on epistemic goods, such as knowledge, truth, and evidence,[10] rather than on those involving us as members of a moral community or political citizenry, such as to life, liberty, bodily autonomy, the pursuit of happiness, property, freedom of speech, voting, and so on. One of the most frequent occurrences is in legal settings where there are laws that mandate the sharing of evidence. For instance, the Brady rule in the United States requires prosecutors to disclose with the defense materially

[9] This was written by "the independent expert to update the Set of principles to combat impunity, Diane Orentlicher."

[10] Later in this chapter, I expand what is included in the notion of "epistemic goods."

exculpatory evidence in the government's possession.[11] We might say, then, that it is a right of defendants to have something epistemic—the State's exculpatory evidence. But this is a legal right that depends on the context of the rights-bearer in question and can be repealed, modified, or restrained by other human laws. This brings us to the third feature: the UN is here talking about *inalienable* natural rights that involve not just the sharing of evidence, but the transmission of knowledge. The idea is that there are natural epistemic rights, not dependent on law, culture, or government, that cannot be repealed. Finally, these rights *are connected to gross violations and injustices*, often perpetrated by states, governments, or groups. In particular, those most directly impacted by the violation and injustice in question, such as the victims, family members, and communities, have the right to the corresponding knowledge. Moreover, the knowledge is specific—it regards the occurrence, causes, circumstances, and perpetrators of gross human rights violations and breaches of international humanitarian law.

Crucially, however, this framework provided by the UN is powerful not only for what it includes but also for what it leaves out. In particular, absent from this picture is another dimension of rights and duties that is arguably just as significant as those highlighted in the report from the Commission on Human Rights: what I call *the right to be known* and the corresponding *duty to know*.

To make the distinction between the right to know and the right to be known clearer, let's consider some important differences. The right to know involves a knower and a proposition or propositions and thus need not be interpersonal. A community's right to know what happened when an unarmed Black man was seriously injured by police violence, for instance, can be fulfilled by the police department releasing impersonal body-worn camera footage of the officers involved. In this way, the voice and the story of the survivor himself need not play any role in the historical record of the event. In contrast, the right to be known is an overtly interpersonal phenomenon. Given that it doesn't make sense to be known by an impersonal object,

[11] See, for instance, Daughety and Reinganum (2018). Another example from the criminal legal system is "Marsy's Law," which involves amendments to state constitutions that protect the rights of victims of crime (Marsy's Law n.d.). One component of Marsy's Law declares that victims have the right "[t]o be heard, upon request, at any proceeding, including any delinquency proceeding, involving a post-arrest release decision, plea, sentencing, post-conviction release decision, or any proceeding in which a right of the victim is at issue" (Cal. Const. art. I, § 28(b)(8)). This "right to be heard" might be understood as a legal variant related to the "right to be known."

being known requires at least two persons at the most fundamental level—the knower and the one being known.[12]

The right to know has the corresponding duty to tell. Since people have a right to know about gross human rights violations, for instance, the State has a responsibility to do things to enable the creation, preservation, and transmission of knowledge. Here there is the implication of at least partial ignorance on the part of those most harmed. That is, victims, their families, and communities have a right to know about gross human rights violations, so the State has the duty to investigate, remember, and archive so as to uncover and make available what really happened and who was involved. Since victims, their families, and communities are typically singled out as special bearers of this right, the idea is that there are truths to which they do not have access, and it is the responsibility of the State to make sure they are informed.

The right to be known, in contrast, has the corresponding duty to know. It is not just that people have a right to know what happened to victims in certain contexts; it is also that these victims themselves have a right to be seen and heard—to have their stories be given proper uptake and to be contributors to the historical record. There is no implication here of ignorance on the part of the victim; they do not need to be given access to truths or facts. Instead, they need to be able to be givers of knowledge, and this requires the listening and corresponding changes in epistemic states of others.

Of course, when the UN talks about the right to know, there is a sense in which bearing witness to victims and their families is included. We cannot know all of the details of what really happened regarding human rights violations without the testimony of those most impacted by the crimes. However, learning from the victims is only one way to fulfill the rights of those who are ignorant. As stated in the report, if a complete picture of a breach of international humanitarian law could be created, preserved, and made available without talking to a single victim, there would be no violation of rights according to the Commission on Human Rights. Otherwise put, hearing the stories of victims on the view found in the UN report is a means to a different epistemic end—fulfilling the rights of individuals and communities to know. On the view developed here, listening to and learning from the testimony of victims is an additional end itself.

[12] As I discuss in later chapters, this is compatible with knowing the dead as well as with collectives or groups knowing and being known, such as the Canadian government knowing Residential School survivors.

What I am proposing, then, is the crucial expansion of the UN's framework for understanding the rights that victims of gross violations and injustices have to include not only the right to know, but also the *right to be known*. Consider, again, the TRC of Canada for survivors of the IRS system. We saw that the TRC's goals reflect the right to know, but they also include dimensions of what we are calling the right to be known in the following ways:

- Acknowledge Residential School experiences, impacts and consequences;
- Provide a holistic, culturally appropriate and safe setting for former students, their families and communities as they come forward to the Commission;
- Witness, support, promote and facilitate truth and reconciliation events at both the national and community levels.[13]

In addition to actions that promote the creation, preservation, and transmission of knowledge about the IRS system, then, the TRC of Canada also recognizes the need for those who were impacted by the system to be themselves known. The TRC requires, for instance, acknowledging experiences, impacts, and consequences of the Residential Schools, which includes the experiences of the survivors. It also calls for providing appropriate spaces for their stories to be shared and for truth and reconciliation events to take place.

While the right to be known parallels the UN's conception of the right to know in that it arises out of gross human rights violations and injustices, often perpetrated by states or governments, there are also important extensions of the core framework. The cases of James Soto from the Introduction and of Lewis "Jim" Fogle discussed at the start of this chapter, for instance, are ones in which they suffered gross miscarriages of justice perpetrated by the State and have the right to be known, despite not involving paradigmatic human rights violation. Indeed, the gross violations and injustices need not be the result of State involvement in order for victims to have the right to be known. Consider the case of Larry Nassar, the USA Gymnastics national team doctor and osteopathic physician at Michigan State University who sexually abused 332 gymnasts.[14] Even if Nassar, USA Gymnastics, and Michigan State are the primary bearers of responsibility for these gross violations—and not

[13] Government of Canada, *Schedule N: Mandate of the Truth and Reconciliation Commission of Canada*.

[14] Associated Press (2019b).

the State—we may still argue that the victims have the right to be known. Moreover, as with the right to know, the right to be known can belong to individuals and to collectives or "a people." A single victim of gross injustice might possess this right, such as James Soto or Lewis "Jim" Fogle, but so, too, can a group of people, such as South African survivors of apartheid-era violence.

Taking a step back, it is important to recognize that the force and impact of being known is wide-reaching. We are all powerfully aware that we are seen by others. In her discussion of reputation, Gloria Origgi writes, "[e]very social interaction brings forth an evaluative dimension of reciprocal judgement, a perception of who we are that we leave in the eyes of others. Every social interaction brings forth also a mastery of this presentation of ourselves, a consciousness of the image of ourselves we want to leave track of through our behavior" (2012, p. 401). Indeed, according to the influential "looking-glass self" theory developed by sociologist Charles Horton Cooley in 1902, our conception of self is formed as a reflection of the responses and evaluations of others in our environment. If this is true, then who we are is fundamentally shaped by how we think we appear to those around us.[15]

Around the same time as Cooley, W. E. B. Du Bois writes in *The Souls of Black Folk*: "It is a peculiar sensation, this double-consciousness, this sense of always looking at one's self through the eyes of others, of measuring one's soul by the tape of a world that looks on in amused contempt and pity" (1903, p. 3). But it is crucial that Du Bois is *not* discussing here a universal or equally shared experience:

> One ever feels his two-ness,—an American, a Negro; two souls, two thoughts, two unreconciled strivings; two warring ideals in one dark body, whose dogged strength alone keeps it from being torn asunder. The history of the American Negro is the history of this strife—this longing to attain self-conscious manhood, to merge his double self into a better and truer self. In this merging he wishes neither of the older selves to be lost. He does not wish to Africanize America, for America has too much to teach the world and Africa. He wouldn't bleach his Negro blood in a flood of white Americanism, for he knows that Negro blood has a message for the world. He simply wishes to make it possible for a man to be both a Negro and

[15] Cooley's view is a descriptive one, describing how our identities are in fact formed, but Lindemann (2016) develops what might be seen as a moral counterpart, which I will discuss later in this chapter.

> an American without being cursed and spit upon by his fellows, without having the doors of opportunity closed roughly in his face. (1903, pp. 3–4)

In contrast to Cooley, Du Bois argues that there is an asymmetry in seeing ourselves through the eyes of others, with the racist and unjust structure of the United States forcing Black Americans to see themselves through the perspectives of those in power in a way that it does not for whites, resulting in the "double consciousness" of "two unreconciled strivings." Moreover, the dual perspectives of double consciousness are directly connected to the desire and possibility of being known. As Orlando Hawkins and Emmalon Davis argue:

> At its core, double consciousness involves entertaining or embodying dual perspectives. Du Boisian double consciousness emerges within a structure of racial domination in which white perspectives are *publicly available and coercively promoted*—that is, white perspectives are widely disseminated and maintained through explicit and subtle political, social, educational, legal, economic, and linguistic practices. It is through these practices that white perspectives are reliably *made known* to whites and non-whites alike. This structural asymmetry raises a related question of channels of access through which the perspectives of Black people and other racial minorities are reliably made known to white people. (2024, pp. 66–67, original emphasis)

The desire to be and to be known as "both a Negro and an American" with respect and dignity, and to have this perspective made reliably accessible, thus lies at the heart of the "lived contradiction attendant to the Black struggle"[16] described by Du Bois.

Relatedly, neither the benefits of being seen by others nor the burden of doing the seeing is equally distributed among members of our communities. James Baldwin makes this point vivid when he says, "I have spent most of my life, after all, watching white people and outwitting them, so that I might survive" (1993, p. 217). Similarly, in discussing the work of David Roediger (1998), Charles Mills highlights "the fundamental epistemic asymmetry between typical white views of blacks and typical black views of whites: these are not cognizers linked by a reciprocal ignorance but rather groups whose

[16] Hawkins and Davis (2024, p. 62).

respective privilege and subordination tend to produce self-deception, bad faith, evasion, and misrepresentation, on the one hand, and more veridical perceptions, on the other hand" (2007, p. 17). Mills continues: "[o]ften for their very survival, blacks have been forced to become lay anthropologists, studying the strange culture, customs, and mind-set of the 'white tribe' that has such frightening power over them, that in certain time periods can even determine their life or death on a whim" (2007, pp. 17–18).

There are, then, at least three points that emerge here. First, our selves are powerfully shaped by how we think we are seen by others and, thus, interpersonal relations are fundamental to our identities. Second, being seen or known is not an equally distributed good—those with less power are often seen or known far less than those with more. Third, the labor involved in doing the seeing and knowing is not equally shared among members of communities, as those in relative positions of powerlessness frequently need to know those who have power in order to navigate the world around them, but those in power can often avoid this epistemic work. Putting these points together provides the start for understanding why we might think that being known is something that can lie in normative space in the first place: while being known can be a tremendously valuable good that has the power to shape a person's life, it is often unjustly distributed and the work of doing the knowing is often unfairly shouldered. Moreover, when these goods and labor are distributed within communities in massively unequal ways, epistemic wrongs can be inflicted. This is particularly powerful as a comparative phenomenon: when whites are generally seen and heard and known, and Black people are not, then whites have goods and positions within the epistemic community that are illegitimately denied to Black people. When Black people have to do so much seeing and hearing and knowing in order to navigate spaces that were designed by whites for whites, they are unfairly burdened with epistemic labor that whites can avoid.

But what, it might be asked, is involved in "knowing someone?"[17] At the very least, since knowledge is factive, being known involves the knower having at least some true beliefs about the person who is known.[18] Of course, within such a minimal constraint, being known can be construed in a

[17] This question will be discussed in detail in Chapter 4.

[18] While this will be taken up in Chapter 4, it is important to note that one can certainly be known even when there are falsehoods sprinkled throughout the narrative of one's life, as is surely the case with all of us. I might, for instance, incorrectly remember that a dog bit me when I was five when I was in fact six, or that my car was stolen on a Friday rather than a Saturday, or that I was angry when I was stopped by the police when I was actually terrified. None of these falsehoods should prevent me from being known, or you from bearing witness to me, in epistemically significant ways.

number of different ways. You may be known, for instance, in the sense of achieving *popularity or fame*, which involves a lot of people knowing who you are, and may be realized along a variety of dimensions, such as by having celebrity status or in terms of the number of TikTok, Facebook, or Instagram followers you have.[19] Or you may be known in the sense of having *intimacy*. This way of being known involves others knowing who you are in a deep and meaningful way and may be determined by feeling truly understood or appreciated by another, as when we say, "she really knows who I am." Or you may be known in terms of others having had *causal contact* with you. This sense of being known can be achieved by others having some sort of interaction with you, even if it is quite minimal.[20]

None of these seem to be exactly what is at work in the above cases. Sure, we might understand Sikwepere, Kossola, the victims from El Salvador, and Fogle desiring to be known in all three of these ways: they may want fame, especially in light of how they suffered; they may want to have relationships where they are truly understood; and they may want others to have causal interaction with others. But there seems to be something else that they desire that goes beyond all of this—namely, for the members of their communities to *see or hear them* for who they are, to *bear witness* to their injustices, and to thereby have their *status restored* in their communities. In order to get a better grasp of what is being called for here, let's explore different ways someone might fail to be known that involves being epistemically wronged.

## 2. Not Being Known

In all of the cases of not being known discussed so far, the gross violation or injustice in question has clear normative force morally, politically, and legally. Sikwepere, for instance, was egregiously wronged not only by living through apartheid in South Africa, but also by his experience of police violence and, arguably, by the amnesty granted to his perpetrators. Similarly, the wrongful conviction and incarceration inflicted by the hands of the State robbed Fogle of his home, family, and freedom for decades. That apartheid and wrongful

[19] I am distinguishing *being known* from a person's *reputation*, where the latter need not involve true beliefs. For instance, one might care very much about having a positive reputation, while caring very little if anyone really knows who one is. For more on reputation, see Origgi (2012, 2018).

[20] This is similar to what is being captured by the "causal accounts" of knowing someone discussed in Chapter 4.

convictions are morally, politically, and legally wrong, and that their victims are deserving of redress, are hardly deniable. But what I want to focus on here are the distinctively epistemic wrongs that arise out of violations of this sort.

Let's take a closer look at the case of Fogle: not only was he convicted of murder and incarcerated, he was also falsely believed to be a liar, a rapist, and a murderer for over three decades. The community both failed to know who he was and believed him to be something altogether different—someone who is a pariah in the eyes of others and is alien to Fogle himself. Because of this, he was doubted, silenced, and forbidden from playing a role in the narrative of his own life, thereby fracturing his relationship within the epistemic community. Justice for Fogle involves not only release from prison, exoneration, and financial compensation, but also repairing the damage done by the epistemic wrongs inflicted on him. We need to hear him and see him for who he truly is, not as the person presented to us by the State. We need, that is, *to know him.*

More generally, there are at least three epistemic wrongs that involve not being known that are relevant here: those concerning *invisibility*,[21] *vilification* and *demonization*, and *systematic distortion*.[22]

In Ralph Ellison's *Invisible Man*, for instance, the narrator discusses how white people "... refuse to see me.... When they approach me they see only my surroundings, themselves, or figments of their imagination—indeed, everything and anything except me" (1995, p. 3). Invisibility is one way of not being known—if I don't have any relevant beliefs about you because you are invisible to me, especially *as a person*, then *ipso facto* I don't know you. There are, of course, different kinds or degrees of invisibility. *Targeted invisibility* involves knowing some facts about a person, but lacking relevant beliefs in particular domains, especially ones that are important to the person, such as *qua* coworker, political participant, member of the moral community, and so

[21] While discussions of not being known owing to invisibility are not widespread in epistemology, there is a long history of writers connecting the Black experience with invisibility. See, for instance, Williams (1905), Ellison (1952/1995), Lorde (1984, 1990), Hurston (1950), Crenshaw (1989, 1992), Mills (1997, 2007, 2015), Wanzo (2009), Dotson and Gilbert (2014), and Dotson (2017). Mills (2007), Dotson and Gilbert (2014), and Dotson (2017) explicitly frame their projects in epistemological terms. There is also epistemological literature on beliefs or evidence that one should have, or facts that one should know, including about people. See, for instance, Lackey (2008), Medina (2013), and Goldberg (2017).

[22] I should note that while I focus on these three ways of not being known when there are gross violations and injustices, as they capture some of the most widespread and prevalent ways of being epistemically wronged, I leave open the possibility that there are others that similarly demand epistemic reparations. For examples of some other kinds of epistemic wrongs, see Dotson (2011, 2014), Berenstain (2016), Davis (2016, 2018), and Leydon-Hardy (2021).

on. *Complete invisibility* involves lacking beliefs about a person *qua* person, which is often found in cases of the dehumanization of a racial or ethnic group during times of mass genocide.

To make the kind of epistemic wrong involved in invisibility vivid, let's compare it with the widely discussed phenomenon of testimonial injustice, where a hearer affords less credibility to a speaker than the evidence supports because of a prejudice about the speaker's social identity.[23] For instance, if a male scientist regards a female coworker as less reliable than the men in the lab simply because he is sexist and she is a woman, then she is the victim of testimonial injustice. But now suppose that, because of his sexism, the male scientist simply doesn't form any beliefs at all about his female coworker's reliability, as he takes her to lie entirely outside the realm of the scientific community. The problem here is not that she is afforded a credibility deficit, even a massive one, *but that she is not regarded as the proper subject of such an evaluation in the first place.*[24] *Qua* scientist, she is invisible to her coworkers. This is a case of targeted invisibility, but there are general ones, as well. Suppose that members of a despised racial or ethnic group are regarded by some as so outside the realm of personhood and agency that they are not even appropriate candidates for credibility assessments. When Nazis referred to Jews as "rats" or Tutsis were called "cockroaches" or "snakes," for instance, there was a call to see the group in question as not human or person-like.[25] More precisely, during the peak of the Rwandan genocide, the problem wasn't that Tutsis were regarded as less credible than the evidence dictated, but that they weren't even credibility-bearers in the first place. Language of "cockroaches" and "snakes" is telling: we don't call insects and reptiles untrustworthy or unreliable. The idea of evaluating them for credibility just doesn't even arise, as they are entirely erased from the epistemic community.[26]

[23] See Fricker (2007). Fricker also discusses hermeneutical injustice, which involves "having some significant area of one's social experience obscured from collective understanding owing to a structural identity prejudice in the collective hermeneutical resource" (2007, p. 155). This could be understood as a kind of epistemic invisibility whereby a group's epistemic resources fail to get uptake, thereby leaving a hermeneutical lacuna in the mainstream knowledge economy where these resources could be.

[24] I develop this point in greater detail in Lackey (2018a).

[25] See Tirrell (2012). See also Goff et al. (2008).

[26] Dotson draws on the notion of "Jane Crow" to develop an "unknowability problem" that is "characterized by a trifold structure of disappearing" involving "the occupation of negative socio-epistemic space, reduced epistemic confidence, and heightened epistemic disavowal" (2017, p. 418). Dotson's view provides one framework for understanding the invisibility dimension of not being known at work in this chapter.

Another kind of invisibility is found in Simone de Beauvoir's work, where she writes that of all myths about women:

> none is more firmly anchored in masculine hearts than that of the feminine "mystery." It has numerous advantages . . . . [F]irst of all it permits an easy explanation of all that appears inexplicable; the man who "does not understand" a woman is happy to substitute an objective resistance for a subjective deficiency of mind; instead of admitting his ignorance, he perceives the presence of a "mystery" outside himself: an alibi, indeed, that flatters laziness and vanity at once . . . . [I]n the company of a living enigma man remains alone—alone with his dreams, his hopes, his fears, his love, his vanity. This . . . is for many a more attractive experience than an authentic relation with a human being. (1988, pp. 285–286)

Drawing on this, Rae Langton discusses how women are not known by men on this view because they are regarded as *unknowable*, with this unknowability sometimes taken to be "distinctive of, even essential to, one's being as a woman" (2000, p. 130). This can then be used to justify not only a disregard of the experiences and thoughts of women as enigmatic, but also a singular focus on the familiar subjectivity of men, which ultimately leads to women being invisible precisely because they are deemed unknowable.

In addition to invisibility, not being known can involve vilification and demonization. Instead of not seeing a particular dimension of someone or not seeing her at all, this epistemic wrong involves replacing the image of the person in question with a vilifying or demonizing version. This is the sort of epistemic harm experienced by Fogle and one that is also widespread in the United States where Black Americans are systematically represented and treated as "criminals" or "thugs."[27] In this sense, they are not invisible at all, for it is not that they are erased from consciousness, but massively overrepresented in inaccurate and vilified ways.[28] Image upon image of especially young Black men depicts them in handcuffs, in the back of police cars, or behind bars. José Medina powerfully connects this with the previous way of not being known when he writes, "[a]lthough people of color are rendered invisible in a racist white world that ignores them and proceeds as if they didn't exist, they are at the same time rendered *hypervisible* as imagined

[27] See, for instance, Smiley and Fakunle (2016).

[28] As I will argue in the next chapter, while being epistemically wronged often involves inaccurate beliefs, it need not, as we see in cases of what I call "misknowing."

social threats and criminals" (forthcoming, p. 3).[29] The criminalization of Black Americans, both in representation and in over-policing and over-incarcerating, is thus not only a political and moral wrong, but also an epistemic one.

A third sense of not being known is powerfully captured in Audre Lorde's discussion of the struggle that Black women face in public narratives: "It's not that we haven't always been here, since there was a here. It is that the letters of our names have been scrambled when they were not totally erased, and our fingerprints upon the handles of history have been called the random brushing of birds" (Lorde 1990, p. xi). Lorde is here drawing our attention to a way in which Black women fail to be known, not through erasure or demonization, but through *systematic distortion*.[30] Black women's experiences are often misunderstood, their identities are misrepresented, and their contributions are misattributed. In her *Sister Citizen: Shame, Stereotypes, and Black Women in America* (2011), for instance, Melissa Harris-Perry discusses "Jezebel's sexual lasciviousness," "Mammy's devotion," and "Sapphire's outspoken anger," as persistent stereotypes of Black women in the United States. In a similar spirit, Patricia Hill Collins identifies a number of "controlling images" that socially dominate perceptions of Black women in America, including "mammies, matriarchs, welfare mothers, mules, or sexually denigrated women" (2000, p. 99). While these stereotypes and images are not all vilifying or demonizing, and so do not straightforwardly fall under the previous epistemic wrong, they reduce the rich and complex lives of Black women to one-dimensional distortions. Even if there is nothing negative about being a "matriarch," for instance, to regard all Black women as matriarchs not only conceals the diversity within this group, it also obscures the uniqueness of those Black women who are matriarchs.[31]

[29] That Black Americans are invisible in some contexts and "hyper visible" in others is widely noted across different disciplines. In discussing healthcare, for instance, Gilbert et al. write, "paradoxically . . . black men are hypervisible . . . in the criminal justice system, and they increasingly have fatal encounters with police officers . . . while remaining invisible in research and policies at improving their health" (2016, p. 300).

[30] Developing Lorde's work, Kristie Dotson and Marita Gilbert say that one of the ways in which "Black women have had problems maintaining a public presence in common narratives and narratives for common consumption within the US" is through "obfuscation" (2014, pp. 873–874), which seems to be similar to systematic distortion. Dotson and Gilbert also discuss "erasure" and "blatant indifference," both of which are versions of the phenomenon of invisibility as outlined above.

[31] There are various phenomena that would fall under systematic distortion. For instance, unwarranted and systematic infantilization of a person or persons would be subsumed within this category, as would what I call "misknowing" that is fueled by the "flat stories" told about certain groups and individuals, which I develop in Chapter 2.

Of course, there is a sense in which every single one of us is distorted in the eyes of someone or other. A one-off interaction at a grocery store, for instance, can lead a cashier to falsely believe that you are a rude or impatient person when in fact you are simply having a very bad day. But clearly this is a far cry from the way in which Black women are treated in just about every corner of their lives. This is why I emphasize "systematic" in the discussion of distortion. It is not that a one-off distortion cannot inflict an epistemic wrong on another person; rather, it is that the depth and widespread occurrence of systematic distortion prevents those who are victimized from being properly recognized as members of the epistemic community.

To appreciate at a deeper level how not being known in one of these three ways wrongs a person epistemically, let's return to some of the earlier thoughts. Recall Cooley's claim that how we think we are seen by others shapes who we in fact are. Even if we don't accept this "looking-glass self" theory in its entirety, regarding ourselves as invisible, demonized, or systematically distorted by other members of our community will very likely have a metaphysical impact on who we in fact become. If, for instance, I think that those in my community regard me as worthless, I may embrace it or overcompensate for it. Cooley's view is a sociological one about the way our identifies are in fact formed, but Hilde Lindemann (2016) argues that there are powerful moral connections between narratives that others have about us and our own identities. She writes:

> We are initiated into personhood through interactions with other persons, and we simultaneously develop and maintain personal identities through interactions with others who hold us in our identities. This holding can be done well or badly. Done well, it supports an individual in the creation and maintenance of a personal identity that allows her to flourish personally and in her interactions with others. Done badly, we hold people in invidious, destructive narratives. Some such narratives identify the social group to which someone belongs as socially and morally inferior, and in that way the stories uphold abusive power relations between "us" and "them." (2016, p. x)[32]

[32] Mills (1997) arrives at a similar conclusion, but focuses on how the "racing" and "norming" of people are connected to the "racing" and "norming" of spaces: "You are what you are in part because you originate from a certain kind of space, and that space has those properties in part because it is inhabited by creatures like yourself" (Mills 1997, p. 42).

Lindemann's notion of *holding* is instructive here: when we hold others well—in accurate and healthy narratives—we allow the development of their personal identities and the formation of flourishing relationships. When we hold others badly—in inaccurate and harmful narratives—we stunt the creation of their personal identities and either prevent positive relationships or promote violating and abusive ones. Given this, we are normatively called upon to not only avoid having destructive narratives about others, but also to have healthy ones. Indeed, on Cooley's and Lindemann's views, failure to do so can literally create a reality that reflects the invisible, vilifying and demonizing, or systematically distorting narratives we have about others, as the identities of victims will be shaped by our beliefs about them.[33]

We have seen that in addition to victims of gross violations and injustices having the right to know, the report provided by the UN should be expanded to include the right to be known. We have also seen that there are at least three ways in which a victim may fail to be known that epistemically wrongs: invisibility, vilification or demonization, and systematic distortion. I will now connect these two claims within the framework of what I call *epistemic reparations*, arguing that victims of gross violations and injustices that result in epistemic wrongs of invisibility, vilification or demonization, or systematic distortion have the right to be known as an act of epistemic reparations.

## 3. Epistemic Reparations

According to Margaret Urban Walker, "reparations are intentionally reparative actions in the form of goods . . . given to those wronged by parties who acknowledge responsibility for wrongs and whose reparative actions are intended to redress those wrongs" (2010, p. 529). It is standard to divide reparations into those that offer a benefit to *individuals* and to those that offer a benefit to *collectives or communities* who have been wronged. In addition, reparations are usually understood as being either *material* or *symbolic*, involving, for instance, monetary payments, health and social

[33] Carter Godwin Woodson draws a connection from how we think we are seen by others, to how we see ourselves, to how we act. As he writes in *The Mis-Education of the Negro*: "When you determine what a man shall think you do not have to concern yourself about what he will do. If you make a man feel that he is inferior, you do not have to compel him to accept an inferior status, for he will seek it himself. If you make a man think that he is justly an outcast, you do not have to order him to the back door. He will go without being told; and if there is no back door, his very nature will demand one" (Woodson 1933, pp. 84–85).

services, and restitution of property, on the one hand, and public apologies and memorials, on the other.[34] Thus, reparations involve actions made to acknowledge and redress wrongs to individuals or collectives in the form of material or symbolic goods. Martha Minow invokes the ideal of "restorative justice" to understand reparations: the goal of reparations is to repair injustice, or to "make up for" it, and to implement future changes to correct the injustice.[35]

The traditional picture understands the aims of reparations as falling into three general categories:[36] legal/political, psychosocial, and moral. Legal and political aims include making victims whole;[37] "measures that seek to reestablish the victim's status quo ante," such as the restoration of citizenship and liberty, the reinstatement of job and benefits, and the restitution of property (de Greiff 2006, p. 452); ensuring public status and recognition;[38] and "the formation or the restoration of trust among citizens" (de Greiff 2006, p. 461). Psychosocial goals include relieving suffering, distress, anger, powerlessness, and the sense of violation experienced by victims and their family members. In the context of discussing Native American reparations, for instance, Rebecca Tsosie writes:

> There is . . . an intangible, psychological component [to reparations]. At a minimum, it is important to emphasize the humanity of victim and offender, to repair social connections and instill a sense of peace rather than ongoing conflict. There is an emphasis on healing. For example, victims need to move beyond a sense of powerlessness. (2007, p. 51)[39]

Finally, moral factors include recognizing and restoring the dignity of victims and reaffirming or reestablishing the moral order of a community. As Debra Satz notes:

[34] See, for instance, Tsosie (2007). Walker (2010) challenges this distinction, arguing that all reparations, including material ones, are symbolic and have an expressive dimension of, for instance, acknowledgment. While I agree with Walker, my central aims in what follows do not depend on settling whether to accept or reject this traditional way of carving up the reparations landscape.

[35] See Minow (1998). Similarly, Walker argues on behalf of restorative justice as "a framing ideal for reparative practice where there is a need to *establish* a governing understanding of 'right relationship' and to approach its realization, rather than to intervene episodically to correct deviations from an existing standard" (2006, p. 379). I will discuss the connection between a restorative justice framework and reparations in more detail in Chapter 3.

[36] See Walker (2010).

[37] See Walker (2010, p. 531).

[38] Walker (2010, p. 531).

[39] See also Herman (1992).

> Consider the example of reparations paid to victims of the Holocaust and their descendants. Jews who were sent to concentration camps were robbed of many goods, but this is hardly the worst of the injustices they suffered. The outright denial of their most basic human rights, the fact that they were treated worse than animals, the cruelty and humiliation they suffered, the rapes, beatings, and forced labor—these were more serious than the theft of material goods. (2012, p. 144)

While many discussions of reparations focus on material goods, Satz is here highlighting the importance of the moral domain in which measures need to be taken to recognize not only the dignity and moral worth of victims, but also their standing and role as members of the moral community.

Despite this crucial addition of the moral, however, there is another normative dimension missing from all discussions of reparations: the *epistemic*. We are members of an epistemic community in addition to a legal/political and moral community. We are not just agents in a political and moral sense, but also an epistemic one. We have epistemic duties distinct from our legal and moral obligations. We can be wronged not only legally/politically, psychologically, and morally, but also epistemically.[40]

While talk of reparations that are distinctively epistemic did not occur before my (Lackey 2021a),[41] it is important to first recognize that traditional reparations often involve distinctively epistemic goods without identifying them as such. For instance, between 1972 and 1991, over 120 people, predominantly Black, were tortured under the command of notorious Chicago Police Department Commander Jon Burge.[42] In May of 2015, Chicago became the first city in the United States to provide reparations for racially motivated police violence when the Chicago City Council unanimously passed the Reparations Ordinance. While the ordinance includes material reparations, such as free tuition at the City Colleges of Chicago, specialized psychological, family, substance abuse, and other counseling services, and job placement in programs offered by the City, it also crucially involves distinctively epistemic reparations.[43] In

[40] Even more expansive conceptions of reparations, such as Tsosie's—which includes the "emotional and spiritual, political and social" (2007, p. 43)—do not include the epistemic.

[41] While the first instance of the term "epistemic reparations" can be found in Lackey (2021a), it is developed in greater detail in Lackey (2022). There are related, but importantly different, epistemic concepts in the literature, which I will discuss in Chapter 5.

[42] Chicago Torture Justice Center, "History of Chicago's Reparations Movement."

[43] Chicago Torture Justice Memorials, "The Reparations Ordinance."

particular, the ordinance includes a formal apology from the Mayor and City Council of Chicago for the torture inflicted on victims; a permanent public memorial acknowledging the torture; and inclusion of a lesson on the Burge torture cases in the Chicago Public Schools 8th and 10th grade U.S. History curriculum.[44]

These are specific instances of three general categories of reparations that have crucial epistemic dimensions: (1) public apologies, (2) memorialization, and (3) education, all of which are clearly connected to the right to know. Communities and future generations have a right to know about gross violations and injustices inflicted upon them and their community members, especially those perpetrated by the State, and (1)–(3) aim to achieve these ends. Public apologies, for instance, have straightforward moral features, including restoring the dignity of victims, promoting healing, repairing relationships, and cultivating reconciliation.[45] But apologies also have equally vital and yet less recognized epistemic dimensions. In his influential work on apologies, Aaron Lazare identifies "acknowledging the offense" as the "most important part of any apology," which, in turn, requires "an explanation" of what happened and why it happened (2008, p. 256). It is crucial that victims understand, say, who was involved in the harm they suffered, whether it was intentional or accidental, whether its impact is fully appreciated, and so on. This is why a vague "I apologize" is often ineffective or even potentially harmful, with Lazare himself classifying this as only a "seeming acknowledgment" (2008, p. 258) rather than an actual one. Successful apologies have substantive content. Consider, for instance, part of Prime Minister Justin Trudeau's 2017 apology on behalf of the Government of Canada to former students and family members of the Residential Schools of Newfoundland and Labrador:

> To all of you—we are sorry.
>
> Children who returned from traumatic experiences in these schools turned to their families and communities for support only to find that their practices, cultures, and traditions had, in their absence, been eroded by colonialism.

[44] Chicago Torture Justice Center, "History of Chicago's Reparations Movement."

[45] According to Martin P. Golding (1984), for instance, the purpose of an apology is to make moral amends where the wrongdoer expresses other-oriented moral regret and appeals for forgiveness.

> For far too many students, profound cultural loss led to poverty, family violence, substance abuse, and community breakdown. It led to mental and physical health issues that have impeded their happiness and that of their family.
>
> Far too many continue to face adversity today as a result of time spent in residential schools and for that we are sorry.
>
> We are sorry for the misguided belief that Indigenous children could only be properly provided for, cared for, or educated if they were separated from the influence of their families, traditions, and cultures.
>
> We are sorry for a time when Indigenous cultures were undervalued—when Indigenous languages, spiritual beliefs, and ways of life were falsely deemed to be inferior. (2017)

Trudeau's public apology clearly includes acknowledgements that are substantive and explanatory. He names the "Government of Canada" as the perpetrator of the wrongdoing, identifies the false beliefs and misguided values of colonialism as the driving forces of the Residential Schools, and recounts in detail some of the specific harms suffered by the victims. It is crucial that we appreciate the distinctively epistemic dimension of these sorts of reparations. Victims and their communities need to be made whole, not just materially, legally/politically, psychologically, and morally, but epistemically as well. They need the wrongs to be acknowledged, they need to be told the truth, they need to know what happened, and they need to have an accurate history documented and remembered, not only for themselves, but for future generations. Indeed, in many cases, other kinds of reparations are dependent on the epistemic ones. Legal reparations cannot be pursued, for instance, without the relevant parties knowing the relevant facts; victims might not be able to psychologically heal without knowing the truth, and so on.

As we have seen, however, there is a prior, and just as important, epistemic reparation that has been far less frequently acknowledged explicitly—the right to be known. Before we can properly acknowledge and apologize, memorialize, and educate, we need to listen and bear witness. We need to know victims, not as merely a means to the ends of fulfilling the right of others to know, but as an end itself. In the same apology, Trudeau himself gestures in this direction when highlighting then Prime Minister Stephen Harper's omission of members of the Residential Schools of Newfoundland and Labrador in his 2008 public apology:

> For too long, Canada has let you carry this burden alone.
>
> In 2008, the Government of Canada issued an official apology to the former students of Indian Residential Schools, but they failed to tell your story.
>
> We know that the delay has caused you greater pain and suffering. The absence of an apology recognizing your experiences has been an impediment to healing and reconciliation.
>
> After years of feeling the sting of exclusion in residential schools, after decades of feeling like you were left behind, I can only imagine the devastation you must have felt in that moment of omission.
>
> I hope that you will continue to tell your stories—in your own way and in your own words—as this healing and commemoration process unfolds. (Trudeau 2017)

While the exclusion of the Residential Schools of Newfoundland and Labrador may have involved the omission of some relevant information to which victims have a right, what Trudeau focuses on here is what I have been calling the right to be known: to have the stories of victims be told, to have their experiences recognized, to not force them to carry the burden of the harms they suffered alone, to ensure that they are not left behind. In his work specifically on postconflict societies, Joram Tarusarira argues that what is needed is a "transformative apology" that "demonstrates an appreciation of the epistemic foundations and conditions that form the bedrock of and facilitate the wrongdoing" (2019, p. 213), including "foreground[ing] rupturing the discourses, narratives, ideas and ideologies in the perpetrator that led to or permitted the wrongdoing" (2019, p. 216). To this end, a transformative apology places "victims' voices and experiences at the centre," encouraging them "to tell their stories" without "burdening them" (2019, p. 222). In this way, Tarusarira highlights not only the distinctively epistemic dimension of a successful apology, especially in postconflict societies, but also how it must involve both the right to know and the right to be known, for it is only through listening to and learning from victims themselves that the narratives forming the epistemic foundation of the wrongdoing in question can really be acknowledged and disrupted.[46]

The expanded framework from the UN that includes both the right to know and the right to be known can thus provide the foundation for an account of epistemic reparations, which can be understood as follows:

> Epistemic Reparations: Intentionally reparative actions or processes that aim to restore, coproduce, or create epistemic goods for those who have been epistemically wronged by parties who acknowledge these wrongs and whose reparative actions are intended to redress them.

While much of this book is aimed at clarifying and deepening our understanding of epistemically reparative work, especially in the sense of satisfying the right to be known, there are some central points to highlight about this account at the outset.

Let's begin with dimensions along which it differs from Walker's general account of reparations. First, I focus on both "actions and processes" so as to make clear that just as the epistemic wrongs in question are often ongoing, so, too, are the corresponding epistemic reparations. In this way, although the account accepts that actions can be epistemically reparative in their own right, it also accommodates the fact that they will frequently function as steps in ongoing processes. Second, I replace "given" with "restore, co-produce, or create" to emphasize that reparations are not provided to victims from perpetrators as unidirectional "gifts." Rather, they can involve returning epistemic goods to those from whom they were stolen, co-producing such goods through direct agential engagement with victims, or developing entirely new goods. Third, Walker focuses on parties acknowledging *responsibility* for the wrongs in question, whereas the account here involves parties merely acknowledging the wrongs in question. This distinction is crucial, as epistemic reparations can and should be undertaken by perpetrators and non-perpetrators alike. Of course, the nature of the duty will differ for the two groups,[47] but the crucial point is that engaging in epistemically reparative

[46] I will discuss the role that narratives about others play in the perpetration of gross violations and injustices in detail in Chapter 2.

[47] I develop this point in Chapter 5 where I argue that perpetrators have perfect epistemic duties to engage in epistemic reparations while non-perpetrators have imperfect epistemic duties to do so.

work can and should be undertaken by all of us, even if we are not directly involved in the perpetration of the epistemic wrong in question.

Since the focus here is on developing an account of epistemic reparations, the goods in question are specifically epistemic in nature. At the same time, I am understanding "epistemic goods" very broadly, and so this account captures both the right to know and the right to be known possessed by survivors of gross violations and injustices. Knowledge is, of course, an epistemic good, and thus when someone has the right to know or the right to be known, epistemic goods—both for oneself and for others[48]—are at issue. More precisely, the satisfaction of both rights involves providing the conditions for the creation and conveying of knowledge and related epistemic goods, such as truth, evidence, justified belief, understanding, wisdom, and so on. Fulfilling a survivor's right to know whether the State was involved in the assassination of her husband, for instance, may involve providing her with crucial pieces of evidence that impart a deeper understanding of the events leading up to his murder. But how, it might be asked, does fulfilling a survivor's right to be known provide epistemic goods *to him*? In particular, repairing the three epistemic wrongs identified earlier seems most likely to generate knowledge or understanding *in others* rather than in the victim. So, for instance, rendering a person visible when he has been wrongly made invisible through a gross violation or injustice, or supporting the creation and sharing of a more accurate and fuller narrative about a person who has been vilified or distorted, promotes the creation and sharing of knowledge *about* the survivor rather than *within* him. In what sense, then, is this epistemically reparative for the survivor, who is owed the epistemic reparations?

There are at least three responses here, each of which will be developed in more detail throughout this book. First, sharing our stories can generate knowledge not only in our listeners, but also in ourselves.[49] More precisely, talking our narratives through can help us make sense out of our own lives, which can, in turn, be directly impacted by the responses of our listeners. An event that was confusing may become clearer as you try to share it with others, and respectful or compassionate responses from listeners may help you no longer see yourself as being responsible or blameworthy for a violation you experienced. So, empowering a survivor to be able to tell the true

[48] In Chapter 5, I argue directly that epistemic duties go beyond duties regarding one's own beliefs and extend to the epistemic lives of others.
[49] See Chapter 3.

account of events in his life can lead to the generation of even traditional epistemic goods, such as knowledge, in the survivor himself.

To be sure, not every case of epistemic reparations will be generative in this sense. A person who is wrongfully convicted of murder may learn nothing new by sharing his story with his friends. But there are epistemic goods that go beyond the traditionally recognized ones, which brings us to the second way that being known can be epistemically reparative: repairing the epistemic wrongs identified above is fundamentally interpersonal and crucially involves relations between the survivor and others. To be made invisible in one's community, or to be falsely regarded as a murderer, negatively impacts one's relations, sometimes in life-destroying ways. Relations may be damaged, forced, broken, circumvented, erased, or never even formed in the first place. To be wrongfully incarcerated, for instance, is to be literally separated from one's family, friends, and community, but also to have one's name, standing, and connections destroyed or severed. This is why the heart of restorative justice, which is often regarded as an illuminating framework for understanding reparations, lies in relations.[50] As Robert Yazzie, Chief Justice Emeritus of the Navajo Nation, writes, "'restorative justice' . . . puts people in good relations with each other, and in continuing relationships. . . . There is a Navajo maxim which describes the healing and the restoration of good relations. It is *hozho nahasdlii*. It means something like, 'now that we have done these things we are again in good relations'"[51] (1996, pp. 120 and 124).[52] Crucially, however, relations do not involve only moral or legal ones. Epistemic relations of acknowledgment, respect, trust, credibility, authority, advising, and related notions also matter for justice. Indeed, in some cases, other forms of repairing relations depend upon addressing the damaged epistemic ones. If a victim isn't even acknowledged as a person, or as a member of a community, or as having a particular kind of standing, or as being a voice that should be listened to, it will be difficult if not impossible to restore his

[50] See Minow (1998), Walker (2006), and Almassi (2020).

[51] While Yazzie speaks about "again" being in good relations, many cases where restorative justice is practiced do not involve prior "good relations." Because of this, we can follow Walker, who proposes "that we understand 'restoration' in all contexts as normative: 'restoration' refers to repairs that move relationships in the direction of *becoming morally adequate*, without assuming a morally adequate status quo ante" (2006, p. 384). When we are talking about epistemic relations in particular, we can adapt Walker's proposal and understand "restoration" as involving repairs that move relationships in the direction of *becoming epistemically adequate*, without assuming an epistemically adequate status quo ante.

[52] In a similar spirit, Walker writes, "In restorative justice, what demands repair is a state of relationship between the victim and the wrongdoer, and among each and his or her community, that has been distorted, damaged, or destroyed" (2006, p. 383).

relations among other normative dimensions. Fulfilling a survivor's right to be known, then, is to take steps to ensure that he is able to stand in *right epistemic relations*[53] within his communities,[54] which is a powerful epistemic good—perhaps even more powerful in many cases than the creation or transmission of particular instances of knowledge.

The third way that being known can be epistemically reparative is by promoting the cultivation, restoration, or repair of a survivor's *epistemic agency*.[55] Invisibility can deny epistemic agency to survivors by failing to even recognize them as storytellers; vilification can erase it by extracting or creating stories for victims; and systematic distortion can damage it by exploiting, coopting, or distorting their narratives.[56] Fulfilling a survivor's right to be known centrally involves recognizing and centering his epistemic agency from the beginning—including whether he tells his story, what is told, to whom it is told, how it is told, where it is told, and so on—to the end—who has access to his story, how it is shared, how it can be updated, and so on. To be clear, epistemic reparations will always be a matter of degree, and so promoting the conditions necessary for victims to exercise their epistemic agency can be done with more or less success. But at a minimum, a survivor is not known in an epistemically reparative sense if his epistemic agency hasn't been cultivated or restored in some sense.

It is also important to emphasize that the right to be known as it is being understood here is not a right that is possessed by everyone. Rather, it is a right that is triggered by gross violations and injustices. Compare it with the UN's right to know. Not everyone has the right to know, for instance, who murdered Laurencia Mukalemera's husband during the Rwandan genocide and where his body is buried. This is a right that Mukalemera has because of the gross violation she suffered. Similarly, not everyone has the right to be known in the sense at issue for epistemic reparations. Instead, this is a right that victims or survivors have in virtue of gross injustices they experienced.

Finally, it should be noted that the acknowledgement of wrongs and intention to redress them can be done implicitly—there is, that is, no need

[53] For an insightful discussion of epistemic relations, see Boult (2024).

[54] I am using "communities" very loosely here. It may pick out a local, national, international, or even global community.

[55] I provide a discussion of how to understand epistemic agency in the Introduction. See Reed (2001) for the first use and development of this concept.

[56] I discuss these sorts of effects on epistemic agency in detail in Lackey (2023).

for them to be done publicly or explicitly. At the same time, in order for the actions or processes to be epistemically reparative, they have to be connected to the violations and injustices in question. To see this, consider the difference between, on the one hand, someone listening to an album created by a wrongfully incarcerated person on death row entirely because she likes jazz with, on the other hand, her listening to it is because of the story being told through the music about the gross injustices in question. While neither might involve an explicit acknowledgment of the wrong or intention to redress it, the latter is an act of epistemic reparations while the former is not. This is because happening to hear a survivor's story while pursuing a wholly different end is not, by itself, epistemically reparative. Of course, the listener might shift during the process from merely taking in jazz to bearing witness to a survivor, in which case epistemic reparations can emerge. But what is crucial is that there is at least a tacit acknowledgment of the gross violation and injustice at issue and an intention to redress it through the action or process in question.

It is instructive that many TRCs specifically acknowledge something very much like the right to be known, in addition to the right to know, even if it isn't presented in these terms. We saw this above with the goals of the TRC of Canada, which legal scholar Jennifer Llewellyn understands through a restorative justice framework, noting that the "commission is . . . clearly charged with *seeking the truth* about residential schools. They are then tasked with *ensuring this truth is widely known* and understood" (2008, p. 186, emphasis added). Crucially, however, "seeking the truth" requires that the Commission "create spaces in which Survivors, their families, and communities can come together to *share their stories*, relate the harms they have suffered, and think about what is required to heal these harms and to create new relationships in the future" (2008, p. 185, emphasis added). Llewellyn writes:

> The commission's mandate is focused largely upon the work of finding truth . . . . Restorative justice places significant weight on truth-telling as a necessary step towards restored relationships . . . . The process is predicated upon parties telling their truths about the nature and extent of the harms they have suffered, their needs with respect to redress and recovery, their role and responsibilities for what occurred, and their capacity to assist in repairing the harms and restore relationships. *It is also through the sharing of their truths that parties come to know and understand one another's*

> *experiences, perspectives, and needs.* Such understanding is crucial to reconciliation. (2008, p. 191, emphasis added)

The charge of the TRC of Canada, then, is both to create spaces in which survivors, their families, and communities can share their truths and come to be known, and to ensure that these truths are then made known to others. Viewed through the restorative justice lens that Llewellyn provides, this cannot be done without bearing witness to the experiences, perspectives, and needs of those most impacted by the wrongdoing in question.

Similarly, the South African TRC recognized "factual and forensic truth," which involves "bringing to light factual, corroborated evidence" (1998, p. 111) and preparing a comprehensive report that covered two essential areas: first, the Commission was "required to make findings on particular incidents and in respect of specific people. In other words, what happened to whom, where, when and how, and who was involved?" (1998, p. 111). Second, the Commission was charged with making "findings on the contexts, causes and patterns of violations. In this respect, the Commission was required to report on the broader patterns underlying gross violations of human rights and to explore the causes of such violations" (1998, p. 111). These mandates of the Commission clearly focus on the right to know that South Africans have of apartheid-related gross violations and injustices.

Importantly, however, the Commission also recognizes "personal and narrative truth," "social truth," and "healing and restorative truth." Personal and narrative truth involves victims and perpetrators telling their stories so as to give "meaning to the multi-layered experiences of the South African story" (1998, p. 112). This facilitates reconciliation "by ensuring that the truth about the past included the validation of the individual subjective experiences of people who had previously been silenced or voiceless" (1998, p. 112). "Social truth," which is "the truth of experience that is established through interaction, discussion and debate," (1998, p. 113) concerns the way in which truth is to be found. According to the South African TRC, "the process whereby the truth was reached was itself important because it was through this process that the essential norms of social relations between people were reflected" (1998, p. 114). Finally, "healing truth" is "the kind of truth that places facts and what they mean within the context of human relationships, both amongst citizens and between the state and citizens" (1998, p. 114). All three of these truths center the importance of the right to be known—victims have the right to tell their stories through interaction and discussion and to have their experiences be placed within the broader context of relationships, including with the State.

Of course, one might bear witness to another person's experiences for all sorts of reasons—because he is your friend, because you are a generous community member, because someone asked you to, because it promotes various kinds of goods, and so on. But I am here focusing on bearing witness as a step toward *redressing an epistemic wrong that arose from or constitutes a gross violation and injustice*. This is one of the crucial ways in which epistemic reparations are different from, say, epistemic benevolence. One might listen to the stories of others as an act of kindness in which one aims to promote epistemic goods in one's community. However, in order for the act of bearing witness to be epistemically reparative, there needs to be a backward- or present-looking epistemic wrong that is being acknowledged and addressed. Importantly, this is not to say that repairing past wrongs cannot *also* have a future-oriented dimension. As Naomi Roht-Arriaza says, "[r]eparations serve multiple functions. They are both backward- and forward-looking. They aim to recompense for loss and to restore the good name of those defamed, but also to reintegrate the marginalized and isolated into society so that they can contribute to the future rebuilding of the [society]" (2004, p. 122).[57] The forward-looking function highlighted here is still connected to the past in that the aim is to *reintegrate* survivors into society to address their past marginalization and isolation, which is distinct from bearing witness to another person's violation entirely to promote epistemic goods independently of backward- or present-looking wrongs.

It is also important to recognize a feature of the epistemic reparations framework developed here that may be missed: the right to be forgotten or to be "unknown."[58] While it is not uncommon to hear the command to "never forget" gross violations and injustices that have been perpetrated against other people, some victims do not want to be known. After suffering trauma and exploitation, for instance, some people might want to move on with

[57] This is to be distinguished from Olúfẹ́mi O. Táíwò's "constructive view" of reparations, which does not have a backward-looking aim at all that focuses on harm and relationship repair. In his *Reconsidering Reparations*, for instance, he writes, "[t]he moral impetus for the project is the past and present treatment of enslaved people and their descendants. But the target of the project—the difference it wants to make in the world produced by those moral crimes—is neither a project of reconciliation nor redemption. It is a forward-looking target, a future goal to remake the world map, in this case by adding a self-determining country" (2022, p. 72).

[58] I discuss the right to be forgotten in more detail in Chapter 2.

their lives and not be the focus of any attention at all. A survivor of sexual assault, for instance, might want the anonymity provided by moving forward as "Jane Doe" in the media and in the legal system. To have her identity be made public without her consent, or to have others bear witness to her suffering, might be revictimizing. But notice that on the framework developed here, being known is a right and, as with other rights, it can be waived. I have the right to bodily autonomy and others have the duty to respect this, but I can waive this right when, for instance, I consent to get my hair cut. When I waive this right, I release my stylist from the corresponding duty to not touch me. Similarly, while victims of gross violations and injustices who have been epistemically wronged in the relevant ways have the right to be known, they can waive this right when, for instance, they prefer privacy or anonymity. In such cases, others are released from the corresponding duty to know the victims. This is crucial, as while some victims seek privacy and do not want to be known, many others do. For instance, after five years of being known as "Jane Doe 1," one of the victims of Harvey Weinstein, Evgeniya Chernyshova, revealed her identity in 2023, saying, "I'm tired of hiding. I want my life back. I'm Evgeniya, I've been raped. This is my story" (Keegan 2023). The rights framework developed here provides space for respecting the desires of Chernyshova both as Jane Doe 1 and under her own name as Evgeniya Chernyshova, which is exactly as it ought to be. To be sure, rights are not always respected, and there are countless cases where victims have been further violated by unwanted publicity. But this is a problem with people failing to respect the rights of others rather than with anything inherent to the view developed here.

While the opening pages of this chapter involve passages that include expressions of the *desire* to be known, such as by Sikwepere and Kossola, what we see is that survivors of gross violations and injustices in fact have the *right* to be known. This is important, as it is crucial to appreciate the true normative force at work here both in terms of what victims are owed and what others must do by way of response.[59] At the same time, the fact that survivors express these as desires is not without significance for at least two reasons. First, as was discussed above, the right to be known can be waived, just as other rights can be, and so the expression of the relevant desire can be helpful in determining whether a survivor would like to exercise his right to be known. Second, in order for fulfilling the right to be known to be an

[59] I discuss the duties there are to know survivors extensively in Chapter 5.

act of epistemic reparation, it has to be epistemically reparative for the survivor himself. Like Sikwepere, who described being able to tell his story to the South African TRC as feeling like he "got his sight back," Kathleen Horne, who is a Residential School survivor and a member of the Tsawout First Nation, says that after she talked about her experience for the first time at a 2013 TRC hearing, she "felt like it was gone, it was lifted off of me and I didn't carry that around with me anymore . . . . I'm not scared anymore of telling people what happened" (Romphf 2021). Rose Grace Miller, who is a survivor of the Kamloops IRS, notes that she chose to come forward about the abuse and trauma she suffered because she wants "non-Indigenous people to know . . . how painful it was and how the colonization hurt us so badly" and how it is "still hurting us with the racism" (CBS News 2021). All three survivors make vivid some of the epistemically reparative work of the storytelling. Both Sikwepere and Horne communicate the impact of being known on their sense of themselves, using language that is suggestive of having their epistemic agency partially restored—such as being able to see again and of no longer being afraid to share what happened to them. Miller emphasizes the connection between being known and her relations with others—such as non-Indigenous people knowing the depth of the violations and pain that she and other Residential School survivors experienced, as well as how they continue to suffer these injustices through racism. These cases are to be distinguished from those in which a victim shares his story entirely out of duty or regard for the needs of others. Elder Clifford Quah, who is a survivor of the Lejac Indian Residential School and is from the Sts'ailes First Nation, notes that "non-Indigenous people . . . must know they must learn more about the schools" and that he is sharing his story of emotional, physical, mental, and sexual abuse to "educate the public about what happened in residential schools" (CBS News 2021). In a similar spirit, Miller emphasizes that she wants "the history to be known" (CBS News 2021) of what happened to Indigenous people in Canada. While this educative component is only part of the motivation for Quah and Miller sharing their stories, it is helpful for clarifying instances of being known that are not epistemically reparative in the sense at issue in this book. Suppose that Quah and Miller are focusing entirely on the epistemic needs of others in choosing to come forward. Perhaps they even find talking publicly about such horrific violations to be further violating but nonetheless do so out of a deep sense of duty or regard for others, especially for future generations. In such a case, their storytelling may be fulfilling the rights that others have to know what happened—such as their own descendants—or may be generous acts of epistemic benevolence, but their being known would not be acts of epistemic reparations *for them*. Connecting this back with the earlier point, a survivor expressing his desire to be known can be helpful for determining whether coming to know him is an act of reparation for him, for others, or for no one at all.

Of course, this is not to say that a survivor expressing a desire to be known is necessary in order for others to properly undertake epistemic reparations. Sometimes, as is the case with those who are deceased, it would be very difficult if not impossible to access this information. Rather, it is to say that what survivors want not only can serve as a useful guide to whether they would like to waive or exercise their right to be known but also can shed light on the broad and complex range of motivations for engaging in the sharing of stories.

To sum up: victims of gross violations and injustices that result in epistemic wrongs of invisibility, vilification or demonization, or systematic distortion have the right to be known as an act of epistemic reparations. Indeed, as we see with Sikwepere and Fogle, survivors themselves are often clear about this epistemic wrong needing to be redressed. When people are the subject of false or distorted narratives, for instance, we often hear them say that they want to "set the record straight," or "get their story out there," or have others "know what really happened." Even when there are no monetary, legal, or social consequences, the call to be known often lingers. Thus, just as we need to take political, legal, and moral measures that seek to reestablish the status of victims, so, too, do we need to take epistemic ones—we need to listen to victims, we need to know them, we need to "say their names."

## 4. Epistemic Reparations: Absences and Deficiencies

In order to develop the kind of epistemic reparations called for within this framework further, it will be helpful to explore some of the different ways in which the epistemically reparative work that is normatively required in a given context may be lacking.

First, there may be the complete *absence* of the requisite kind of epistemic reparations. Consider, for instance, the case of 43-year-old Andrew Royer, who has an intellectual disability and no prior criminal record and was convicted in 2004 of a 2002 murder of a 94-year-old woman in Elkhart, IN.[60]

[60] Lazzaro (2021).

According to the director of the Exoneration Justice Clinic at the University of Notre Dame, Jimmy Gurulé, Royer's case wasn't one "of some inadvertent error, some eyewitness mistakenly identifying the defendant.... Andy's conviction was the result of a coerced, involuntary, illegal confession—make no mistake about it" (Lazzaro 2021). Moreover, following a 2019 evidentiary hearing regarding Royer's case, Kosciusko County Judge Joe Sutton found that "the state withheld evidence including paying a witness for testimony and putting a fingerprint expert on the stand who was not an expert, but instead just a sheriff's deputy" (Lazzaro 2021). While Royer was exonerated in July of 2021, Gurulé said that the Elkhart County prosecutor's office should also "apologize and accept responsibility for the wrongful conviction" (Lazzaro 2021). When Vicki Becker, who is currently county prosecutor and was the lead prosecutor in Royer's 2004 case, was asked about this, she responded, "Certainly, no apology would be appropriate or even ethical" (Lazzaro 2021). What we see here, then, is the complete absence of epistemic reparations that are clearly normatively demanded. Regardless of Becker's prosecutorial plans moving forward, there is no doubt that the state of Indiana wronged Royer both morally and epistemically through his coerced confession and wrongful conviction[61] and that an acknowledgment of this wrongdoing and an apology are therefore called for.

This form of absence involves overt refusal, but there can also be epistemic reparations that are missing because of ignorance or indifference. There are countless cases of deep, pernicious, widespread exclusion of many different individuals and groups who have suffered gross violations and injustices. Not even recognizing an individual as a person or a group as people, or that they are missing from the conversation, or that they have been wronged, or that they are owed reparations are all cases of absent epistemic reparations.

A second way in which epistemically reparative work may be lacking is when epistemic reparations are made but they are *deficient*, which can happen in a variety of ways. One way is when the epistemically reparative work is *illegitimately blocked or constrained*. For instance, a common criticism of the TRC in South Africa—and the more general official response to apartheid-era violations—is that victims felt pressured to forgive perpetrators in the name of healing for the nation. Sisonke Msimang, for instance, writes that "forgiveness has enjoyed a special place in the story of

[61] For a detailed discussion of the distinctive epistemic wrongs inflicted on suspects and defendants who are coerced into confessing to crimes they did not commit, see Lackey (2016, 2020a, 2023).

our remarkable transition out of apartheid . . . .the capacity to pardon one's oppressors is . . . seen as part of the miracle of our country" (2016). Msimang discusses Limpho Hani—the wife of former anti-apartheid leader Chris Hani, who was assassinated in front of their teenage daughter—and her refusal to forgive Janusz Walus, the man responsible for her husband's death. When Walus was granted parole in 2016, the judge told Hani and her family that they should "move on." Msimang writes:

> Women in particular have been expected not only to forgive, but also to nurture the healing process; not to be bitter and outraged.
>
> And so, by rights, Limpho Hani should have spent the last two decades cutting ribbons and opening memorial centres in her husband's name. She should have been gracious and pleasant, or serious and reflective; but always, always, forgiving.
>
> Good apartheid victims wept, they did not rage. They cried out but they dared not swear. The ugly side of grief—vengeance and the nihilism of loss—have had no place in the vocabulary of the new South Africa. We are a nation founded on the benign principles of tolerance and forgiveness, not on the craggy rocks of fury. (2016)

Archbishop Desmond Tutu, who was the chairman of South Africa's TRC, famously said, "there is nothing that cannot be forgiven, and there is no one undeserving of forgiveness" (Tutu and Tutu 2014, p. 3).[62] Against this background, then, Hani's "public refusal to forgive, indeed her flagrant disregard for this founding promise" is seen by many as "almost heretical" in post-apartheid South Africa. But when victims of gross violations and injustices are given space to tell their stories as a form of redress, the epistemically reparative work is deficient when they are pressured to do so in a way that conforms to previously formed expectations, especially when these come from the perpetrators or oppressors themselves.[63] Not only does

[62] Despite this, Archbishop Tutu also said at a hearing of the Commission in Port Elizabeth on May 21, 1996, "[t]his Commission is said to listen to everyone. It is therefore important that everyone should be given a chance to say his or her truth as he or she sees it. . . . " (South African Truth and Reconciliation Commission, *Report*).

[63] A similar criticism is made of Rwanda's "Reconciliation Villages": "A quarter century after the 1994 genocide that killed 75% of the country's ethnic Tutsis, Rwanda has six 'reconciliation villages' like Mbyo, where genocide survivors and perpetrators live alongside each other. Convicted killers

this fail to repair the moral and epistemic damage that has been done, but it can also exacerbate existing wrongs or lead to entirely new ones. A victim who feels pressured or compelled to forgive, or to swallow her anger, may have fresh wounds from being treated unjustly twice over. As Limpho Hani said in an interview, "Janusz murdered my husband in cold blood . . . . [The judge] told me and my family to move on . . . . It's a very sad day in South Africa and I am highly irritated that this white woman can tell me how to feel" (Msimang 2016). In addition to the loss of her partner and the father of her children through an act of violence, Limpho's internal life and story are being subject to the control of those in power—she is being told how to grieve, what emotions to experience, when to show mercy, and what to share. Moreover, a victim might feel rendered further invisible when her true emotional response to the wrong perpetrated against her is ignored, distorted, or stifled. If Hani's rage at Janusz and the South African criminal legal system is dismissed as inappropriate, for instance, then not only is the full scope and nuance of the injustice she has faced neither seen nor repaired, but her story is relegated to the margins of the community twice over. This is an example of a constraint on the *content* of the story that is permitted in a space that purports to be epistemically reparative, thereby leading to the victim facing a choice to either conform to the expectations and tell a distorted story[64] or to reject the script in question and risk being silenced, ignored, or punished. This is why the epistemic agency of the survivor—its creation, cultivation, and/or restoration—lies at the heart of epistemic reparations.

Another way in which epistemic reparations can be constrained or blocked is when the *manner* of bearing witness is deficient. For instance, land

re-integrate into society by publicly apologizing for their crimes. Survivors profess forgiveness. The villages are showpieces of President Paul Kagame's policy of ethnic reconciliation, although some critics say the communities are forced and the reconciliation is artificial . . . . Sam Nshimirimana, a Rwandan genocide expert and survivor, said forgiveness would be more meaningful if it were initiated by the survivors and perpetrators themselves and not promoted by the government or charitable organizations. 'The government tells perpetrators that once they apologize to the victims, they will be released' from prison . . . 'Obviously, they apologize in order to be released. This is an artificial apology'" (Associated Press 2019a).

[64] This might involve a form of what Kristie Dotson calls "testimonial smothering," which is the "truncating of one's own testimony" so that the testimony offered "contains only content for which one's audience demonstrates testimonial competence" (2011, p. 244). However, many cases of deficient epistemic reparations through the constraining of the testimony in question involve neither a truncating of the speaker's story nor a lack of competence on the part of the audience. If, for instance, Hani conforms to the judge's demands, it is not that she will cut her story short but, rather, that she will offer an entirely different one that focuses on forgiveness rather than anger. Moreover, the judge certainly has the competence to understand Hani's rage; it is just not what she wants to hear, given the broader goals of healing for the nation.

acknowledgments can be seen as aiming, in part, at epistemic reparations. As Lambert et al. note, "[a] land acknowledgment should be a *truth-telling*, a demand for accountability, and a call to action" (2021, p. 6, emphasis added).[65] However, increasingly, land acknowledgments have been criticized as being "rote,"[66] "hollow,"[67] "performative,"[68] and instances of "moral exhibitionism."[69] They are often "read verbatim," with no deeper understanding or discussion of the history of the land and people in question, resulting in relieving "the speaker and the audience of the responsibility to think about Indigenous peoples, at least until the next public event."[70] If one of the aims of epistemic reparations is to render the one who has been wronged—whether an individual or a group—visible, and this is failing because of the manner in which land acknowledgments are being made, then the reparative work is deficient.

It is also important to recognize that the pathways toward being known in an epistemically reparative way may differ across cultures, communities, and individuals. Some may prefer to share only through oral storytelling, which would necessitate creating living spaces for talking and listening in real time.[71] Others may prefer music or painting or poetry. Again, what is crucial for the acts in question to truly be acts of epistemic reparations is to center the epistemic agency of the survivor. To engage in purportedly epistemically reparative work but only in a manner suited to the expectations of the listener is to risk not only a total failure of fulfilling the survivor's right to be known, but also the infliction of further epistemic wrongs. If, for instance, space is created for indigenous survivors of Residential Schools in Canada to share their stories, but they are kept to time limits that are foreign or constraining, or they are offered only the option of written rather than oral communication, then there will very likely be further harm rather than repair.

Two further ways in which epistemically reparative work might be illegitimately blocked or constrained is through the *space* in which epistemic reparations are undertaken and the *make-up of the decision-making*

[65] See also: "Across North America, [land] acknowledgments gained momentum after the report of the TRC of Canada in 2015, particularly in response to the commission's finding that the IRS system was cultural genocide. After that, Indigenous-settler state relations shifted in Canada, with the government beginning to systematically acknowledge the existence of First Nations people, *in an effort to right past wrongs*" (Cleaves and Sepulveda 2021, emphasis added).

[66] Cleaves and Sepulveda (2021).

[67] Kaur (2021).

[68] Kaur (2021).

[69] Wood (2021).

[70] Wood (2021).

[71] As Yazzie writes, "For the most part, Navajo traditions are oral . . . .The Navajo legal procedures is based on 'talking things out' so that everyone can have their say, and when someone is out of line, they get a 'talking to' by a *naat'aani*" (1996, pp. 121–122).

*participants*. Imagine, for instance, that an oppressed group is invited to speak about their experiences at a truth and reconciliation event, but the only public space offered to them is at an institution that has been the central cause of the wrongdoing in question rather than, say, a center in their own communities. Or suppose that the members of this group who have been wronged are offered a platform for sharing their experiences, but they are not involved in the decision-making process about how it will unfold.[72] In both cases, epistemic reparations are undertaken but are deficient due to barriers or constraints that impede their efficacy.

In addition to epistemically reparative work being *illegitimately blocked or constrained*, it can also be deficient through what Veli Mitova (2025a) calls *epistemic authority whitewashing* and *tokenizing epistemic reparations*. The former involves putative reparations that undermine the reparative project by making it seem like epistemic authority is restored while it is in fact being further eroded. For instance, Mitova discusses how the Council of Traditional Health Practitioners of South Africa was formed in part to recognize the epistemic authority of traditional healers, but because the government hasn't set up the right regulatory bodies, in practice employers end up not being required to accept medical certificates from them.[73] Thus, every time a medical certificate is denied as legitimate by an employer, the aim of the South African government to engage in epistemically reparative work not only fails but the epistemic authority of traditional healers is further eroded. Mitova's notion of *tokenizing epistemic reparations* involves reparations that putatively restore epistemic authority but in fact only tokenise the victim. As an example, Mitova discusses efforts to "decolonize" the philosophy curriculum by merely inserting African philosophy readings here and there and then regarding the work as being complete. She argues that this practice not only essentializes African philosophy by assuming that there is just one kind of philosophy in the face of complex and vastly differing African philosophy traditions, but also tokenizes particular African philosophers by making them represent African philosophical traditions in general.[74] Again, if the

[72] For instance, see Townsend and Townsend (2020) for a powerful discussion of how two participatory rights widely recognized for Indigenous communities regarding greater inclusion in decision-making processes that directly affect their land and livelihood—the right to consultation and the right to free, prior, and informed consent—are often implemented and interpreted in ways that, in fact, silence them.

[73] "In short, until such a time as the Minister of Health has promulgated the relevant regulations in order to bring traditional healer certificates in line with the requirements of the BCEA [Basic Conditions of Employment Act], employers are not obliged to accept a medical certificate from their employees that has been issued by a traditional healer" (Coetzee n.d.).

[74] This is not intended to be an exhaustive list of the ways in which epistemic reparations can be deficient.

aim is to engage in epistemically reparative work, then decolonizing efforts are deficient when African philosophy and philosophers are tokenized in this sort of way.

It is worth highlighting that among these various ways that epistemic reparations can be deficient, there are important differences. Some are deficient in being inadequate or "not enough." A sincere and substantive land acknowledgment, for instance, might be regarded as merely a "first step" toward proper recognition of Indigenous peoples, but might be criticized for being woefully insufficient for repairing the epistemic wrongs of colonialism without also centering the voices of Indigenous peoples, bearing witness to their stories, recognizing their epistemic authority, and so on. Moreover, epistemically reparative work is often clearly inadequate by itself and should be accompanied by other kinds of reparations, such as legal, political, and moral. A land acknowledgment, for example, might be regarded as hollow—even if sincere—if there is no intention to take steps to also return the land itself. *First-step deficiencies*, however, are importantly different from *wrong-causing deficiencies*. In the case of Limpho Hani, for instance, the problem is not that the epistemic reparations in question are partial or inadequate but, rather, that they are themselves epistemically wronging her. To be given space to tell the story of the violence her family suffered through her husband's assassination, but to be handed a script by a white judge for what she should say and how she should say it, is to not only ignore the original epistemic wrongs but to also inflict new ones. It is to try to render her refusal to forgive her husband's murderer invisible, to vilify or demonize her justified anger, and to hijack her epistemic agency so that she turns into a puppet of the State by telling the story that they want to hear.[75]

Much of my focus here has been on identifying various kinds of epistemic reparations, with a specific focus on the right to be known since this dimension has been entirely ignored in discussions of what victims of gross violations are owed. But I want to again emphasize that many of the examples used are instances of only *partial* epistemically reparative work. Consider, for instance, a wrongful conviction that resulted from a racially motivated coerced false confession. Sure, I may bear witness to this victim's

[75] It should be noted that contextual factors will often be relevant to determining the kind of deficiency that is at issue. Tokenizing, for instance, might be a first-step deficiency if it is only an initial attempt at the inclusion of voices that have previously been marginalized, but it might instead be a wrong-causing deficiency if it is taken to adequately represent a vastly diverse group of perspectives and people.

experiences and may even have the ability to facilitate a larger platform for him to share his story. Holistic epistemic reparations in such a case, however, would be massive and multifaceted. Perhaps it would involve epistemically reparative work not only from individuals—such as the investigator who coerced the confession, the prosecutor, the judge, and so on—but also from collectives, such as the community, the United States criminal legal system, white Americans, and so on.[76] It would certainly involve epistemically reparative work on both the side of the right to know, including access to information about racially motivated coerced false confessions in general and in his particular case, and the right to be known, including providing platforms for him to share his story so that others can bear witness to the injustices he faced. While this is true even in a case of a single wrongful conviction of this sort, the scope and scale of the required epistemic work will grow exponentially when multi-generational, collective epistemic wrongs are at issues, such as the impact and effects of colonialism.

## 5. Conclusion

Let's return to the voices of those who opened this chapter. When Sikwepere, Kossola, the victims from El Salvador, and Fogle express a desire to be known, and when those who are protesting the systemic racism of policing in America cry out to "say their names," it is crucial that we see the true normative force at work here. These are not expressions of mere personal preferences or demands to simply utter words. Rather, these are statements of powerful and legitimate epistemic claims being made by, or on behalf of, those who have suffered serious wrongs. In this chapter, I provided some first steps for understanding the nature of these claims. Those who suffer gross violations and injustices that result in invisibility, vilification or demonization, or systematic distortion have been epistemically wronged and have the epistemic right to be known. We, in turn, owe them epistemic reparations, the most fundamental of which is to know them. It is only by listening to and bearing witness—by saying their names—that we can truly begin to repair the wrongs of the past and present and lay the foundation for a more just future.

[76] For more on epistemic reparations involving groups both as victims and as wrongdoers, see Mitova (2025a).

# 2
# Stories That Wrong and Stories That Repair

Stories[1] play a powerful and pervasive role in our lives, extending far beyond fiction in particular and literature more generally.[2] History, for instance, is said to be "complex storytelling,"[3] narratives are "ubiquitous in the sciences,"[4] and telling stories is said to be the "real work" of museums.[5] But narratives of this sort do not merely reflect the world—they can shape reality in both small and large ways. Nobel Prize-winning economist Robert J. Shiller, for instance, provides an account of how stories help drive economic events, which he coins *narrative economics*—"the study of the viral spread of popular narratives that affect economic behavior."[6] This view of economics

[1] I will use "stories" and "narratives" interchangeably and will focus on only those that purport to be true.

[2] While there is a fair bit of literature on the formal structure and features of narratives, I will be relying on a pre-theoretical notion that is loose and expansive. This is not uncommon. In her account of narrative testimony, for instance, Rachel Fraser writes:

> Which formal features . . . make for a narrative? I won't provide anything like a list of necessary and sufficient conditions; rather, I consider narratives to be just those texts and utterances which have the form of a story. I take it that we have a robust pre-theoretic grip as to when that condition is satisfied. (2021, p. 4027)

Drawing on work by Amsterdam and Bruner (2000), Fraser goes on to say:

> Nonetheless, it's helpful to say a bit about what paradigmatic stories look like. Paradigmatic stories:
>
> i describe the doings of humans or human-like characters,
> ii which take place over a period of time
> iii encode a goal structure, viz., the characters have aims,
> iv recount an obstacle, viz., the characters are blocked or impeded or face some barrier to the achievement of their aims
>
> Of course, some stories will lack at least some of these features. (2021, p. 4027)

Like Fraser, I will take paradigmatic stories to have (i)–(iv), though I will not be understanding them as necessary and sufficient conditions. Moreover, I will often talk about features of stories, such as labels, pictures, and so on. The label "criminal" or a mugshot may not be a story by itself but may nonetheless be a part of a story that carries powerful information about the main characters and obstacles the characters are facing.

[3] Welsch (1998).

[4] Morgan (2022, p. 3).

[5] Bedford (2001).

[6] Shiller (2019, p. 3).

*The Right to Be Known*. Jennifer Lackey, Oxford University Press. © Oxford University Press 2026.
DOI: 10.1093/9780197833988.003.0003

can be understood as an example of the widely cited Hopi proverb, "Those who tell the stories rule the world." If someone has control of a given narrative, power in the world itself often follows. Michele Moody-Adams has recently developed this insight in relation to socially significant narratives, especially the "grand narratives" that aim to provide a unified story about a society's origin. She argues that socially significant narratives can have a powerful grip on a society, often rendering it impossible to remedy injustice without first getting a society to repudiate the narratives that legitimize the injustice. For instance, the "great replacement narrative," according to which nonwhite immigrants are systematically "replacing" white European-descended groups, has been invoked to justify hate-filled violence across the globe. Moody-Adams argues that until this narrative itself is rejected, it will continue to fuel social injustice.[7] As she says, "[t]he idea that narrative has the power to shape the world, and govern conduct, rests on a critical insight: narrative is the most important tool that we have for giving meaning to diverse actions, events, and states of affairs" (2022b).

But storytelling is critical not only for capturing the big-picture questions about history, economics, and the origin of societies. Narratives also shape us as individuals: what we do, how we live, how we interact with one another, and even who we are. Robert Burns, for instance, writes that:

> narrative forms the deep structure of human action. In other words, the bedrock of human events is not a mere sequence upon which narrative is imposed but a configured sequence that has a narrative character all the way down. To act at all is to hold an immediate past in memory, to anticipate a goal, and to organize means to achieve that goal—analogously, the 'beginning, middle, and end' of a well-constructed story. (1999, p. 222)

In a similar spirit, Barbara Hardy says, " . . . we dream in narrative, daydream in narrative, remember, anticipate, hope, despair, believe, doubt, plan, revise, criticize, construct, gossip, learn, hate, and love by narrative. In order really to live, we make up stories about ourselves and others, about the personal as well as the social past and future" (1968, p. 5). Indeed, the fertile area of narrative psychology focuses on how stories provide human lives with a sense of unity, moral purpose, and temporal coherence, centering on the concept

[7] See Moody-Adams (2022a).

of a narrative identity,[8] which is "a person's internalized and evolving story of how he or she has become the person he or she is becoming" (McAdams 2019, p. 2).[9] These stories have the power to shape not only the trajectories of our life, but also who we ultimately become, with Marya Schechtman maintaining that " . . . a person creates his identity by forming an autobiographical narrative—a story of his life"[10] and Jerome Bruner writing that "[i]n the end, we become the autobiographical narratives by which we 'tell about' our lives" (1987, p. 15).[11]

Crucially, however, we are not the sole authors of our own stories. As we saw in the previous chapter, in all sorts of ways we are depicted and viewed through the eyes of others. And just as narrative psychology explores how our own stories about ourselves impact who we become,[12] so, too, do the stories that others have about us shape who we are and what our futures can be. How the unfolding of events is presented in a narrative, for instance, or the layers of a person's character are sketched, can have monumental consequences for the people involved in them. In this chapter, I focus on how stories themselves can rise to the level of inflicting a gross violation or injustice on those at their center.[13] Taking the role that narratives play in the United States criminal legal system as a paradigmatic case, I show that stories that erase, demonize, or systematically distort a defendant through a wrongful conviction can result in catastrophic epistemic wrongs and that "counterstories" can function as a crucial form of epistemically reparative work. I then argue that wronging another person in a way demanding of epistemic reparations does not necessarily involve having false or even unwarranted beliefs about him. I support this through the introduction of the concept of "misknowing," which applies when only a narrow, one-dimensional set of facts are centered about a person or persons, often focusing on those that are most injurious. I show

[8] For objections to the narrative view of the self, see Strawson (2004).

[9] "By the early 20s, most people have constructed a narrative identity for their lives—an internal story that explains how the individual has become the person he or she is, and where his or her life may be going in the future. The story affirms a sense of temporal coherence in life, integrating the reconstructed past with the imagined future, and it typically provides the person with a sense of wholeness, psychic unity, and moral purpose" (McAdams 2019, p. 14).

[10] Schechtman (1996, p. 93).

[11] "[T]he culturally shaped cognitive and linguistic processes that guide the self-telling of life narratives achieve the power to structure perceptual experience, to organize memory, to segment and purpose-build the very 'events' of a life" (Bruner 1987, p. 15).

[12] The very title of McAdams's (2019) article reflects this: "First we invented stories, then they changed us: The evolution of narrative identity."

[13] I should emphasize that the arguments in this chapter do not depend upon any of these specific views, such as of narrative psychology or of narrative identity. I include them to support the far more general point that storytelling plays a powerful role in our lives.

that misknowing is often fueled by "flat stories" about the person in question, which are agentially closed and depict him in static, one-dimensional, and psychologically simplistic terms. When such stories are grounded in or constitute gross violations and injustices, epistemic reparations require "rounder stories," which are agentially open and portray a person in dynamic, multidimensional, and psychologically complex terms. In this way, while stories can epistemically wrong a person in life-altering ways, they can also be the source of the life-restoring epistemic reparations that are demanded in response.

## 1. Storytelling and the Criminal Legal System

In nearly every aspect of the United States criminal legal system, storytelling plays a fundamental role. Robert M. Cover, for instance, argues that the law itself is derived from "the sacred narratives of our world" (1985, p. 180) and that "[n]o set of legal institutions or prescriptions exists apart from the narratives that locate it and give it meaning" (Cover 1983, p. 4).[14] Philip Meyer maintains that lawyers are "storytellers . . . [where] effective storytelling . . . sometimes . . . is literally a matter of life and death" (2014, p. 2).[15] With respect to trials more specifically, Saira Mohamed claims that they are the "means by which judges or juries or the public at large try out different narratives—of a particular crime or of the larger world—and select one" that "prevails" or "emerges triumphant" (2015, p. 1678) and Samuel R. Gross writes that "[i]t is commonplace that most successful courtroom advocacy is structured as storytelling rather than logical proof" (1998, p. 852). According to Andrew E. Taslitz, "it is the narrative itself that determines a trial's outcome" (1996, p. 393) and Aviva Orenstein argues that in the case of jury trials, "jurors try to piece together a coherent narrative of the events" (1998, p. 677, note 51) and so "story credibility and structural coherence are better explanations of juror reasoning than logical proof" (1998, p. 677). This is supported by the Court's opinion in *Old Chief v. United States*, where it is said that the government "may fairly seek to place its evidence before the jurors, as much to tell a story of guiltiness as to support an inference of

[14] In a similar spirit, James Boyd White maintains that law is "the open hearing in which one point of view, one construction of language and reality, is tested against another" (1985, p. 104).

[15] Similarly, J. Christopher Rideout writes that "storytelling lies at the heart of what lawyers do. Every legal case starts with a story—the client's story—and it ends with a legal decision that, in effect, offers another version of that story. . . . In between, in the middle, lies the story told at trial—or, rather, the stories told at trial, since most trials contain competing narratives" (2008, p. 53).

guilt, to convince the jurors that a guilty verdict would be morally reasonable as much as to point to the discrete elements of a defendant's legal fault" (*Old Chief v. United States*, 519 U.S. 172 (1997)). Indeed, Lisa Kern Griffin discusses a 2010 habeas case,[16] in which "the Seventh Circuit went so far as to suggest that the failure to present a coherent narrative rises to the level of ineffective assistance of counsel. In the case of a defendant adjudged 'guilty but mentally ill' in a murder trial, Judge Posner wrote that a narrative richer than the 'bare facts of his bizarre behavior' was necessary to effective representation" (2013, p. 296). Even in the presentation of expert testimony, Orenstein maintains that "[t]he expert does not tell the jury who or what to believe, rather the expert fills in gaps based on scientific knowledge and clinical experience that allows the jury to fashion a coherent story" (1998, p. 712).

These claims are supported by empirical studies of jury behavior.[17] Nancy Pennington and Reid Hastie (1993), for instance, show that juries choose among competing narratives by focusing on three central features: coverage, coherence, and uniqueness. "Coverage" picks out the extent to which a story explains the evidence presented at trial. "Coherence" refers to consistency, plausibility, or completeness.

> A story is "consistent" to the degree that it does not contain internal contradictions with other credible evidence or other parts of the story. A story is "plausible" to the extent that it does not contradict our knowledge about what typically happens in the world. A story is "complete" when the expected structure "has all of its parts," according to the rules of episodic structure. (Taslitz 1996, p. 438)

Finally, a story is "unique" if there is only one coherent story as defined by these standards. According to Pennington and Hastie, jurors reason and deliberate through the lens of stories, and so the more powerful the narrative is in terms of coverage, coherence, and uniqueness, the more likely jurors are to convict. What this research shows, then, is that the mechanism by which jurors assess the explanatory power of the admissible body of evidence presented in court is driven, in large part, by storytelling.

[16] *Wilson v. Gaetz*, 608 F.3d 347, 352 (7th Cir. 2010).

[17] "Experimental research has yielded the insight that jurors do not, by and large, estimate probabilities when determining the events that transpired in a case; rather, they draw conclusions based on whether information assembles into plausible narrative" (Griffin 2013, p. 293).

Despite the critical role that narratives play in the criminal legal system, defendants rarely have the opportunity to use their own voices during the legal process.[18] Alexandra Natapoff expresses this point powerfully when she writes, "[t]he United States's criminal justice system is shaped by a fundamental absence: Criminal defendants rarely speak" (2005, p. 1449). This is the result of a number of factors, including that trial by jury is on the verge of extinction in America,[19] with 97.4% of federal felony convictions in the United States obtained through guilty pleas[20] and state felony convictions not far behind.[21] Moreover, even when defendants go to trial, they are often discouraged from taking the stand to avoid aggressive cross-examination, prejudices and biases of the juries, and so on. Against this background of silence, then, an area in the criminal legal system where defendants seem to have a robust role to play in their own destinies is at sentencing hearings. In particular, the "right of allocution" permits a criminal defendant to speak at his own sentencing hearing prior to the sentencing itself, which is detailed in Rule 32 of the Federal Rules of Criminal Procedure: "before imposing sentence, the court must... address the defendant personally in order to permit the defendant to speak or present any information to mitigate the sentence" (32(i)(4)(A)(ii)). The importance of this right is clear: "[i]n a system where so few people go to trial, let alone testify, sentencing is often the only opportunity for defendants to speak during the legal process in a way that is even nominally unconstrained" (Burger-Caplan 2017, p. 41).

As presented in the Federal Rules of Criminal Procedure, the central function or rationale of allocution is mitigation. Defendants are allowed to personally address the court and present information that might lessen their sentence prior to it being imposed. There may, however, be other, related purposes of allocution as well. In *United States v. Li*, for instance, the right of allocution is said to allow "a defendant ... [an] opportunity to plead for mercy...." (115 F.3d 125, 133 (2d Cir. 1997)), quoting *United States v. Barnes*,

[18] The material in this section relies heavily on Lackey (2023) where these and related issue are discussed in far more depth and detail.

[19] See New York State Association of Criminal Defense Lawyers (2021).

[20] United States Sentencing Commission (2019).

[21] As Jed S. Rakoff (2014) says, "While corresponding statistics for the fifty states combined are not available, it is a rare state where plea bargains do not similarly account for the resolution of at least 95 percent of the felony cases that are not dismissed ...." Similarly, according to the New York State Association of Criminal Defense Lawyers, "Recent data shows that in New York State 99 percent of misdemeanor charges and 94 percent of felony charges are resolved by a guilty plea. New York is by no means an aberration. Across the country criminal trials are vanishing at an alarming rate" (2021, p. 3).

948 F.2d 325, 328 (7th Cir. 1991). To the extent that pleading for mercy is distinct from the presentation of mitigating information, this is an additional function of allocution. A further purpose of allocution is the individualization or humanization of the defendant: "[t]he sentencing hearing, and the defendant's allocution in particular, is an opportunity for the court to learn details about the person to be sentenced. The court uses these nuances to impose a just sentence that is appropriate to the particular defendant" (Thomas 2007, p. 2644).[22]

For a defendant who is innocent, however, the right of allocution can be a source of further victimization. Note, first, that regardless of whether allocution's rationale is mitigation, mercy, or humanization, the actual innocence of a defendant ought to be relevant. Mitigating reasons, for instance, are those that show that the defendant should be viewed as less responsible for his acts or that the acts themselves should be seen as less severe.[23] A story of innocence should then be understood as an extreme version of mitigation insofar as lack of guilt warrants neither responsibility nor punishment.[24] Moreover, when one has the power to punish or harm another, mercy involves showing that person compassion or forgiveness. If a defendant is actually innocent and yet has been wrongfully found to be guilty, then the court has a final opportunity to hear that mercy may be called for before sentencing. And certainly individualization and humanization involve listening to a defendant's particular story of innocence. In *Williams v. New York* (1949), for instance, it is noted that "[h]ighly relevant—if not essential—to [a judge's] selection of an appropriate sentence is the possession of the fullest information possible concerning the defendant's life and characteristics" (337 U.S. 241, 246). That the innocent defendant is in fact innocent seems to be a feature about his life and characteristics that is relevant to his sentencing. Yet, this is not in any way the reality in the current criminal legal system. As Kimberly A. Thomas says, "[c]ourts do not want to hear allocution stories of innocence. Most judges assume, often consistent with the evidence they have heard, that the person before them actually has committed the offense and any innocence tale is fiction" (2007, p. 2661). Similarly, Mary Margaret Giannini writes, "[c]ourts appear willing to hear from remorseful and apologetic defendants, but are quick to cut off defendants who use their allocution

[22] See also Chan (2009).
[23] Thomas (2007, p. 2655).
[24] See Thomas (2007, p. 2661).

right to reargue their case; to challenge the court, judicial system, or government; or to continue to protest their innocence" (2008, pp. 463–464).

The mere fact that courts silence innocent defendants and their allocution stories of innocence is violating by itself. Consider, for instance, the perspective of an innocent defendant who has just been wrongfully convicted of murder. The only point at which he has spoken in the process may have been in the interrogation room when a confession was coerced. After that, he may have been found guilty at trial because of the massive weight afforded to his false confession or pled guilty because he felt trapped by manufactured evidence against him. In all of the proceedings since the confession or the guilty plea, he has been silent—spoken for and about—but never heard from by the court through his own, in-real-time voice. He finally arrives at the sentencing hearing and is aware that this is his final opportunity to make a case to the court for justice and mercy. And now he is told that no one wants to hear that he is actually innocent. As Natapoff says, "[s]entencing is the last stage of silencing: Between hostile judges, instrumentalist lawyers, and the threat of heightened punishment, the defendant's final day in court is one in which he will be told in numerous ways to be quiet.... Since this day will also often be his last day of freedom, for millions of defendants the silencing of the courtroom is the dress rehearsal for the silencing of incarceration" (2005, p. 1469). The innocent defendant is thus told to swallow the truth, to silence his cries of innocence, and to bury the facts that would warrant no sentence at all.

But the violation doesn't stop here. In addition to being silenced about his actual innocence, the defendant is then essentially provided with a script of what he should say: " . . . judges . . . have archetypes of ideal allocutions in mind. They want the allocution to express 'genuine remorse,' 'sincerity,' 'realistic and concrete plans for the future,' 'apology to the victims,' and an 'understanding of the seriousness of the offense'.... With such clear goals for what should and should not be said in an allocution, continuously reinforced as judges gain more experience with allocutions and sentencing, it stands to reason that the further a defendant ventures from these archetypes, the angrier and less sympathetic that judge is likely to become" (Burger-Caplan 2017, p. 55). Even if the defendant is in fact innocent and was the victim of unjust circumstances of a coercive interrogation or plea-bargaining process, the court does not want to hear this. Instead, the defendant should admit guilt, express remorse, be sincere, apologize to the victim and the community, and display an understanding of the seriousness of the crime. So, the innocent defendant is not only told to swallow the truth and eat his cries of innocence, he is also handed a script of what he should say to the court. William Peeples, a graduate of the Northwestern Prison Education Program, powerfully describes the pain of following a script at his sentencing hearing for a crime he didn't commit:

> to stand before that judge and "perform" as this repentant "would be rapist" truly made me sick! My public defender literally coached me on how to stand, how to appear, what to say, and how to say it! I was terrified of doing 30 years. I wanted to be free, I missed my family, and the system played on that, coercing me to forever "brand" myself as someone I could never be, would never be. (personal correspondence)

More perversely, the innocent defendant is told, impossibly, to be both "sincere" and yet to express life-shattering and identity-destroying falsehoods. He should somehow feign remorse for a crime he didn't commit—one that is often for him unimaginable to have committed—and to utter words that are in the shape of an apology but have no authenticity, as he cannot be truly sorry for doing something that he simply didn't do. This is an attack on him as a person, for he is being told to follow a script that has no grounding in truth and to repair fractured relationships in the moral community that he didn't disrupt in the first place.

The assault continues, for defendants who maintain their innocence at sentencing hearings[25] "... risk and receive harsher sentences because of their perceived failure to accept responsibility, lack of candor with the court, or failure to acknowledge the validity of the fact-finder's decision" (Thomas 2007, p. 2661). In *United States v. Burgos-Andújar*, for instance, the defendant, who was a legislator in the Puerto Rican Senate, was found guilty of criminal trespass in United States naval territory. When she exercised her right to allocute, she maintained her innocence and challenged both the court's authority and the evidence it relied upon in her guilty conviction.[26] "As a result of the defendant's allocution, the judge raised her sentence from that which the court had originally contemplated" (Giannini 2008, pp. 463–464). On appeal, the reviewing court supported this decision: "appellant essentially declared herself innocent of crime and thus was refusing to acknowledge the impact of her illegal action ... [which] may have legitimately

[25] See Ward (2006) for a discussion of how both silence and professions of innocence are interpreted as a lack of remorse and aggravate the defendant's sentence.

[26] Giannini (2008, pp. 463–464).

led the sentencing judge to increase appellant's sentence" (275 F.3d 23, 30 (1st Cir. 2001)). What we see here is not only the pressure to silence claims of innocence, the imposing of a script, and the threat of a harsher punishment for failure to abide by it—we see the court following through on the threat. Moreover, this is not in any way unique or anomalous.[27] Indeed, harsher sentences are handed out not only for claims of innocence, but also for simply failing to follow the court's script to the judge's satisfaction. In an interview with a defendant who "chose to incorporate speech into his allocution that went beyond areas typically thought of as acceptable," Burger-Caplan notes that the "gamble did not pay off":

> So being that I was arrogant, being that I challenged [the judge], being that I told him that this whole thing was like an illusion, okay, that this happened, dah, dah, dah, dah.... [S]o he actually says it... that he increased [the sentence] because of my arrogance, because he felt that I wasn't taking responsibility.

As Burger-Caplan says, "because his expression did not comport with the judge's expectation or desires for the allocution, his sentence was increased" (2017, pp. 53–54). More generally, Richard Weisman notes that in his observation of court conduct, "[t]here is . . . some evidence . . . of moral economism in which the more serious the offense, the more dramatic must be the offender's suffering in order for it to be validated" (1999, p. 127). So defendants are told not only what not to say, but also what to say and how to say it, and failure to comply will literally result in more time behind bars.

Thus, while storytelling plays a powerful role in the American criminal legal system, defendants rarely have a voice in their own narratives. This especially impacts innocent defendants, who are systematically silenced when telling the truth, resulting in who they actually are being largely invisible to the public. The invisibility here can involve both kinds discussed in Chapter 1: when people who are convicted of crimes are regarded as "monsters," for instance, then they may not be seen as a person and so may be completely invisible. When people who are convicted of crimes are regarded as not capable of being political participants or members of the moral community, then they may be invisible in targeted domains. Against

[27] "If [the defendant] does speak outside the expected script of acquiescence and remorse, he will be punished more severely" (Natapoff 2005, p. 1469).

this background of invisibility, then, the script that innocent defendants are told to follow, which not only demonizes and distorts them but is also foreign and fracturing to their moral identity, is poised to play an oversized role in shaping who they are taken to be and who they are able to become.

## 2. Epistemic Reparations and Counterstories

As we have seen, the violations and injustices inflicted on a person through a wrongful conviction are deep and multifaceted. In addition to the horrors of being convicted and incarcerated for a crime he didn't commit, his actual story of innocence is silenced, his true self is rendered invisible, and the official story about him cultivated, extracted, and promoted by the State is often unrecognizable, vilifying, and distorting. In this way, the State's official story inflicts an *additional* violation and injustice on a wrongfully convicted person, one that profoundly impacts who he is and, often, who he can become. As we saw in the Introduction, Northwestern Prison Education Program student Scot Miller compellingly makes this point when he writes, "[a]n extracted false confession creates a false narrative of that person's life. In other words, the extracted confession turns a person's life into a lie. That lie is then believed over the truth of that person's life, victimizing him over and over again. This seems to be the ultimate crime—stealing the essence of someone's life while they yet breathe" (personal correspondence). It is, then, unsurprising what we saw in Chapter 1: that after wrongfully convicted Jim Fogle was both released from prison and exonerated in 2015, he reported in an interview: "I want people to know the truth about my case" (Innocence Project in Print 2015, p. 16). As we noted then, knowing the truth about Fogle's case is to *know him*. Justice for the wrongfully convicted requires, then, not only traditional reparations, such as material ones—including release from prison, exoneration, and financial compensation—but also epistemic reparations.

One way of engaging in the epistemically reparative work required in knowing someone is through the stories that are told about him—autobiographically or otherwise. In the context of discussing the absence of autobiographical narratives of female captives who survived the Middle Passage, for instance, Saidiya Hartman writes, "[l]oss gives rise to longing, and in these circumstances, it would not be far-fetched to consider stories as a form of compensation or even as reparations, perhaps the only kind we will ever receive" (2008, p. 4). Here, Hartman is talking about the stories that haven't been told, making clear that she endeavors to "represent the lives of the nameless and the forgotten, to reckon with loss, and to respect the limits of what cannot be known" (2008, p. 4). Drawing on the discussion from the previous chapter, Hartman aims to repair the epistemic wrong of invisibility through telling the stories that are missing, either through indifference or through intentional exclusion. But often the absence of stories—and the corresponding invisibility—is accompanied by the presence of false, vilifying, or distorting ones. When this rises to the level of a gross violation or injustice, epistemic reparations require replacing these narratives with truer, respectful, and fuller ones. Consider, for instance, Hilde Lindemann Nelson's notion of a "counterstory," which is:

> a story that resists an oppressive identity and attempts to replace it with one that commands respect . . . . The counterstory positions itself against a number of master narratives: the stories found lying about in our cultures that serve as summaries of socially shared understandings. Master narratives are often archetypal, consisting of stock plots and readily recognizable character types, and we use them not only to make sense of our experience . . . but also to justify what we do . . . . As the repositories of common norms, master narratives exercise a certain authority over our moral imaginations and play a role in informing our moral intuitions. (2001, p. 6)

While Nelson's central example of a counterstory involves a group of nurses weaving together a collective counterstory through sharing "histories, anecdotes, and other narrative fragments," history is replete with members of oppressed or marginalized groups creating, telling, and sharing various kind of counterstories, especially as acts of collective resistance. Moreover, a counterstory of even a single person's life can begin to do some of the reparative work that is required. Consider, again, the case of Fogle. Extending Nelson's concepts,[28] we can understand the master narrative of his life being the one created and promoted by the State—that Fogle raped and murdered a child, that he lied about his own actions, and that he failed to have the appropriate normative responses of taking accountability for his

[28] I say that this is an extension of the original concepts because I am using "master narrative" and "counterstory" more liberally than Nelson does.

actions and committing to repairing the damage he caused. This narrative exerted a tremendous amount of epistemic and moral power over the community. It enabled them to make sense of their experiences of, say, hatred for Fogle, to justify incarcerating him, to constrain their imagination over how he deserves to be treated, and so on. The reparative counterstory here—first told by Fogle himself and then promoted by the Innocence Project and others—resists this false narrative and replaces it with one that is accurate and restorative of Fogle's status in his community. It not only makes clear the truth about his innocence and the grave injustice he faced through being wrongfully convicted and incarcerated for decades, but also the duty we have to know him for who he truly is.[29]

The importance of this particular epistemically reparative work is made even clearer against the background of empirical work on wrongful convictions. According to a systematic review of research by Brooks and Greenberg, the impact of being wrongfully accused of a criminal offense "is frequently complex and long-lasting," with participants reporting negative impacts on a broad range of aspects of their lives, including, among others, "their self-identity, reputation, psychological and physical health, [and] relationships . . . ." (2021, p. 50). For instance, participants in these studies reported permanent changes to their personality, being less confident and more mistrustful, a loss of dignity and credibility, a loss of hope and purpose for the future, a loss of their pre-accusation self, damaged reputations or feeling stigmatized by others, feeling that their standing in the community had been affected negatively, and feeling labeled and vilified by others.[30] Negative impacts on family members were also reported, such as being stigmatized, socially rejected, blamed, labeled, and stereotyped by others in the community.[31] Crucially for our purposes here, the authors note that "[i]t was particularly difficult for participants to regain their previous sense of self if they received no formal apology or public statement of innocence effectively 'delabelling' them" (Brooks and Greenberg 2021, p. 47). This is a clear

[29] Of course, there may be a host of challenges in actually coming to know who someone is, including because of the impact of the violations or injustice in question on the one being known. In his discussion of the consequences of incarceration on those who are incarcerated, for instance, Craig Haney writes that "[m]any develop an impenetrable, defensive shell to prevent anyone from ever truly knowing them, because prison is a place where others readily exploit such knowledge to manipulate or harm them (or threaten to do so)" (2006, p. 13). I will take up the question of how to understand knowing a person in far more detail in Chapter 4.

[30] Brooks and Greenberg (2021, p. 47).

[31] Brooks and Greenberg (2021, p. 48).

and compelling acknowledgment of the importance of epistemic reparations in this context. Without a counternarrative, the victims in question are left not only with the stigma and loss of standing within their community that comes with a wrongful conviction, but also with a damaged sense of self that impacts who they are and who they can become. Amanda Knox, who was wrongfully convicted of the 2007 murder of her roommate, Meredith Kercher, in Perugia, Italy, makes this point powerfully when she writes, "[o]nce you become a figure in a story, your story doesn't belong to you anymore. And that is the sort of shocking experience that I've had that I noticed other people having all the time . . . and so it seems like the only thing to do is to try to give people their stories back" (Burbank 2021).

Even still, "[r]esearch suggests public perceptions of exonerees tend to be negative and not dissimilar to perceptions of actual offenders, despite knowing they had been exonerated" (Brooks and Greenberg 2021, p. 51). So, even when there is an acknowledgment of wrongdoing by the State through an exoneration, and an accurate story added to the public record through the court's decision, exonerees still face an uphill struggle for epistemic reparations. According to Brooks and Greenberg, "[t]his may be because the public are concerned that the exoneration process itself was flawed, and they prefer to believe the veracity of the original conviction, despite the outcome of the legal review process" (2021, p. 51). They recommend that "[f]uture research . . . consider ways of improving public perception. Otherwise, the wrongfully accused will continue to be stigmatised by others, which is likely to worsen the psychological impact of their experience" (Brooks and Greenberg 2021, p. 51). Heather Weigand argues that part of this work involves educating the public on the causes of wrongful convictions, as well as being sensitive to the way stories of innocence are told "by limiting sensationalism from becoming the overwhelming form of communication regarding the wrongfully convicted. Those working with exonerees should limit media's ability to create detailed, sensitive and sensational stories that do not benefit but potentially harm the exonerated" (2009, p. 436). At least one way that this can be done is by providing tools and spaces for those who have been wrongfully convicted to tell their own stories and to create platforms for others to bear witness to them as they do so. As exonerees are increasingly empowered to effectively use their own voices, the public will learn about the many ways in which the criminal legal system makes mistakes in a way that is authentic, humanizing, and non-sensational.

## 3. Misknowing

Crucially, harming or wronging another person in a way demanding of epistemically reparative work does not necessarily involve having false or even unwarranted beliefs about him. Consider what I will call "misknowing," where only a narrow, one-dimensional set of facts are centered about a person or persons, often focusing on those that are most injurious, resulting in the erasure or distortion of other relevant truths.[32] Misknowing *is* a form of knowing, but in virtue of its singular or excessive focus on the facts in question, it obscures as much as it reveals. It is not, for instance, misknowing your dentist to know very little about him other than that he is your dentist. But if you center this fact about him in your cognitive architecture in a way that conceals or crowds out your ability to see anything else about him, then it is. While there are many versions of misknowing, here I will discuss cases where someone is in fact guilty of a crime, but his entire identity is reduced to this one action. He is regarded as, for instance, nothing more than a "murderer" both in the sense that he is *only a murderer*—there is nothing of interest or normative value about him other than this fact—and he is *always a murderer*—there are no agential possibilities open to him for being or becoming more than the identity associated with this singular act.

As a paradigmatic case, let's return to William Peeples. William admits that he murdered his neighbor in a burglary gone terribly awry in May

[32] Since I am interested in misknowing that is connected with epistemic wrongs that deserve epistemic reparations, I will focus on the centering of negative facts about a person. As suggested above, however, this phenomenon can also involve knowledge of what we might otherwise regard as positive truths. For instance, just as systemically driven stories that vilify or demonize can depict a group or person in one-dimensional, static, and psychologically simplistic terms, so, too, can idolization or valorization do this. Regarding someone as, say, only a hero, saint, role model, or celebrity can result in the erasure or distortion of other important truths about him, including those connected to his personhood and agency. While dehumanization involves treating someone as less than human, "superhumanization" involves treating someone as more than human, and both can obscure who someone really is. For the idolized, the effort of accomplishments and the agony of challenges may be invisible, leading to, among other consequences, unmeetable or unreasonable expectations placed on them as well as indifference to the reality or depth of their struggles. Perhaps this is how to understand the way sports heroes are seen by young fans—consider Charles Barkley's famous resistance to this with his "I am not a role model" Nike commercial (1993)—and celebrities are seen by the paparazzi. An interestingly different kind of misknowing can be seen by considering this sort of case: suppose that the only fact you know about Christopher Columbus is that he sailed the ocean blue. This is not a fact that is injurious to Columbus, but it is a form of misknowing, as it involves a narrow, one-dimensional perspective of him that leaves out relevant, important truths, including ones that are harmful to others. Indeed, given the epistemic impact that this knowledge has on others, it may be helpful to think of it as a relational or interpersonal form of misknowing, where only a narrow, one-dimensional set of facts are centered about a person or persons, resulting in the erasure or distortion of important truths about others. (I am grateful to comments from an anonymous reviewer, Rory Aird, and Christopher Willard-Kyle that led to the inclusion of this note.)

of 1988.[33] Today, well over three decades later, William is a deeply valued member of the Northwestern Prison Education Program community who mentors those in need, lifts up those around him, lives an exemplary life of love and service, and made history as one of the first incarcerated students in the United States to receive a bachelor's degree from a top ten university. To know William through the lens of only one—albeit true—action in his nearly six decades of life is to misknow him. It is to center one moment in his full, rich life and to relegate features that are now crucial to his identity, such as student, friend, published author, mentor, and visionary, to the margins. It is to allow this one truth about him to squeeze out knowledge of other, deeply important truths about William as a person.

Of course, not every instance of misknowing calls for epistemic reparations. So when is it grounded in, or does it rise to the level of, a gross violation or injustice that does? To answer this, let's explore a paradigmatic case of misknowing that calls for epistemic reparations. In particular, I will argue that systemic forces targeting certain groups lead to the public or "master" narratives of many defendants in the American criminal legal system—both collectively and as individuals—resulting in a kind of misknowing which, in turn, amounts to a gross violation or injustice demanding of epistemic reparations.

At the outset, the way that criminalized actions are interpreted can have a profound impact on how justice-impacted people are seen, the treatment they are thought to deserve, and even who they can become.[34] To see this, consider the *fundamental attribution error*, which is the tendency to prefer or overvalue dispositional explanations of behavior, such as a person's personality traits or character, and undervalue situational explanations, such as the context in which the behavior occurs.[35] For instance, rather than looking at a defendant's drug use or the financial desperation of his family to explain him robbing a gas station attendant, there is a tendency to instead see him as

[33] This murder took place after the wrongful conviction mentioned earlier. For more on these details, see Peeples Jr. (2020).

[34] These consequences can be exacerbated for juveniles, where research shows that contact with the juvenile justice system "stigmatizes adolescents and initiates a process that redefines one's self-concept, reduces prosocial opportunities, and leads to changes in interpersonal relationships conducive to criminal behavior" (Rowan et al. 2023, p. 732).

[35] See Jones and Harris (1967), Snyder and Jones (1974), and Miller (1976). There are two aspects of the fundamental attribution error: "[d]ispositionalism is the tendency to prefer dispositional attributions over situational attributions. Correspondence bias is the tendency to infer that dispositions correspond to behavior" (Krull 2001, p. 211). Regarding the "correspondence bias" in particular, see Gilbert and Malone (1995).

a violent or "deviant" person.[36] Perhaps unsurprisingly, this has a host of negative consequences. With respect to the criminal legal system in particular, dispositional attributions can lead to investigators and juries engaging in racial profiling when initially encountering witnesses and defendants,[37] and studies show that how crime is explained directly affects beliefs and policies about legal and social responses:[38] when a defendant's behavior is attributed to his circumstances, judicial officials are more likely to advocate for rehabilitation than punitive responses, whereas when a defendant's behavior is understood as "the result of internal factors," he is regarded as "dangerous" or "treatment resistant" (Kubota et al. 2014, p. 122). Moreover, research by Kubota et al. shows that acute physiological stress increases dispositional attributions, not only of mundane behaviors, but also specifically of criminalized behavior. Indeed, even when extenuating circumstances are present, increased stress is accompanied by more dispositional judgments of the behavior of criminal defendants. The authors conclude that "stress may make people more likely to commit the [fundamental attribution error] and less favorable in their evaluations of others . . . when making socially consequential judicial decisions" (Kubota et al. 2014, p. 117).

Given that criminal proceedings largely occur in contexts that are stressful for all involved, the above results suggest that arrests by police officers, charges brought by prosecutors, verdicts made by juries, and sentences given by judges may all be distorted by tendencies to see the actions of suspects and defendants as resulting from character traits rather than contingent circumstances. This can then lead to them being regarded as "criminals" and ultimately as "prisoners"—which are highly stigmatized labels associated with delinquency, deviance, or moral deficiency[39]—resulting in a broad range of discrimination and mistreatment.[40] Indeed, "criminality labelling alone is sufficient to activate stigma-related processes"[41] with people who are labeled as "criminals" being subject to social rejection, loss of social status, and discrimination in housing and employment.[42] Even in areas like health

[36] To foreshadow the next section, many of these features of misknowing directly contribute to the "flat stories" of defendants and suspects as both collectives and individuals in the criminal legal system.

[37] Sommers and Ellsworth (2000).

[38] Cullen et al. (1985).

[39] See Harding (2003), Hirschfield and Piquero (2010), and LeBel (2008, 2011).

[40] Even "suspect" can trigger bias. As Edwin Meese III famously said in 1985 while he was Attorney General of the United States, "you don't have many suspects who are innocent of a crime. That's contradictory. If a person is innocent of a crime, then he is not a suspect" (Kurtz 1985).

[41] Boutet et al. (2022, p. 2).

[42] See Pager (2007) and Boutet et al. (2022).

care, studies show that the label of "formerly incarcerated" results in patients being 41% less likely to be given appointments with primary care providers who are currently accepting new patients in their practices.[43] And recent research on reactions to the pain of individuals with a criminal history reveals that people are less willing to help those who are labeled as criminals.[44]

As is widely known, the media also contributes to the distorted images, labeling, and stories of many criminal suspects and defendants in the legal system in the United States. For instance, Black people, especially young men, are "over-represented as crime perpetrators [in the media]. Blacks are also more likely than Whites to have their mug shots displayed on local news, be shown handcuffed, be on 'perp walks', and have prejudicial information aired about them (for example, as having a criminal record)" (Adamson 2016, p. 192).[45] These findings are supported by a 2021 report published by the Global Strategy Group in collaboration with the Equal Justice Initiative on the role of racial bias in the media regarding coverage of people prosecuted in the criminal court system.[46] In a section titled "A Picture Is Worth a Thousand Words," the report notes that mugshots were used in coverage of 45% of cases involving Black people accused of crimes compared to only 8% of cases involving white defendants. At the same time, white victims were nearly four times more likely to be presented in photos with friends and family than Black people victimized by crime. In another section, "Labels Matter," the report found that more personally descriptive words are used for white defendants, while more crime-related descriptions are used for Black defendants. White defendants, for instance, were characterized as a father, son, or man while Black defendants were referred to as the arrested or accused. In a case study of *Florida v. Howell Emanual Donaldson III*, 57% of the pre-trial coverage characterized Donaldson as a "serial killer" in article headlines, with his name rarely mentioned in them. In general, media coverage was 50% more likely to refer to white defendants by name as compared to Black defendants. As the report notes, "[e]xclusion of a defendant's name, particularly in favor of a label like 'serial killer,' is yet another way we see defendants—especially Black defendants—dehumanized and reflexively criminalized in coverage, even before trial" (Global Strategy Group 2021). This dehumanization is exacerbated by the fact that quotes from family

[43] Fahmy et al. (2018).
[44] Boutet et al. (2022).
[45] See also Entman and Rojecki (2000) and Dixon (2017).
[46] Global Strategy Group (2021).

members and friends were nearly twice as likely to be found in articles about white defendants than in those about Black defendants. Founder and Executive Director of the Equal Justice Initiative, Bryan Stevenson, concludes, "News media have often reinforced a presumption of guilt and dangerousness assigned to Black people when reporting on crime while devaluing the lives of Black people and the harm they suffer when victimized. American media can and should do better in eliminating racially biased coverage" (Global Strategy Group 2021).

There is arguably no clearer instance of the connections between distorted labeling and stories, the media, and the impact on human lives than the role that "superpredator" played in American history. Indeed, the very title of this 2020 article from NBC News and *The Marshall Project* conveys this: "How the media created a 'superpredator' myth that harmed a generation of Black youth: Twenty-five years ago this month, the word 'superpredator' spread in the media like wildfire, shaping criminal justice policy for decades" (Bogert and Hancock 2020). The authors go on to trace how the term was introduced in 1995 by an academic named John J. Dilulio Jr. who "warned that by the year 2000 an additional 30,000 young 'murderers, rapists, and muggers' would be roaming America's streets, sowing mayhem. 'They place zero value on the lives of their victims, whom they reflexively dehumanize as just so much worthless "white trash"' (Bogert and Hancock 2020). Not only was the "superpredator" theory a "racist trope" that dehumanized young people of color, but it was not supported by crime statistics. "Juvenile . . . crime . . . had already started falling when Dilulio's article was published. By 2000, when tens of thousands more children were supposed to be out there mugging and killing, juvenile murder arrests had fallen by two-thirds" (Bogert and Hancock 2020). Despite this, the damage was already done, with much of the media wholeheartedly embracing the label,[47] spreading it with sensationalist stories, and ultimately driving policies that irrevocably altered the lives of countless young Americans, especially young Black men.

This is not new. So-called danger narratives, which portray racially "oppressed groups as innately violent, uncivilized, and threatening" to the public and are used to "justify state-sanctioned and vigilante forms of violence against oppressed communities while also functioning to assert the

[47] As the authors note, "[o]f the 281 media mentions of 'superpredators' we found from 1995 to 2000, more than three in five used the term without questioning its validity" (Bogert and Hancock 2020).

'rightful' place of White men in positions of power,"[48] have been told "since the first Europeans arrived in North America" (Webb 2021, p. 132).[49] Such narratives distort and vilify entire communities and groups of people and, unsurprisingly, often result in laws, policies, and practices that reflect them. Drawing on Khalil Gibran Muhammad's 2010 book, *The Condemnation of Blackness*, historian Jill Lepore powerfully summarizes the recent history of modern day American policing as follows: "[p]olice patrolled Black neighborhoods and arrested Black people disproportionately; prosecutors indicted Black people disproportionately; juries found Black people guilty disproportionately; judges gave Black people disproportionately long sentences; and, then, after all this, social scientists, observing the number of Black people in jail, decided that, as a matter of biology, Black people were disproportionately inclined to criminality."[50] Avlana K. Eisenberg discusses a related "danger narrative," according to which policing is viewed as "inherently dangerous," and officers are "under constant threat of grave physical harm at the hands of those . . . they police,"[51] and shows how such a narrative is at the core of police training, dominates police self-image and professional protocols, and is codified and reinforced by courts. With respect to routine traffic stops in particular, Jordan B. Woods maintains that narratives that such stops are "fraught with grave and unpredictable danger to the police" permeate police training.[52] And Ben Grunwald and Jeffrey Fagan argue that officers' assessments of what they call "high-crime areas" are only "weakly correlated with actual crime rates," that the "racial composition of the area and the identity of the officer are stronger predictors of whether an officer deems an area high crime than the crime rate," and that officers may even be using high-crime areas as "cover to bolster the appearance of constitutional validity in their weakest stops" (Grunwald and Fagan 2019, p. 396). These danger narratives and resulting consequences are then connected to a kind of "hypervisibility" of Black Americans, where white Americans "disproportionately attend to Black Americans"[53] under certain

[48] Rondini (2018, p. 60).

[49] "The media construction of Blacks as thugs or criminals is nothing new. Negative representations have been evident ever since Western colonization of the New World, when colonial newspapers ran slave advertisements and devoted ink to Black insurrections and crimes in columns entitled 'The Proceedings of the Rebellious Negroes'" (Adamson 2016, p. 192).

[50] Lepore (2020).

[51] Eisenberg (2023, p. 476).

[52] Woods (2019).

[53] Brown-Iannuzzi et al. (2024, p. 584).

circumstances, especially when feeling threatened.[54] There is a great deal of research supporting this, including studies that show that white people have enhanced capacities for recognition and remembering angry Black faces,[55] rate the speed of Black faces moving toward them in ways consistent with experiencing threatening events,[56] "have a bias to perceive young Black men as bigger (taller, heavier, more muscular) and more physically threatening (stronger, more capable of harm) than young White men,"[57] and are faster both to shoot armed Black targets and to have a "don't shoot" response to unarmed white targets.[58] Danger narratives thus not only reflect the overpolicing, overcriminalizing, and overincarceration of Black people in America but also fuel them by shaping perceptions, actions, practices, and policies.[59]

As we saw in the discussion of the role of storytelling in the criminal American legal system, criminal defendants rarely speak and when they do, they are often expected to follow a script provided by the court. While we earlier focused primarily on those who are innocent, a guilty defendant faces similar pressures that may find him silenced or losing control over his own narrative. At a sentencing hearing, for instance, he may quite reasonably feel that it is inappropriate and inauthentic to follow the court's script and simply admit guilt, express remorse, and apologize. A guilty defendant may have ended up in front of the judge for countless reasons, including in large part because he is consistently profiled by police, a victim of abuse or neglect, poor, a Black male, or addicted to drugs. He may feel that he has been victimized himself by many people and systems in a multitude of ways. For instance, in a study of interviews with drug sellers in Philadelphia, all but one started selling drugs when they were between 11 and 17 years old and most reported "facing dire economic circumstances such as food and housing insecurity, drug-addicted family members, and teen parenthood," which forced them to assume adult economic responsibilities early in life

[54] "Social cognition research has demonstrated that under some circumstances African Americans are 'hypervisible': they draw significantly more visual attention than do Caucasian Americans" (Brown-Iannuzzi et al. 2014, p. 33). This is a different form of hypervisibility than discussed in the previous chapter, where what was meant there is more akin to massive overrepresentation, as seen with Black men in the criminal legal system.

[55] Ackerman et al. (2006).

[56] Kenrick et al. (2015).

[57] Wilson et al. (2017, p. 59).

[58] Senholzi et al. (2015).

[59] Even the genre of true crime media, which is defined as including both storytelling and a commitment to truth-telling as essential aspects, is used to "justify and support institutions of racial control" (Webb 2021, p. 133).

(Fader 2019, p. 62). If one of these drug sellers were to be at a sentencing hearing, wouldn't it be understandable for him to not feel fully responsible for his actions? Moreover, perhaps his anger, sadness, and resentment at his own circumstances push out feelings of remorse or regret. Nevertheless, these facts and emotions should be swallowed so that the allocution story is one that fits the narrative prescribed by the court. One of the defendants interviewed by Burger-Caplan expresses this point powerfully:

> It's tough, right, because it's like, you know, it is a desperate-ass time, and people are probably going to say anything that they can say. It's like, shit, somebody has a gun to your head, and you know, "Tell me what you want me to say so. . . ." Or, "Tell me something, you know, why I should keep you alive." You know what I mean? It's like, you'll say anything. . . . (2017, p. 75)

As this passage notes, the desperation invoked at a sentencing hearing will drive a defendant to say just about anything, including admitting guilt and apologizing when this is entirely or largely unwarranted. These scripted and coerced allocutions not only contribute false and distorted content to the public narratives of criminal defendants in America, they also lend legitimacy to them: "If even the defendant himself admits guilt and shows this much remorse, we are clearly getting things right."

Moreover, many aspects of the United States result in people who have been convicted of a crime having their identities largely reduced to this one act in their lives. For instance, while crimes, especially high-profile ones, are often covered heavily by the media, rarely do we see similar attention paid to the accomplishments, virtues, and growth of people who are incarcerated. This results in the publicly accessible information about incarcerated people often being limited to only their criminal activity. We see the mugshots of people who are incarcerated rather than photos of them in classrooms or hugging their children during visits, and we read about their possession of a gun rather than their publication of a work of poetry or their leading a restorative justice circle. In addition, prisons are often geographically isolated so that the institutions and the people inside of them are rendered invisible to most of the public,[60] and communication is highly restricted and monitored within carceral settings so that incarcerated people have very few options for having their own voices heard beyond the bars of their cells. All of this

[60] See Vanden Bosch (2020).

contributes to a systemically driven, unwarranted focus on only the criminal acts of incarcerated people in the United States. This, in turn, leads to a sort of narrative entrapment where they are vilified and distorted as nothing more than, for example, "a cold-blooded murderer" or "a monster."

Of course, the way that misknowing is generated and sustained can vary for both individuals and groups. Sometimes, a single, injurious fact is quite literally the only truth known about a person, as when readers of a news article know only that someone is, say, "a serial killer." This can be generated by reductive stories told by the State and the media and the absence of any additional publicly available information. Other times, further facts are available about a person, but they are ignored, dismissed, relegated to the margins, or swamped. Zara Bain's development of the concept of white ignorance introduced by Charles Mills is helpful here, as Bain distinguishes between Mills's "propositional ignorance," which is the "absence of belief, [or] a set of false beliefs" (Mills 2015, p. 217) and "dispositional ignorance," which involves "the cultivation of epistemological practices and dispositions to ignore important information," (Bain 2023, p. 20) such as "self-deception, bad faith, evasion and misrepresentation" (Mills 2007, p. 17). Since white ignorance is typically understood as an active process, Bain characterizes dispositional ignorance in terms of the cultivation of practices, but we can extend this notion to have both passive and active dimensions. Passive dispositional ignorance might involve, for instance, failures to question or inquire further about the reductive stories told about incarcerated Americans because of indifference, while its active counterpart might involve tendencies to dismiss positive facts about them or push fuller information to the periphery because of bias or hatred. Consider, for instance, a news story highlighting William Peeples as one of the first incarcerated students to graduate from a top ten university in the United States. A person who generally scrolls past these kinds of articles might be passively dispositionally ignorant of fuller stories of incarcerated Americans, but a member of the public who generally reads them and writes in the comments, "yes, but he is a murderer" may be actively dispositionally ignorant of them. This commenter may be resistant to any updating of information about William, even when it is right in front of his eyes, and may hold fixed the centrality of this one action of his life, ensuring that every other fact about him is swamped by or viewed through the lens of it. Otherwise put, this one action in William's six decades of life is in bold and is the framing device according to which everything else about him is filtered and in grayscale.

Misknowing, then, is often caused, fueled, and exacerbated by the stories told about suspects and defendants. Despite the powerful space that narratives occupy in our lives, especially for those swept up in the criminal legal system, defendants—whether innocent or guilty—rarely play even a marginal role as authors of their own public stories. They are silenced, handed a script to follow, and punished severely for failing to follow it. They are then vilified and distorted by the media, relegated to isolated carceral settings that are under nearly constant surveillance, and afforded very few avenues for communication with the outside world. This results in these images, labels, and master narratives, developed and promoted by the criminal legal system and the media, socially locking defendants into these stories, sometimes for life.

## 4. Flat Stories and Round Stories

Consider some of the different ways in which a typical case of misknowing within the criminal legal system impacts the misknown's stories. There are stories that demonize or distort him—perhaps as being a liar, a murderer, irredeemable, or monstrous. There are stories that render who he truly is invisible—perhaps marginalizing his loving relationships or ignoring facts about his honest and trustworthy character. There are stories that are extracted from him by prescribed scripts—perhaps of heightened levels of responsibility, blameworthiness, and remorse that fail to take into account backwards looking mitigating or explanatory factors. There are stories that he is prevented from telling due to his isolation and surveillance—perhaps about who he is today or who he plans to be tomorrow. There are stories that attempt to justify how he is treated—perhaps as deserving of the brutal and inhumane conditions of many carceral settings. There are stories that are taken from him—perhaps of who he could have been had he not lived in a racially driven, overpoliced community. In each case, the misknown's epistemic agency is compromised in deep, violating, and unjust ways.

I now want to make the case that just as invisibility, vilification, and distortion involving a false or unwarranted narrative requires a counterstory as a form of epistemic reparations, so, too, misknowing requires what I call a *rounder story* as a kind of epistemic reparations for some of the stories that have and have not yet been told.

E. M. Forster's famous distinction between flat and round characters is a foundational lesson of many writing courses. Flat characters, according to Forster, are static and "constructed round a single idea or quality" with none of the psychological desires and "aches that . . . complicate [even] the most consistent human lives" (1954, pp. 67–68). Gerald Prince's *A Dictionary of Narratology* defines flat characters as "endowed with one or very few traits and highly predictable in behavior,"[61] and Philip Meyer writes that flat characters are "monochromatic or one-dimensional, often cast onstage to express a single idea or to serve a specific plot function . . . . [They] may have some aspect or trait that makes (and keeps) them interesting or compelling, but what they lack, typically, is psychological complexity or the ability to change; they are fixed entities and typically do not develop or change in the course of the plot" (2014, pp. 75–76). In contrast, round characters are dynamic, complex, and multidimensional[62] with sufficient information conveyed about their " . . . internal tensions, contradictions, and complications"[63] so that their actions are understood as "the product of several different drives or conflicts derived from more than one level of the personality" (Lodge 1992, p. 183). In addition to this psychological complexity, round characters are "not static" and "evolve or change internally . . . as the plot develops" (Meyer 2014, p. 77). This multidimensional, dynamic aspect of round characters, and the one-dimensional, static aspect of those that are flat, is so fundamental to their nature that some scholars have proposed alternative labels that more clearly focus on this distinction. Paul Pickrel, for instance, argues that *essentialist* and *existential* are better suited to capturing what is importantly different about these characters, where the former are those "whose 'essence precedes existence', whose nature is a given that remains largely (essentially) unchanged by the experience it passes through, where [the latter] is the reverse—for him or her 'existence precedes essence'; his or her nature is shaped by experience" (Pickrel 1988, p. 182). In what follows, I will stick with "flat" and "round" since these terms are widely used in the literature but keeping in mind "essentialist" and "existential" may shed additional light on what they are aiming to capture.

I would like to extend this distinction between flat and round characters to apply to stories themselves and the resulting knowledge that is conveyed. So, a *flat story* is one that depicts a person in static, one-dimensional, and

[61] Prince (2003, p. 12).
[62] Prince (2003, p. 85).
[63] Meyer (2014, p. 77).

psychologically simplistic terms and the knowledge that is then conveyed about him is correspondingly flat, while a *round story* is one that portrays a person in dynamic, multidimensional, and psychologically complex terms and the knowledge that is then conveyed about him is correspondingly round.

As should be clear from what was developed above, many of the master narratives told about justice-impacted people, especially when they are Black, are flat. Suspects and defendants—as both a group and as individuals—are distorted by a tendency to view their criminalized actions as reflecting something deep or important about their character rather than as arising out of contingent circumstances. The media then center on the one day of a person's crime, depict the person in a mugshot, avoid the use of his actual name, and label him as the "accused," a "serial killer," and so on. The criminal legal system then provides virtually no avenues for the defendant to tell his own story in his own words. Moreover, with the rise of social media use, the lines between the media and the broader criminal legal system are increasingly blurred. Law enforcement agencies, for instance, are beginning to take on the role traditionally reserved for journalists, with a recent study showing that more than 14,000 law enforcement agencies communicate directly with their communities.[64] This same study also found that crime involving a Black person was overrepresented by 138% on Facebook. As one of the researchers, Julian Nyarko, writes, "The arm of the state that's principally responsible for controlling crime also shapes public views about character and incidence" (Itoi 2023). Once this story of a person's life is created, told, and promoted, the defendant who is convicted is then locked away in an American prison, often in a rural community far from his loved ones, with his public narrative similarly locked in time. As far as most of the world knows, he will always be nothing more than that one awful day of his life. This is a paradigmatically flat story—one that depicts a person in static, one-dimensional, and psychologically simplistic terms.

This brings us to a further dimension of flat and round stories that bears similarities to the distinction between being static versus dynamic but that is worth focusing on in its own right. A flat story is *closed*, meaning that the story—or at least the part of it that is seen as worth telling—is regarded or portrayed as finished. This is distinct from being static, as a person and his story can remain unchanged for any number of reasons, not all of which

[64] See Itoi (2023).

involve the story being finished. Moreover, a flat story is often agentially closed, meaning that there are no future options available to the main character that are regarded as potentially relevant to his story. For those swept up in the criminal legal system, for instance, many of the forces at work in shaping their master public narratives are shouting, "You're a criminal and that's all you'll ever be." This is supported by the fundamental attribution error, where criminalized activity is seen as reflecting something deep about a person's character and is connected to Pickrel's use of "essentialist" and "existential" to capture flat and round characters. If a person's nature remains essentially unchanged by his experiences, then his story can be largely completed by focusing on him as a criminal since not only is that who he is, but that's also who he will always be. In contrast, a round story is *open*, especially agentially, with the story's future having many different possible directions and outcomes, sort of like the "Choose Your Own Adventure" books where the reader could make choices about how the story unfolds and ends. If a person's actions can be impacted by contingent circumstances in life-altering ways, and his nature can be shaped in deep and important ways by experiences, then the story of who he is should leave open agential possibilities, even radical ones. In other words, while his choices may not necessarily reflect who he is today, they can affect who he becomes tomorrow.

Summarizing, then, a flat story is one that is closed and depicts a person in static, one-dimensional, and psychologically simplistic terms, while a round story is one that is open and portrays a person in dynamic, multidimensional, and psychologically complex terms.

To develop this further, notice that the misknowing connected to a flat story also often begets further downstream epistemic wrongs. The flat story of the criminal defendant, for instance, is typically massively *impoverished*. From a backwards-looking perspective, it paints a dramatically incomplete picture of the person's past, leaving out highly valuable information that would help understand his motives, actions, and character, such as a history of abuse, neglect, drug addiction, living in an overpoliced community, being subject to racism, attending a poorly funded school, and so on. From a current point of view, it fails to include relevant information about the person's relationships, community connections, educational accomplishments, activism, mentoring, and so on. It is also *distorting*, often including labels that are powerful and memorable, such as murderer, rapist, drug dealer, and so on, that swamp other facts about a person. The combination of the knowledge being impoverished and distorting can then give rise to future-looking inferences and conclusions that are false, misleading, and close or limit possibilities. To make this vivid, let's return to William Peeples. There are many flat stories that can be told about his life, but the one that is favored by the criminal legal system focuses on that single day in 1988 that led to his current incarceration. It portrays his actions as the result of some deep, important truth about his character and it depicts him as static—William is still the same person now that he was on that fateful day—despite the fact that nearly 40 years have passed. A flat story fueling misknowing will then lock him into the label of being "nothing more than a murderer," leading to life-destroying inferences about what can be expected of him in the future, such as that he is a violent person, that he poses a threat to his community, that he is not an ideal candidate for clemency, that he should not be employed or housed in a particular location, and so on.

Returning to the unjust, systemic forces at work in the creation and promotion of the flat narrative of William's life, it should be clear that he is owed epistemic reparations, with one kind being the creation and promotion of a rounder story of who he is. What might such a rounder story look like? Just as the exonerees in the study cited above report that their sense of self cannot be restored without a counternarrative "delabelling" them, so, too, many people swept up in the criminal legal system need a rounder narrative delabelling them, even when they are guilty of committing the crime in question. The concept of misknowing, combined with the fundamental attribution error and labeling, adds an important dimension here. While some dispositional attributions may be false—for instance, I mistakenly judge you to be a rude person for honking your horn at me rather than leaving room for the stress of your recent medical diagnosis to be the cause—some are true. Strictly speaking, for instance, it may be correct to say that William is a murderer or a criminal, but these labels not only fail to be explanatory of his actions, they are also obscuring and distorting.

Consider, for instance, William's early years in Chicago, which involved neglect, abuse, and violence.[65] After charges against him for gang intimidation and assault were dismissed, his mother moved them to suburban Schaumburg to get him away from the problems in the city. On the night after they moved in, he was on his way back home from buying cigarettes for his mom when he was stopped and searched by a police officer who said, "We don't like you city n-----s in our town, so you be careful, boy." After this

[65] See Peeples Jr. (2020). All details and quotes about William's early years are taken from this story.

experience, William describes remembering the stories his "granny used to tell of black boys and men being lynched" and says he went home "scared and humiliated." Later, a neighbor called the police because of a loud argument William was having with his sister and after standing between his mother and an officer to protect her, the sergeant at the scene said, "There's no reason for us to get involved. Let the n-----s handle their own problems." The next day, William was arrested on his way to the store because he allegedly fit the description of a Black boy who attempted to rape a white girl. He was denied counsel, was choked and beaten until he signed a typed confession, and was advised by his public defender to take a plea deal rather than go to trial and face a 30-year sentence. William writes, "I took the plea! An 18-year-old has no business being confined with seasoned criminals. But there I was, and if I wanted to survive I'd better learn the art of war. I learned too well. By the time I was paroled, I was a sociopath."

These backwards-looking events in William's life are inseparable from what led to his current incarceration. Interpreting his actions, which arose in a context of violence, racism, and injustice, as reflecting his character in some important sense, and then reductively labeling him accordingly—"he's a murderer" or "he's a criminal"—is to misknow him. It is to know some truths about William, but only those that are most injurious, which conceal and obfuscate deeper and more explanatory truths. Part of the rounder story owed to William, then, crucially includes these chapters of his life.

The present story should involve recentering William's humanity, emphasizing who he has become through decades of growth, and pushing facts about the worst day of his life to the periphery. In the report discussed above on the role of racial bias in the media regarding coverage of people prosecuted in the criminal court system, the authors provide recommendations for the media, some of which provide minimal guidelines for rounder stories, such as forgoing images that drive perceptions of guilt and avoiding labels that carry negative connotations. In particular, they write that reporters credentialing defendants by crime is "dehumanizing" and that "journalists should provide quotes from family members, friends, coworkers, and community members, so that they do not remain singularly associated with the offense with which they have been charged," especially in the case of Black defendants.[66] This is an explicit call for rounder stories in the media coverage of defendants in the American criminal legal system.

[66] Global Strategy Group (2021).

The rounder story of William, for instance, might include images of the people and projects that are most important to him, such as of him hugging his loved ones, offering public lectures, and engaging in restorative justice work, and of labels that reflect these values, such as "father," "Northwestern graduate," "published author," and "restorative justice practitioner." As J. C. Buitelaar notes, "[m]any people find their most important interests in 'life-time transcending interests' and they put much value on *becoming known through these projects*. Once undertaken, these projects can become part of these persons and, in fact, they provide them with a unique identity" (2017, p. 137, emphasis added).

More generally, there are four points to emphasize here regarding rounder stories as epistemic reparations. First, notice that I focus on *rounder* stories rather than *round* ones. This is to make clear that roundness is on a spectrum and that we may never succeed in providing a fully round story of any of our lives. Nevertheless, there are many steps, both big and small, that can be taken to ensure that rounder stories are told about those who are owed them. This may involve everything from a published biography or a full-length documentary, at one end of the spectrum, to the replacement of a label with a fuller description of the person—such as William being known as a "Northwestern graduate" or "restorative justice practitioner" rather than "murderer"—at the other end of the spectrum. Each takes steps of varying degrees to provide rounder stories and while some may be more complete or successful than others, it is important to engage in the work even when there are limitations. Sharing a rounder story of a survivor on Instagram, for instance, takes radically less time and effort than creating a documentary does, but both may be epistemically reparative in important and different ways.[67] The Instagram post may have greater reach and impact in restoring the survivor's status within the community, and the documentary may have a small audience but provide a deeper and richer narrative of the person's life. The fact that one end of the spectrum is capacity prohibitive does not normatively license doing nothing at all in such cases.

Second, a rounder story does not involve providing just any additional information about a person, but nor does it necessarily require the addition of positive facts or details about him.[68] Instead, it is one that contributes to

[67] I discuss who has the duty to engage in this epistemically reparative work in Chapter 5, but I should note here that all of us, regardless of whether we are perpetrators of the violation or injustice in question, have work to do.

[68] I explore this point in more detail when I consider "unsympathetic perpetrators" later in this chapter.

portraying a person in agentially open, dynamic, multidimensional, and psychologically complex terms. A flat story about a person as, say, a "murderer" does not become rounder by piling on more information that contributes to this closed, static, one-dimensional, and psychologically simplistic picture of him. Emphasizing how he murdered his victim, for instance, or how evil he must be to have done such a thing, may fill out the story but it does nothing to *round* it out. It simply adds more detail to a story that remains entirely flat. What the rounder story needs to do in order to be an act of epistemic reparations is to target the distinctively epistemic wrong that either arose from or constitutes a gross violation or injustice. So if the epistemic wrong is the flat story of being regarded as "only a murderer," then the rounder story needs to target the invisibility and vilification of failing to be seen as so much more than this one act. This doesn't necessarily mean providing only positive information about a person, such as his virtues or accomplishments. It may instead involve filling in background about his challenges or struggles, current relationships, projects, and so on. Similarly, the flat story of being "always a murderer" or a "perpetual perpetrator"[69] depicts a person in static and agentially closed terms, either rendering invisible transformation and growth or erasing them through vilification—for example, "he is just trying to manipulate the court for leniency." The rounder story here needs to show the capacity for authentic change even if not every detail is unqualifiedly positive.[70] Perhaps it involves years of him making harmful choices in prison before committing to rewriting his own narrative to be one where love and accountability are at the center. Indeed, rounder stories often show the layers and nuances of people and their relations with others, and so sharing how incarceration has led to someone being estranged from his daughter, or how he struggles to be patient even when the weight of living in a cage with another person threatens to crush him, may still contribute to seeing him as dynamic, multidimensional, and psychologically complex.

Third, I have emphasized the importance of centering the epistemic agency of survivors when engaging in epistemic reparations and while I fleshed out some of what is involved in this, it may be helpful to distinguish epistemic agency with respect to *telling a story* from epistemic agency *within a story*.[71]

[69] Jain (2024, p. 128).

[70] While she is not discussing this in the context of epistemic reparations, Neha Jain makes a similar point about flat stories in international criminal trials, emphasizing the need to "recognize the defendant as a complex moral agent who possesses the capacity for self-transformation" (2024, p. 159).

[71] I am grateful to a question from Michael Bratman that led to the inclusion of this point.

We started this chapter by looking at how the criminal legal system silences the true stories of suspects and defendants and extracts false ones, and so one way of engaging in epistemic reparations is to give people back their stories. This may involve creating and promoting the conditions for survivors to tell authentic stories about themselves, either on their own or through others, and by coming to know them through listening to them. But when the epistemic wrong itself involves a story that is closed, one-dimensional, static, and psychologically simplistic, the rounder story that is owed will also often include the creation or restoration of epistemic agency within the story. As a contrast, consider that a true counterstory of a wrongful conviction may focus on how a defendant's rational capacities were bypassed or subverted, and so there may be very little epistemic agency within the story. Indeed, its absence may lie at the heart of what happened. However, when a flat story depicts a person as, say, nothing more than, and perpetually, a murderer, the epistemically reparative work needed involves centering the creation or restoration of epistemic agency as a part of the narrative itself. Growth, transformation, open possibilities, nuance, and complexity might all be crucial elements of the rounder story that ought to be told, and so in addition to epistemic agency in telling his story, there are cases where a survivor is also owed epistemic agency within the story.

Finally, a slightly different form of epistemically reparative work that can be done in the face of misknowing can be seen in the case of Kimyon Marshall, who at 15 years old stabbed and killed 17-year-old Ruben Cotton over an argument regarding a pair of sneakers. Twenty-five years later, Cotton's brother, Darryl Green, decided to forgive Marshall and advocate for his release from prison:

> It was the beginning of their second chapter—together. Green spoke on behalf of Cotton and their family who recommended Marshall be released, and asked the court if he could approach Marshall. "I shook his hand. He was crying, I was crying," recalls Green. "I said to him, 'You've been known for taking a life, now let's go save some lives together.'" (Keating 2023)

Green makes clear that for twenty-five years, Marshall was known almost entirely for being a murderer, an act of a 15-year-old child in a moment of anger that seemed to forever define him, even as a 40-year-old man. The request to "save some lives together" is thus not only a call to collective action, it is also an invitation to rewrite Marshall's story. In particular, epistemically reparative work can involve not only reorienting already existing truths about a person, such as when William Peeples was given space to tell a fuller version of his story for the *Northwestern Magazine*, but also providing opportunities to create new truths that can squeeze out injurious ones.[72] And that is precisely what Green and Marshall have together done since the 2016 launch of their organization, Deep Forgiveness, whose mission is to "analyze the impact of forgiveness, encourage conversation and the healing power thereof . . . [and to] restore wholeness and a spirit of reconciliation as we embody the true meaning of forgiveness" (Deep Forgiveness). By talking about their own experiences, listening to others who are similarly situated, and cultivating a spirit of reconciliation, Green and Marshall make possible a new narrative—one that does not deny or forget the act of violence that originally connected them, but creates new chapters for a fuller, richer story of both of their lives.

One question that may be asked is whether there are cases where what is owed in the name of epistemic reparations is a flat rather than a rounder story. For instance, just as other goods in our communities, such as material ones, are unequally distributed in massively unjust ways, so, too, are epistemic ones. Some groups and individuals have far more or far rounder stories told about them, while others are forgotten, ignored, silenced, and flattened. So as we provide counter and rounder stories of some, should we also be forgetting or flattening others in the name of epistemic justice?

By way of response, notice first that epistemic justice is a much broader category than epistemic reparations, with the latter being part of what is necessary to achieve the former. In taking steps toward distributive epistemic justice, then, one may argue that it is important to not only tell, round out, and center stories that have been sidelined, but to also push those that have been dominant out of the spotlight. Perhaps this is how to best understand efforts to diversify the canon in philosophy, which may involve, say, both the inclusion on a syllabus of some views and stories that have been relegated to obscurity as well as the removal of some that have been disproportionately highlighted. While this may indeed result in a more fair or just distribution of epistemic goods, this does not involve flattening some stories as acts of epistemic reparations. Indeed, even in cases of interpersonal wrongdoing between groups of individuals, this doesn't work. An ethnic group subjected to

[72] This is similar to the discussion of James Soto in the Introduction wanting to become a lawyer focusing on exonerations so that he can "be known as someone who helped."

widespread flat stories of dehumanization, say, is not in any way made visible or humanized or accurately depicted through also telling dehumanizing stories of the relevant perpetrators. In other words, steps are not taken toward repairing the damage to a survivor of a flat story by also making someone else's flat, even if this other person has enjoyed unfair rounder stories and is himself a contributor to the wrongs in questions.

A further question that may be asked is whether a person can misknow or tell a flat story about himself and, if so, if it can rise to the level of a gross violation or injustice that demands epistemic reparations. By way of response, recall that our identities can be powerfully impacted by the stories that are told about us, including the ones we tell about ourselves. According to Dan P. McAdams, for instance:

> If you want to know me, then you must know my story, for my story defines who I am. And if *I* want to know *myself*, to gain insight into the meaning of my own life, then I, too, must come to know my own story. . . . It is a story I continue to revise, and tell to myself (and sometimes to others) as I go on living. (1993, p. 11)

Even if we don't embrace McAdams's narrative identity view in all of its detail, it is clear that stories play a significant role in our lives, especially regarding how we revise our life narratives in the face of traumatic events. Research shows, for instance, that with respect to incarceration in particular, unless the relevant experiences are integrated "into a revised, updated, and meaningful self-narrative," incarcerated people's "sense of ontological order can rapidly descend into existential chaos and narrative wreckage" (Hardie-Bick 2018, p. 575),[73] ultimately leading to "one's whole sense of self" becoming "uncertain" (Hardie-Bick 2018, p. 576).[74] The label "criminal" is particularly damaging, with one study finding incarcerated respondents citing "winning the lottery" and "death" as what would need to happen in order to avoid engaging in future criminal behavior.[75] For one respondent in this study, this self-narrative of the inevitability of future criminal behavior is directly attributed to the master narrative about his life that "because you're a criminal you'll always be so . . . ." (Maruna and Ramsden 2004, p. 137).

[73] See also Frank (1995).
[74] See also Crawley and Sparks (2013).
[75] Maruna and Ramsden (2004, p. 136).

What we see here is the powerful interplay between flat master narratives that generate, shape, and perpetuate systemic violations and injustices of both groups and individuals. The master narrative of "criminals," which is driven by the criminal legal system and the media, is static, one-dimensional, psychologically simplistic, and closed. When this is internalized by an individual justice-impacted person, he can find his own sense of self and his future being fixed by the completed story of his life. He regards himself as a criminal, nothing more than a criminal, and always a criminal, leading to dramatic events outside of himself—such as winning the lottery or death—being regarded as the only avenues for new chapters of his life to be written. This is a clear instance of a person not only misknowing himself through a flat story, but also one that, given the systemic injustices fueling it, rises to the level of deserving epistemic reparations.[76]

While we have discussed general ways of telling rounder stories that are epistemically reparative, there is also research specifically on how incarcerated people can create and rewrite their life narratives.[77] According to James Hardie-Bick, "the challenge is to . . . develop a more life-affirming narrative, . . . [which] can be achieved by examining and re-examining the past, reinterpreting the significance of key events, and understanding previously unacknowledged motivations, aspirations, and beliefs" (2018, p. 583). This includes all of the features of rounder stories—reexamining and reinterpreting the past as well as key events counters both the static and closed dimensions of flat stories, and understanding previously unacknowledged motivations, aspirations, and beliefs addresses the one-dimensional, psychologically simplistic portrayals of the central characters in them. One respondent in the study cited above, for instance, reexamined and reinterpreted his past as follows: "I look back and I think I was misunderstood . . . My intentions was good but methods was wrong, sort of thing . . . " (Maruna and Ramsden 2004, p. 137). Recognizing that he did not have bad intentions but, rather, that his actions were the result of a failure of implementation enables him to reclaim his sense of self as a good person. We see, then, that although being in the grip of misknowing about one's very identity, especially when it is driven by dominant flat narratives about who one is as an individual and as a member of a certain group, can be a powerful

[76] Sarah Wright (2025) has fascinating and important work on epistemic reparations that are owed to oneself, including because of blocked counternarratives of oneself in a dominant story, credibility deficits to oneself, and being cut off from participation in public language.

[77] See Brookman (2015), Presser and Sandberg (2015), and Hardie-Bick (2018).

force, there are concrete pathways for providing the epistemic reparations that one owes to oneself.

## 5. The Right to Be Known Versus the Right to Be Forgotten

An additional virtue of the epistemically reparative impact of rounder stories can be seen by contrasting it with the European Union's "right to erasure"—otherwise known as the "the right to be forgotten"[78]—which gives EU residents the right to have personal information erased from search results and public information databases.[79] Since the 2014 ruling of the European Court of Justice in a high-profile privacy case in Spain that led to the right to be forgotten, Google reports that it has received nearly 1.6 million delisting requests.[80] This is perhaps unsurprising, as Viktor Mayer-Schönberger warned in his 2009 book, *Delete: The Virtue of Forgetting in the Digital Age*, that "with the help of widespread technology, forgetting has become the exception and remembering the default" and asked "[d]o we want a future that is forever unforgiving because it is unforgetting?" (2009, p. 2 and pp. 4–5). With the internet's nearly perfect memory, events that were once embarrassing or damaging in a specific place and time, and to a limited audience, can now be made just about universally and permanently available. Mayer-Schönberger, for instance, opens his book by discussing the cases of Stacy Snyder, whose university denied her a teaching certificate because of an "unprofessional" MySpace photo of her wearing a pirate's hat and drinking out of a plastic cup, resulting in the destruction of her future career goals, and of Andrew Feldmar, a Canadian psychotherapist who mentioned in an article he had written for an interdisciplinary journal that he had taken LSD in the 1960s. In 2006, when Feldmar was crossing the border from the United States back to Canada, a border guard found this article online, questioned him for four hours, and fingerprinted him, leading to him signing a statement that he had taken drugs four decades ago and being barred from further entry into the United States. These sorts of life-altering consequences prompt Mayer-Schönberger to argue for "expiration dates" on information so that we "take steps to ensure we'll remember how to forget in the digital age" (2009, p. 15).

[78] This is Article 17 of the General Data Protection Regulation, which governs how personal data in the European Union is collected, processed, and erased. See European Union (2016).
[79] European Union (2016).
[80] Google (n.d.).

Whether we focus on erasure or expiration, there is widespread support that some information about people that is accessible online should be forgotten. A 2020 study, for instance, showed that 85% of adults in the United States believe that all Americans should have the right to have potentially embarrassing photos and videos erased from online searches and 67% report that this should be a right for all Americans regarding information about employment history or work records.[81] But the percentage drops to 39% when it comes to this same right being applied to data collected by law enforcement, such as criminal records or mugshots.

This tracks debates over how to balance the right to be forgotten in the EU, and privacy laws and interests in the United States—including "Clean Slate" legislation[82] that automatically clears records of eligible convictions, as well as other laws that allow for convictions to be expunged or sealed from public view—with a host of other ones that often pull in competing directions, such as the right to freedom of expression, freedom of the press, and access to information that is of public interest.[83] The right to have a criminal conviction cleared from search results, for instance, is resisted by some who say that this information is of public interest for the purposes of safety. So, while the accessibility of this information may lead to a lifetime of housing, employment, and legal challenges, this may be regarded by some as an unfortunate but necessary consequence of keeping communities safe. In other words, even if people have the right to have some information about them erased or forgotten from public consciousness, this right may be trumped by competing ones. Using the framework developed here, we might say that the right for someone with a criminal conviction to be known through a rounder story may be in conflict with the public's right to know what turns out to be a flat story about him through, say, inclusion on a sex offender registry.

By way of response to this apparent tension between a justice-impacted person's right to be known and the public's right to know, the first point to note is that research shows that people who receive expungements actually have very low recidivism rates and quickly exhibit much better employment outcomes. In particular, because criminal records raise significant barriers to employment and housing, which in turn aggravate poverty and inequality that contribute to crime risk, expungements of criminal records

[81] See Auxier (2020).
[82] See Clean Slate Initiative (n.d.).
[83] See, for instance, Singleton (2015).

actually increase public safety.[84] But the point I want to emphasize here is that the power of rounder stories provides an avenue for repairing the epistemic damage of flat stories even when there isn't legislation available that grants rights like being forgotten or having a clean slate. Telling, promoting, and making accessible rounder stories about a person can swamp the one-dimensional flat ones that socially lock people into one moment in their lives. Consider, again, William Peeples. At a recent event, he reported that when his daughter last Googled him, the first page of search results included links to only his published stories and accomplishments connected with the Northwestern Prison Education Program, with none linking to his criminal record or mugshot. So, while William's past is not erased or deleted, it is nonetheless pushed out of the position of centerstage that it would otherwise occupy on the internet. In this way, not only do the links provide access to rounder stories of William's life—some told by him and some told about him—but his overall search result profile itself is rounder, depicting a multidimensional life of transformation, nuance, growth, and agency.

Moreover, balancing conflicting rights between those seeking erasure and privacy, on the one hand, and those seeking freedom of expression and access to information, on the other, is often complex and dependent on the specific details of the case. The Court of Justice of the European Union, for instance, holds that neither the right to be forgotten nor the right to freedom of expression "takes absolute precedence over the other" and that the "relevant compelling interest—public or private—depends on the facts of the given case" (Singleton 2015, pp. 179–180). Similarly, the "'United States Supreme Court has long held that freedom of speech, as guaranteed by the First Amendment, does not include all modes of communication of ideas' but must be balanced against other interests, including the privacy protection of individuals."[85] Navigating the legal complexities involving such competing rights and interests can lead to lengthy, expensive, and often disappointing results. In contrast, empowering those who have been directly impacted by the sort of wrongdoing demanding of epistemic reparations to tell rounder stories of themselves, or encouraging those with platforms—such as journalists and political leaders—to do so, provides timely, inexpensive, and potentially highly impactful pathways for changing or expanding social

[84] See Prescott and Starr (2020).

[85] Gajda (2018, p. 202, quoting *Hartzell v. Cummings*, No. 150103764, 2015 WL 7301962, at *1 (Pa. Ct. Com. Pl. Nov. 4, 2015).

narratives. In March of 2023, for instance, TikTok announced that more than 150 million Americans are users, which is nearly half of the country's population.[86] Anyone with access to a cell phone with the app can create content immediately for free and with the potential to be accessed by far more readers than traditional news sources.[87]

Still further, even when there are laws that permit deletion or clean slates, narratives that wrong may linger in the news, on social media, on blogs, and in a variety of other spaces. Adding stories that are fuller and deeper, rather than merely subtracting those that are reductive and wrongful, includes information that may be deeply important and illuminating, not only for the main character of the story, but also for people like him. Consider William again. Even if it were currently possible to clear or expunge his criminal convictions from public searches, the decades of work that William has devoted to growing into the man he is today is a part of his story that he not only wants to be told, but also that he is owed having others bear witness to. This can be made even more vivid by considering the availability heuristic, which refers to a mental shortcut that humans take when judging how likely it is that an event will occur based on how easily information about such an event comes to mind or is available.[88] So, for instance, I may massively overestimate the likelihood of getting attacked by a shark after witnessing one on vacation but underestimate my risk of getting in a car accident because so many go unreported. Perhaps unsurprisingly, research shows the availability heuristic at work in judgments about crime, with exposure to media about crime having a biasing effect on people's perception of actual crime rates.[89] This has been impacted by the increased role of social media and neighborhood apps in the reporting of crimes. In particular, a recent study of neighborhood apps like Nextdoor reveals that their use is associated with inaccurate perceptions of higher local crime rates.[90] As psychologist Sue Frantz notes, "for frequent Nextdoor readers, crime information is salient. The availability heuristic leads such readers to think their neighborhoods are crime-ridden when, in

[86] TikTok (2023).

[87] For instance, about eight months after TikTok made the above announcement, the *New York Times* published an article with the headline, "*The New York Times* Passes 10 Million Subscribers" (Robertson 2023).

[88] See Tversky and Kahneman (1973). The salience bias discussed later is a specific instance of the broader cognitive bias found in the availability heuristic.

[89] See Morgan and Shanahan (1997) and Drakulich (2013).

[90] See Fetterman et al. (2023).

fact, the crime rates may be quite low. If only people would also report when they experienced no crime."

Of course, it is highly unlikely that norms will shift so that people begin reporting the absence of crime as often as they report the presence of crime, and it is unclear whether this would even be desirable. After all, information overload[91] is only growing, with some reporting that the amount of information being created every two days in current times is roughly equivalent to the amount of information that was created between the beginning of human civilization and the year 2003.[92] This has real consequences, including stress, burnout, various health complaints, and performance losses.[93] Nevertheless, there is a useful connection between Frantz's ironic suggestion for countering the bias of the availability heuristic in Nextdoor and what is possible here. Consider the earlier discussion of how Black Americans, and Black men in particular, are invisible in some spaces and regarding some social or interpersonal goals and are hypervisible in other spaces and with respect to other goals. Similar considerations are found with incarcerated and formerly incarcerated people: with respect to their accomplishments and loving relationships, for instance, they are largely invisible from public consciousness; regarding their criminal activity, they are hypervisible. While the legislation focusing on being forgotten and clean slates may help with some of the hypervisibility, the telling of rounder stories like William's helps repair both epistemic wrongs. Ensuring that narratives are told of incarcerated people as devoted fathers and college graduates and talented singers and engaged students and loving friends and wise poets and livers of other full and rich lives, despite being in some of the darkest corners of the world, counters their invisibility in spaces traditionally regarded as elite or admirable or worthy of respect. Moreover, if such stories are made widely available, then they have the potential to also counter or even swamp those that focus entirely on the criminal activity of justice-impacted people. Perhaps images of incarcerated people playing with their children during their college graduation ceremony or reciting poetry at a conference would not only more easily come to the public's minds, but, given the availability heuristic, would also impact judgments about how likely it is for justice-impacted people to live these kinds of lives.

[91] See, for instance, Arnold et al. (2023).
[92] Schmidt, cited in Jackson and Farzaneh (2012).
[93] See Arnold et al. (2023) for a comprehensive overview of these consequences.

Taking a step back, we saw earlier that there are master narratives that are flat of both incarcerated people as a group and of particular individuals, such as William. Each of these flat stories fuels the other—those who are incarcerated are regarded as violent or dangerous *people*, so this is taken to be true of William; William is regarded as a dangerous or violent *person*, so this further supports the master narrative of incarcerated people. Interrupting this cycle with rounder master narratives at the level of the group or at the level of individuals can have deeply important ripple effects. Rounder stories of William epistemically repair not only some of the epistemic damage inflicted on him, but also on others like him. While William is indeed an extraordinary person, there are countless others incarcerated across the globe who could similarly achieve what is remarkable if given appropriate support and resources. Hearing his rounder stories and seeing him in his Northwestern cap and gown or teaching writing to a group of students provide dreams for incarcerated people that many of them never even knew were possible. And as more and more stories like William's are told and heard, they can serve as the archetype of a justice-impacted man rather than the flat narratives found in mugshots and much media coverage. These would be some first steps toward epistemic reparations for incarcerated people as a group grounded in epistemically reparative work focusing on the stories of individual survivors of carceral injustice.

The call for narratives that counter those that are wronging is not uncommon. Lindsey Webb, for instance, notes that "[w]e have the opportunity to ask what justice looks like if it is not the justice of the danger narrative or the true crime story. And we can consider how to create a world in which these new tales of justice can be told" (2021, pp. 169–170). Woods "urges institutional actors that regulate the police to abandon oversimplified danger narratives surrounding routine traffic stops in favor of context-rich archetypes that more accurately reflect the risks and costs of policing during these stops" (2019, p. 636). And according to Bryan Stevenson: "We often misunderstand topics. Underneath these topics are narratives—and narratives are what we need to change" (Ramos 2019).[94] What the framework here provides is an understanding of the distinctive epistemic wrongs that flat narratives inflict on others, the right survivors of these injustices have to be known, and how rounder stories can serve as part of the epistemic

[94] See also: " . . . behind every news story advancing a dominant racial ideology lie discarded counter-narratives, ignored cultural meanings, and omitted counter-stereotypical information" (Adamson 2016, p. 278).

reparations they are owed. In this way, each of the calls to action above can be at least partially illuminated. The new tales and changed narratives of the criminal legal system should include rounder stories that are context rich and depict people in dynamic, multidimensional, psychologically complex, and agentially open ways.

## 6. Unsympathetic Perpetrators

A worry that might be raised to this framework is how to handle unsympathetic perpetrators who are regarded as undeserving of a rounder story. For instance, Harvey Weinstein and Bill Cosby might be known as "rapists" and Hitler might be called a "monster" or "pure evil" but surely we do not want to say that they are owed fuller, richer narratives of their actions and lives. Indeed, some might argue for an even stronger claim: not only do such perpetrators deserve the one-dimensional narratives being told about them, it would also be potentially dangerous to provide multidimensional, dynamic ones. In a discussion in *The Guardian* of a 2021 documentary, *The Meaning of Hitler*, Betsy Reed writes that "to try to understand Hitler is to risk humanising him and reducing his culpability" and quotes documentary filmmaker Michael Tucker saying "the more you try to understand him, the more empathy you have" (Smith 2021). Legal scholar Kenworthy Bilz takes this one step further and argues that "[i]f we are rightly contemptuous of a person's unique perspective, not only is it fine to prevent him from presenting it, but it would even be affirmatively wrong to let him" (2010, p. 430).[95] Indeed, with respect to trials in particular, she claims that we should "refuse to hear the stories of those being judged when doing so might lead us to exonerate, or even just empathize, when we ought not" (2010, p. 430). One reason she offers for this is that "our attentions and sympathies are a scarce commodity" and so we should choose to invest these limited resources into survivors and victims who deserve them rather than perpetrators. Another is that the interests of those involved may be incompatible, and recognizing someone as having been wronged or victimized depends on blaming and having negative emotions toward the wrongdoer. As Bilz says, "Outrage at the aggressor is a way of recognizing the victim as a victim. Being angry with

[95] I should note that Bilz's thesis specifically concerns narratives in trials, but her arguments have general application.

the bully engages an alliance with the victim; being an apologist betrays an alliance with the aggressor" (2010, p. 454).

There are, however, several points that can be made by way of response. To begin, many of the widely used cases of unsympathetic perpetrators are not victims of unjustified flat stories in the first place. For instance, we know all about Harvey Weinstein's successful career as a film producer, Bill Cosby's work as an actor and comedian, and Hitler's military and political life. While it's true that we also know about their horrific crimes, they are not reduced to only these actions in any reasonable sense. A slightly different point arises with respect to Brock Turner, who was convicted in 2016 of sexually assaulting a woman in California but was widely identified in media coverage as a "Stanford swimmer." Indeed, even after he served his sentence, *Sports Illustrated*'s headline was "Ex-Stanford swimmer Brock Turner was released after serving half of his six-month sentence" and *Time*'s was "Stanford swimmer Brock Turner to be released from jail Friday."[96] While it may appear that viewing all of Turner's actions through the lens of him being a Stanford swimmer is to cultivate a flat story about him—albeit a positive one—not all labels that are centered in a person's public narrative are equal. We learn a great deal about Brock Turner just from these two words, including that he is a college student, he is smart, he is a talented swimmer, he is athletic, and he has enough support to apply to, be accepted by, and attend such a prestigious university. This does not in any way amount to an agentially closed, static, one-dimensional, and psychologically simplistic narrative about him, and thus he is not deserving of a rounder story as a form of epistemic reparations.

But even for those perpetrators who lack the richer narratives of those who are famous, or whose flat story is itself epistemically injurious, it is a mistake to equate rounder stories with positive ones. If someone is owed a rounder story, there is no guarantee that he will be more sympathetic after it is told. Sure, many rounder stories do have this outcome. Hearing that someone who murdered a rival gang member grew up surrounded by violence and abuse may elicit a sense that he is a victim, too, and that his early trauma mitigates his responsibility. The flipside of this, however, is that learning that someone with seemingly limitless resources weaponized his power and privilege to prey upon vulnerable people can make him seem dangerous and callous and fully responsible for his actions. The rounder story may be owed to

96 See LaChance (2016).

him because he was unjustly known through only a flat one but this does not thereby guarantee sympathy or exculpation. Knowing more does not mean blaming less.

Consider Ethan Couch, who as a teenager killed four people and injured nine others when he drove his pickup in 2013 into a group of people who were helping a woman with a stalled car in Texas. The rounder story that emerged about him drew outrage and condemnation rather than sympathy. We learned that Couch was driving 70 mph in a 40 mph zone and had a blood-alcohol level that was three times the Texas legal limit.[97] Moreover, his attorneys famously invoked an "affluenza" defense at his trial, arguing that his recklessness was due to his wealthy and privileged upbringing, which caused him to have a sense of entitlement and poor judgment. When Couch received 10 years of probation by a juvenile court judge, there was a public outcry that such a lenient sentence was a "grave injustice,"[98] not because of a flat story about him, but because the fuller, richer narrative of his life made him seem more responsible for his actions rather than less. This also bears on Bilz's claim that the narratives of perpetrators should be excluded because outrage at them is a way of recognizing victims as victims, as there is no reason to conclude that rounder stories of perpetrators will lead to less rather than more outrage.

Similarly, there is no reason to infer that a rounder story will result in greater understanding of or empathy with the perpetrator. Understanding is often taken to be connected with an explanation that enables the grasping of the "why" of an event.[99] A doctor explaining to you, for instance, that your fatigue is due to iron deficiency anemia sheds light on something that may have been completely mysterious to you beforehand. In this case, it is because there is a clear causal connection between low iron levels and insufficient hemoglobin, which is needed for red blood cells to carry oxygen through a human body's blood vessels. You learning that you have an iron deficiency thereby enables you to grasp why you have been constantly exhausted. But not all events are like this. In a *New York Times* article about a 2004 film, *Der Untergang*, that takes a deep dive into Hitler's last 12 days in a bunker in Berlin, then editor at *Die Zeit* says, "Showing [Hitler] in intimate situations does not make us understand him better. He remains monstrous

[97] See Strauss (2014).
[98] CBS News (2018).
[99] See Kim (1994), Zagzebski (2001), Riggs (2003), Elgin (2006), Hills (2009), and Grimm (2012, 2014, 2017).

and incomprehensible" (Landler 2004). What is being suggested here is that some actions are so horrific that no matter how much we learn, we will never get any closer to truly comprehending them. Sure, delving into Hitler's childhood or his relationship with his father may shed some light on his capacity for hatred. But unlike low iron levels and fatigue, there is no clear causal connection between anything we might learn about Hitler and the orchestration and perpetration of the Holocaust. This has a direct impact on the concern about empathizing with unsympathetic perpetrators. If empathy involves imaginatively occupying another person's position in an emotionally engaged way,[100] and I cannot grasp the why of that person's action, then it will be very difficult, if not impossible, for me to empathize with him.

In other cases, perhaps it is a question not of what is graspable but of a simple failure of a narrative that adds up, makes sense, or is coherent. If a multidimensional story reveals that someone who is capable of deep love and care nonetheless chose to violate vulnerable people, we may find ourselves more confused than we were with just a one-dimensional picture. Learning, for instance, that Harvey Weinstein was a respectful, loving, devoted husband to Georgina Chapman may make it more rather than less puzzling how he also sexually abused at least 60 women.[101] If a person knows how to interact with some women with dignity, then, it might be asked, how could he at the same time treat others with such violence and degradation? Again, there is a connection to empathy here. It may be easier to take up the perspective of someone who wholly lacks the capacity for love and care and treats everyone in his life in self-serving and exploitative ways than it is to imaginatively adopt Harvey Weinstein's.

This is important because the resistance to rounder stories for perpetrators often stems from a worry that they will lead to greater understanding, which will thereby promote forgiveness. Bilz is clear about this connection, even using the French proverb "to understand all is to forgive all" as the epigraph for her article.[102] But as a general inference this is certainly false. If my friend breaks her promise to pick up my children from school while I'm in the hospital, I may initially be puzzled by this. Where I go from here, however, depends crucially on the content of what I later learn. According to

[100] See, for instance, Hoffman (2000), Oxley (2011), Kaupinnen (2014, 2017), and Bailey (2022). It is worth noting that there is a debate over whether empathy involves me imagining myself in your situation or me imagining you in your situation. A discussion of this issue is complex and lies outside the scope of the present context.

[101] See Russian (2018).

[102] See, also, Mohamed (2015, p. 1632), though she goes on to reject this.

the standard view, forgiveness largely involves giving up negative emotions or attitudes, such as anger, disappointment, or contempt, toward one who has wronged you.[103] If my friend tells me that she was in a car accident on her way to the school, then my understanding of why she failed to pick up my children would indeed lead to me forgiving her. Yet what enables me to move past my anger or disappointment toward my friend in such a case is not simply understanding *why* she broke her promise to me; it is learning specifically that it was bad luck or something that was outside of her control that led to her doing so. If I instead hear that she was having drinks with a colleague and lost track of time, then a fuller grasp of why she broke her promise to me would lead to a deeper sense of anger and disappointment. I would rightly feel that she made some thoughtless and irresponsible choices that resulted in disrespecting our friendship and putting my children in danger, which would deepen the gulf between us. Understanding more can lead to forgiving less.

Empirical work that looks at the impact of perspective-taking is relevant here, which is understood as an other-oriented social cognitive process that involves making inferences about another person's mind—primarily, his thoughts and intentions.[104] Colloquially, this is often phrased as "putting yourself in another's shoes." While the bulk of this research focuses on interpersonal perspective-taking with members of victimized, marginalized, and negatively stereotyped groups, which generally has positive consequences,[105] more recent work has turned to perspective-taking with perpetrators and found greater nuance and complexity in the results.[106] In studies by Lucas et al. (2016), for instance, perspective-taking with perpetrators was shown to both decrease and increase moral condemnation, depending on the nature of the intentions attributed to the perpetrator. In particular, perspective-taking decreased condemnation and fostered forgiveness when benevolent intentions were attributed to a transgressor, but perspective-taking increased condemnation and punishment when malevolent intentions were attributed to a transgressor. This supports what was argued above: there is no necessary connection between rounder stories and understanding, empathy, or forgiveness. In all of these cases, the arrows can go in both directions, with

[103] See, for instance, French (1982), Murphy (1988), McGary (1989), Watkins (2015), and Emerick (2017).

[104] See Lucas et al. (2016).

[105] See Batson et al. (1997), Dovidio et al. (2004), Galinsky and Moskowitz (2000), and Vescio et al. (2003).

[106] See, for instance, Li et al. (2020).

richer narratives leading to more and less understanding and empathy, and greater understanding engendering more and less forgiveness. So, even if an unsympathetic perpetrator is also epistemically wronged and is owed a rounder story, it does not follow that this will thereby lead to deeper understanding, empathy, or forgiveness.

In addition, there are epistemic and moral benefits that are made possible by providing multidimensional narratives of wrongdoers. Consider the depictions of perpetrators of mass atrocity in international criminal trials, who have been described as "malignant forces," "dark shadows," "evil spawn," "hounds from hell," and "beasts of impunity" who committed crimes that are "against nature, against logic, against life itself" (Jain 2024, pp. 131–132). According to legal scholar Neha Jain, flat, one-dimensional "practices, scripts, and narratives of mass atrocity trials erect representative perpetrators who . . . have failed at the project of being human" (Jain 2024, p. 128). They are viewed as "perpetual perpetrators, the moment of their participation in atrocity radiating backwards and forwards to demarcate the juridical bookends of their lives" (Jain 2024, p. 128). But notice that to regard someone like Hitler as being monstrous or as pure evil is to push the fact of his humanity to the margins, thereby denying or obscuring the reality that human beings are indeed capable of committing mass atrocities. Bernd Eichinger, *Der Untergang*'s writer and producer, makes precisely this point in defense of his film: "[t]his whole debate over whether we are allowed to show Hitler as a human being is wrong. Of course he was a human being. You have to make clear to people that he was a human being, and that's the dangerous thing" (Landler 2004). This is what Hannah Arendt refers to as "the terror of the idea of humanity,"[107] which is "the terror that comes with accepting the perpetrator of radical evil as one of us, not a monster or wild animal" (Luban 2018, p. 136). Reductive labels and flat stories enable us to regard perpetrators as so foreign and unlike us that there is no point in even trying to understand them or their actions, but rounder narratives force us to confront the fact that even ordinary people can be recruited to take part in "extraordinary project[s] of radical evil" (Luban 2018, p. 136).[108]

Moreover, in order to properly hold people responsible for their actions, we need to see them as moral agents in the first place. Responding to "malignant forces," "dark shadows," "evil spawn," "hounds from hell," and "beasts of

[107] Arendt (1994, p. 131).

[108] Holocaust historian Raul Hilberg is said to have asked, "[w]ouldn't you be happier if I had been able to show you that all the perpetrators were crazy?" (Bauman 2003, p. 82).

impunity" may require steps to ensure the safety of others, but they would be comparable to how we protect people from viruses, natural disasters, and wild animals. We may, for instance, use quarantines to prevent the spread of COVID and avoid places prone to avalanches and wild polar bears, but it wouldn't make sense to ask questions about motives, responsibility, and punishment in such cases. Martha Nussbaum makes a similar point when she writes, "the further we place the murderer at a distance from us, the less obvious it is that this is a moral agent at all, and the less obvious it consequently is that this person deserves the penalty we reserve for fully responsible agents" (2006, p. 165). It is, then, precisely the fact that Hitler is a human being with agency that enables our moral assessments of him to have a normative grip.[109] Pushing him to the realms of natural disasters, wild animals, and monsters not only ignores the very humanlike forces that can drive someone to commit acts of mass atrocity—such as hatred, power, and ignorance—it also threatens to render senseless our moral condemnation of him and his actions.

A slightly different kind of unsympathetic perpetrator is one whose crime itself is motivated by a desire for fame or popularity, such as a school shooter.[110] In this sort of case, providing a rounder story of him may not only be to give him exactly what he wants, but also risks encouraging others to be copycats. For instance, in an article entitled, "When coverage is what they want: covering mass shootings without perpetuating them," *New York Times* freelance reporter Natalie Yahr discusses the intentionality involved in a "reporting shift" in coverage of school shootings, noting a 2019 case in which the name of the perpetrator "was decidedly absent from the headlines and initial internet search results" (2019). This reflects a response to research on what is often referred to as the "contagion effect," according to which "mass shootings often happen in clusters, with intense media coverage playing a critical role in subsequent attacks" (Liu et al. 2022, p. 1). We see both the desire for notoriety and the role of the media in some of the statements of the shooters themselves, with the teenager who killed 17 people at Marjory Stoneman Douglas High School in Parkland, Florida saying in a cell phone video taken right before the attack, "I'm going to be the next school shooter

[109] David Luban also makes this point when he writes, "[t]he cost of holding an Eichmann to account is accepting him as part of the immense fellowship of the human species, not dismissing him as a monster" (2018, p. 136).

[110] I am grateful to comments from Rima Basu that led to the inclusion and development of this objection.

of 2018 . . . .When you see me on the news you'll know who I am" (James 2018). This has led Caren and Tom Teves, whose son, Alex, was killed along with 11 others in a movie theater in Aurora, Colorado in 2012, to create No Notoriety, an organization that calls on news outlets to follow six guidelines in their reporting of "rampage mass killings," including limiting the name of perpetrators to once per piece, never in the headlines, and with no photo above the fold, refusing to broadcast/publish their self-serving statements, videos, and/or manifestos, and elevating the names and likenesses of all of the victims.[111] Given all of this, there seem to be very compelling reasons to deny rounder stories to at least some perpetrators.

By way of response, notice, first, that in order for a rounder story to be owed to a perpetrator, he also needs to be the victim of a flat story that rises to the level of a gross violation or injustice. The explanation for why someone like William is owed a rounder story despite having harmed someone himself is systemic and multifaceted, involving his earlier coerced false guilty plea for attempting to rape a white woman, the impact wrongful incarceration had on him, and the way law enforcement and the media treat Black suspects and defendants in America. While none of these features is a necessary condition for a flat story rising to the level of being a gross violation or injustice, nor is their presence universal across the criminal legal system, we saw in the discussion in the earlier part of this chapter that they are present in many cases of those who are currently incarcerated. But there is nothing to suggest that anything of the same depth or magnitude of injustice is generally true of school shooters or those who are seeking notoriety more broadly.

Should there be such a perpetrator who is in fact also a victim of a grossly unjust flat story, however, it doesn't automatically follow that he ought to receive a rounder one as an act of epistemic reparations. To see this, notice that as with other rights, most are not absolute in nature, and so they can be limited or suspended under certain conditions, such as for "valid reasons." The International Covenant on Civil and Political Rights, for instance, discusses a number of rights that everyone has—such as "liberty and security of person"—but then notes that they are subject to restrictions that are "provided by law, are necessary to protect national security, public order . . . , public health or morals or the rights and freedoms of others . . . ."[112] It is possible that the contagion effect poses a serious enough risk to others that the

[111] No Notoriety (n.d.).
[112] United Nations General Assembly.

right to a rounder story for a school shooter ought to be restricted or suspended even if a case can be made that he is otherwise owed one.

This still leaves us with Bilz's objection that we should invest the limited attention and sympathy we have into survivors rather than perpetrators. By way of response, note that the distinction between victims and perpetrators is often itself complex, as many of those who inflict harm on others have themselves been harmed in countless ways.[113] Dominic Ongwen, for instance, was a senior commander in the Lord's Resistance Army (LRA) in Uganda and was charged with an "unprecedented"[114] 70 counts of war crimes and crimes against humanity in Northern Uganda.[115] But Ongwen was also abducted by the LRA as a child and forced to undergo military training, where "abductees were often forced to kill adults or other children who transgressed the LRA's strict rules or who tried to escape" (Coalition for the International Criminal Court). So while Ongwen committed acts of mass atrocity, he was himself subjected to horrific neglect, violence, and trauma as a child. In an *Amicus Curiae* submitted to the International Criminal Court on Ongwen's behalf, Erin Baines et al. argue:

> There is an urgent need for the ICC to be consistent, predictable, and principled in assessing and determining the long-term effects of trauma on child soldiers. This means recognizing the painful reality that victims can victimize. It also means not dismissing Ongwen as an exception because he is an accused instead of a prosecution witness. As has been made abundantly clear by the evidence at trial, Ongwen was a victim first. (2021, pp. 6–7)

Ongwen's defense counsel made a similar point, arguing that "[i]t is disingenuous to only recognize the immense suffering of child soldiers and the impact their experiences have on them as victims in one breath while in the other

[113] This is not an uncommon point, especially in the context of gross violations and injustices. The South African Truth and Reconciliation Commission, for instance, notes in its report that "it is important to recognize that perpetrators may in part be victims," writing that "[p]erpetrators may be seen as acting under orders, as subjects of indoctrination, as subjected to threats, as outcomes of earlier doctrinaire education. In the most pernicious situation, askaris (former ANC cadres who were 'turned', frequently through torture, threats, and brutality, into state agents) are themselves transformed into killers and torturers. Military conscripts could view themselves in part as victims of a state system. Kitskonstabels (special constables) could see themselves as victims of poverty, in need of a job" (1998, Volume 5, Chapter 7, 53–54).

[114] Jain (2024, p. 1).

[115] Coalition for the International Criminal Court (n.d.).

breath rejecting the same arguments in relation to Dominic [Ongwen]."[116] Both passages emphasize the fact that Ongwen was a victim himself of the very crimes he perpetrated against others and, moreover, that there is a connection between the two that serves as a mitigating factor. There is, for instance, ample evidence showing that exposure to traumatic events as a child can have a lasting impact on a person's long-term development and cognitive competencies. Given this, the flat narrative of Ongwen as only a perpetrator erases a crucial part of the story that has enormous importance causally, explanatorily, psychologically, morally, and legally.

The powerful sense in which perpetrators are often themselves victims is also seen in the rounder story that William Peeples tells of his early years, which includes past events that are inextricably linked to his current incarceration, including being convicted for a crime he didn't commit. Moreover, as was argued, the flat narrative of William's life told by the criminal legal system inflicts a further wrong on him, one for which he is owed epistemic reparations. To argue that we should not invest our limited attention and sympathy into William because he is a perpetrator is to ignore all of the ways in which he has been wronged and harmed. It is also at odds with the path that many victims choose for moving forward. Consider Jeanne Bishop, whose sister was murdered along with her husband and their unborn child by then teenager David Biro. In her book about forgiveness, including her own personal "change of heart," Bishop writes:

> Many people—there is no shortage of them—are willing to write off the David Biros of the world. I was one of those people. Here was our argument: Look at what he did! It's so evil, so depraved, that only a malignant heart could have concocted it. He is without feeling. Any remorse he might express later is only a sham. He will never change.
>
> It is not true. I know this from my own transformation. God changed my heart. Why not the heart of David Biro? Why not the hearts of the thousands of people languishing in prison who have committed crimes for which we are willing to lock them up forever, without a second thought? (2015, p. 152)

[116] *Prosecutor v. Dominic Ongwen*, Case No. ICC-02/04-01/15-T-23, Transcript of the Confirmation of Charges Hearing, January 26, 2016, at 5–6.

As a victim herself, Bishop is explicitly acknowledging that she earlier relied on a flat narrative of the man who murdered her family, one that focused on his character—he has a malignant heart and is without feeling—and is closed and static—he will never change. Yet, based on her own transformation, she now advocates for leaving open the possibility of rounder stories of change and growth not only of David Biro, but also of the countless other people incarcerated in the world. To follow Bilz's arguments is to disregard or silence the voice of Jeanne Bishop and the many others like her.

There is then no universal normative mandate that we ought to devote our limited time and attention to only those survivors who have not themselves perpetrated any wrongs, or who fit a particular mold, or who are regarded as most deserving according to some standard or other. There are many victims who have been silenced or whose identities have been distorted or obscured, and many worthy stories that have not been told or heard.

## 7. Biases, Perspectives, and Flat Stories

There are a number of cognitive biases and heuristics that can shed light on and deepen our understanding of flat and round stories, not only in terms of what drives them, but also regarding steps forward.

The anchoring bias[117] involves the tendency to rely too heavily on one piece of information or trait, with this "anchor" often being the first piece of information acquired on the subject in question. A close neighbor is the salience bias,[118] which involves the tendency to focus on information that is more emotionally striking or prominent even if it is not the most important or accurate. Suppose, for instance, that the first fact a community leader learns about William, or the most emotionally striking one, is that he murdered his neighbor. Even if the context is such that this is not the most important event in his over six decades of life—perhaps the discussion at issue is regarding his academic record—it may nonetheless anchor the community leader's judgments about him. She may focus on or gravitate toward this one fact, remember only it, and overemphasize its significance. This can then lead to or ground the formation of false beliefs and erroneous

[117] See Tversky and Kahneman (1974).

[118] See Taylor and Fiske (1975) for one of the earliest discussions of what has come to be known as the salience bias.

judgments. For instance, just as a person who recently witnessed a hurricane may overestimate the risk of this happening to her, the community leader who knows only this fact about William may overestimate the risk of him engaging in violence in the future despite ample evidence to the contrary. Or just as voters may respond to an emotionally charged news report of an immigrant harming someone to arrive at a decision about immigration policies more generally, this one event in William's life may sway people's views about his employment opportunities even if there are no corresponding arguments in support of them. Appealing to "but he's a murderer" to form judgments or persuade people when it is irrelevant to the question at issue not only leads to epistemically unwarranted conclusions, but also provides a centrality to this fact and knowledge that is distorting and misleading. This can then lend itself to tunnel vision, which is a "compendium of common heuristics and logical fallacies" (Martin 2002, p. 848) whereby we

> focus on a particular conclusion and then filter all evidence . . . through the lens provided by that conclusion. Through that filter, all information supporting the adopted conclusion is elevated in significance, viewed as consistent with the other evidence, and deemed relevant and probative. Evidence inconsistent with the chosen theory is easily overlooked or dismissed as irrelevant, incredible, or unreliable. (Findley and Scott 2006, p. 292)

Once the fact that William took the life of another person is an anchor in the community leader's cognitive framework, she may filter everything else about him through this lens. Evidence of any sort of conflict while he's been incarcerated may be elevated in significance or taken to support the flat story in question while evidence of growth and transformation may be reinterpreted or dismissed as deception and manipulation. So, while the community leader's acceptance of the flat story of William as nothing more than a murderer vilifies him, renders who he is today invisible, damages or destroys his epistemic relations in the community, and stifles his epistemic agency and future possibilities, she also harms herself epistemically by forming false beliefs, missing out on knowledge, failing to deepen her understanding of important matters, and closing off areas of inquiry. Indeed, there is frequently an epistemic connection between the subject of a flat story and the teller of it. To oversimplify with a slogan, "when I epistemically harm you through a flat story, I often epistemically harm myself, too."

Some of the cognitive biases, or their nearby neighbors, driving flat stories have also been taken up in philosophy in interesting ways. Jessie Munton, for instance, uses the concept of a "salience structure"—which is the ordering of information by accessibility both by an individual's mind and his broader social context—to provide an account of prejudice, which she understands as involving a problematic salience structure. More precisely, it is sufficient for there to be a prejudice if there is a salience structure that is "unduly organized around demographic categories . . . even when the information which falls within the ordering determined by the salience structure in question is not itself inaccurate, and regardless of whether that then manifests in behaviour, or is accompanied by negative affect" (2023, p. 2). In a similar spirit, Ella Whiteley focuses on what she calls a "harmful salience perspective," which involves either attention on things that should not be salient, or not enough attention on things that ought to be made salient. To illustrate this, Whiteley notes that one reason why a high percentage of women who are raped do not want to testify in court may be that they "do not want the fact that they were raped to become the most salient thing about them" (2022, p. 201). More specifically, they do not want it to be the thing that others attend to the most—that "others find most noticeable, memorable, and cognitively accessible" (2022, p. 201). Whiteley discusses the case of Monika Korra, who was kidnapped and raped at gunpoint in 2009 and has spoken publicly about the experience of being known as "Rape victim Monika Korra," saying "I hated that. . . . I was fighting every day to step out of that role. But that's how people were viewing me" (Lopez 2016). Realizing that rape "doesn't have to identify you" and that it is "not who you are" but is instead "something that happened to you—a crime committed against you," Korra arrives at the conclusion that "[w]ho you are is what you are passionate about," which for her is being "a runner." Connecting this with salience perspectives, Whiteley argues that we can be harmed when aspects of our identity that do not reflect our personhood, such as our agency, rationality, and personality, are more prominent in the minds of others than aspects that do reflect our personhood. Attending to Korra as a rape victim "directs our attention" to her "passive status as someone who has been attacked," which is a status she "did not choose" and so does not reflect her individuality, agency, and so on. (2022, p. 202).

Salience structures and perspectives can undoubtedly help us understand flat and round stories. Flat stories, for instance, often involve information that is organized around a single fact about a person, such as that he wronged someone. The centrality of this event relative to everything else about him then gives rise to corresponding patterns of attention, which can, in turn, make various inferences and judgments seem more obvious, justified, or important. For instance, when the fact that William took the life of his neighbor is all that is known about him, or is at the center of his story in bright lights, it may well seem obvious or justified that he should not be employed in spaces with vulnerable populations. But when this fact is replaced with who he is today, with that one day in 1988 being just one awful chapter, it may seem equally obvious or justified that he is ideally positioned to be working with vulnerable people.

At the same time, however, the analysis offered by Whiteley that what makes such perspectives harmful is that they direct our attention to facts about, or features of, a person that do not reflect their personhood or agency does not map on neatly to the framework here.[119] Indeed, for many, including those in some of the paradigmatic cases discussed in this book, there *is* personhood and agency at the center of the flat stories told about them. While William, for instance, shares details about his past that shed some light on who he was on that day in 1988, he has never denied his own role in taking the life of his neighbor. Indeed, many of the ways we harm one another are fundamentally interpersonal and agential—consider betrayal, deception, and cruelty, to name just a few—and so we wouldn't want to rule out the possibility that focusing on only that one event, even if it did reflect personhood, could still be violating or unjust. Especially when it comes to the wrongness of flat stories involving those who are themselves perpetrators, this point is critical, for acknowledging personhood and agency is often fundamental to holding someone responsible or accountable.[120]

But the deeper point here is not unique to perpetrators. When Olympic gymnast Simone Biles shared that USA Gymnastics national team doctor Larry Nassar had sexually abused her, she said, "this horrific experience does not define me. I am much more than this. I am unique, smart, talented, motivated, and passionate. I have promised myself that my story will be much greater than this . . . ." (BBC Sport 2018). Crucially, Biles is not rejecting being known under the description of this violation, saying "I too am one of the many survivors that was sexually abused by Larry Nassar" (BBC Sport 2018). What she wants to make clear, however, is that she is *so*

[119] To be clear, and as I will develop below, this framework has some illuminating features regarding the right to be known.

[120] This is to not to say, of course, that there cannot be responsibility or accountability even when there is limited agency, such as in cases of acts of violence undertaken while severely intoxicated.

*much more than this one truth about her.* Not only does she not want being a survivor to be at the center of her story, or to "define" her, but she also makes an explicit call for what we are calling a rounder story—one that is multidimensional, psychologically complex, and open. She wants the other chapters of her life, including those that have yet to be told, to also be part of her story. There may be a connection here to the earlier discussion about the right to be forgotten—perhaps Korra would prefer that the chapter "Rape victim Monika Korra" be altogether eliminated or erased from her story while Biles would like other chapters of her life to always be included with the chapter about her abuse. But the point that I want to emphasize here is that both the wrongs involved in flat stories and the corresponding epistemic reparations owed are often multidimensional and vary between survivors.

Returning to William, the epistemic wrong of his flat story is not only the centrality that is given to the one fact about him that led to his incarceration. For William is not only believed to be *most fundamentally a murderer*, but also *nothing more than a murderer*, and *always a murderer*. There are three different dimensions of failing to know him here. This one act in his life is given *center stage* in his story, but then nothing else about *who he is* or *who he can be* is included in his narrative. Moreover, these wrongs can be inflicted even when the original salience structure or perspective is one that directs our attention to a fact about a person that reflects his personhood. It can be true both that William's actions in 1988 reflected his agency at that time in his life when he was hurt and angry and broken from the years of neglect and violence he had previously experienced. But it can equally be true that William no longer resembles that person in any way and that his future possibilities are now beautiful and limitless. This is why I focus on flat stories rather than salience structures or perspectives, as the latter include only one-dimensionality while the former are also closed and depict a person in static and psychologically simplistic terms. As we can see in the case of William, this is crucial, for even when the anchoring or centering fact about a person is agential, it can still wrong him to reduce him to this one act, to disregard other chapters of his narrative, and to regard his story as complete.

To be sure, flat stories *can* involve the absence of personhood or agency with respect to the centering fact. We saw this, for instance, in the discussion of perpetrators of mass atrocity, who have been regarded as "malignant forces," "dark shadows," "evil spawn," "hounds from hell," and "beasts of impunity." However, while harmful salience perspectives *require* the absence of backwards-looking agency with respect to the centering fact, flat stories not only do not require this but also regard as relevant present- and future-looking agency. To regard William as nothing more than, and perpetually, a murderer—even if the centering fact involves something he did rather than something that was done to him—is to deny the open, dynamic, multidimensional, and psychologically complex reality of being a person and an agent in the world. Even when we make an irreversibly harmful choice, we can grow and change. At the same time, however, the efficacy of the epistemic reparations of a rounder story is also often connected to personhood and agency. For instance, a story of William that included not only the event that led to his incarceration but also, say, his height and weight would fail to be epistemically reparative in the relevant sense even though it does include additional facts about him. Indeed, since some of the work of rounder stories begins with labels, titles, and headlines, compare "five-foot-seven murderer" with "Stanford swimmer." One crucial difference between the two is that being five feet, seven inches tall fails to reflect anything about the subject as a person or agent, while, as we saw earlier, being a swimmer at Stanford University does. So, personhood and agency undoubtedly play a powerful role in the creation and promotion of rounder stories.

Thus, while familiar cognitive biases and heuristics can help us understand the creation, acceptance, and promotion of flat stories about certain groups and individuals in our communities, we also see that there are some important differences between them. These contrasts illuminate the distinctive normative benefits of the framework of flat and round stories so that we can grasp not only a fuller range of epistemic wrongs perpetrated against members of our communities, but also the steps needed to engage in the ongoing process of providing epistemic reparations.

## 8. Conclusion

Through stories that are false or flat, people can be wrongfully thought to be who they are not, either because they are not even the proper subject of the narrative in question or because they are so much more than how they are depicted. At the same time, we have the power to engage in the epistemic reparations called for in such cases through the generation and cultivation of stories that counter or round out those that are responsible for the wrongdoing. In this way, though the narratives we create and share can, quite literally, shape who people are capable of becoming in life-destroying ways, they can also be the path forward for holding one another in life-restoring ways.

# 3

# Talking, Listening, and Learning

In previous chapters, I argued that victims of gross violations and injustices who are epistemically wronged through invisibility, vilification, or systematic distortion—including those who have false or flat stories told about them that rise to the level of such a violation or injustice—have the right to be known as epistemic reparations. But a natural question that might be asked is what is involved in *coming to know* survivors of gross violations and injustices as acts of epistemic reparations.

The standard view in epistemology is that for all practical purposes, knowledge is essentially the same. What matters is *that* one knows something, not *how* one knows it. For instance, the possession of knowledge is often said to provide the support that is needed for us to be proper epistemic agents in the world—to assert, to engage in practical reasoning, and to act with epistemic propriety.[1] Otherwise put, if I know a proposition, then I am not subject to epistemic criticism for offering it as testimony, using it in my deliberation, and acting on it. This view lends itself to a model of epistemic reparations according to which *how* the knowledge of someone is acquired is insignificant and relegated to the margins.

In previous work,[2] I challenged this general epistemological view, showing that for many practical matters, the origin of the relevant knowledge is an important question. In cases of a specialist offering a diagnosis, for instance, it is not enough epistemically for her to simply possess knowledge; it also matters that *her own expert judgment* is at least part of its basis. In this way, that the knowledge is a particular kind—*firsthand*—is essential to the specialist being able to assert the diagnosis, engage in practical reasoning about it, and act on it with epistemic propriety. In a recent book, Ernest Sosa develops the importance of how knowledge is acquired further by exploring the significance of firsthandedness in the moral domain, arguing that "understanding

[1] See, for instance, DeRose (2002), Reynolds (2002), Hawthorne (2004), and Hawthorne and Stanley (2008).
[2] Lackey (2011).

*The Right to Be Known*. Jennifer Lackey, Oxford University Press. © Oxford University Press 2026.
DOI: 10.1093/9780197833988.003.0004

through firsthand knowledge is salient for . . . moral issues . . . specifically . . . , where we should and do often prioritize firsthand, nondeferential judgment" (2021, p. 9). As a paradigmatic case, Sosa focuses specifically on how a firsthand grasp of why something is morally wrong is preferable to sheer deference to someone's else's testimony, even if the latter is more reliable in reaching the truth about the matter in question. If, for instance, I apologize to someone only because I defer to your advice to do so, with no firsthand appreciation of the moral wrongness of the actions that call for the apology, then my grasp of the situation is deficient in important ways, resulting in what Sosa calls "truncated understanding" (2021, p. 9). I may, for instance, be unable to answer questions about what made the original actions morally wrong, generalize to other morally similar situations, grasp the underlying values at issue, and so on.[3]

Sosa is not the first to argue that firsthandedness is necessary for the acquisition of moral knowledge. Robert Paul Wolff argues that "[the responsible man] may learn from others about his moral obligations, but only in the sense that a mathematician learns from other mathematicians—namely by hearing from them arguments whose validity he recognizes even though he did not think of them himself. He does not learn in the sense that one learns from an explorer, by accepting as true his accounts of things one cannot see for oneself" (1970, p. 13). Similarly, Bernard Williams writes:

> There are, notoriously, no ethical experts . . . . Anyone who is tempted to take up the idea of there being a theoretical science of ethics should be discouraged by reflecting on what would be involved in taking seriously the idea that there were experts in it. It would imply, for instance, that a student who had not followed the professor's reasoning but had understood his moral conclusion might have some reason, on the strength of his professional authority, to accept it . . . . These Platonic implications are presumably not accepted by anyone. (1995, p. 205)

[3] Moreover, Sosa argues that firsthandedness may be desirable for its own sake as a satisfaction of the curiosity of rational beings. Just as I wouldn't want to hit the bullseye in archery simply because my coach guided my hands to the target, so, too, I wouldn't want to successfully complete a crossword puzzle simply because I Googled all of the answers. In this respect, Sosa says, moral judgments ". . . are like crossword solutions. Indeed, given our broad understanding of [such] questions, crossword puzzles constitute a light humanistic domain, where it is preferable and generally preferred to reach one's answers firsthand, not just through deference" (2021, p. 13).

And C. A. J. Coady maintains that "[s]urely morality, unlike perception, is a predominantly, if not purely, rational activity. When someone tells me that what I am proposing to do is immoral, I do not react by asking for his credentials but for his reasons . . . . What the present uneasiness amounts to . . . is an uneasiness with the very idea of a moral expert" (1992, pp. 71–72).[4]

While it is indeed important to consider how one knows something in addition to that one knows it, I show in this chapter that there can be epistemic disadvantages to firsthandedness in the moral domain, as well as epistemic benefits to secondhandedness in this same domain.[5] This is crucial when developing an account of epistemic reparations, as much of what we learn when coming to know someone who has been the victim of a gross violation or injustice is not only secondhand but also moral in nature. Coming to know William Peeples,[6] for instance, might involve knowing largely on the basis of his testimony that he is a victim of injustice, remorseful, worthy of forgiveness, and so on. But there is a deeper point that emerges from this discussion: the full scope of the importance of how one knows something goes beyond the question of what kind of knowledge is at issue and encompasses the *process* whereby it was acquired. More precisely, it can matter epistemically not only that moral knowledge is secondhand in nature, but also that it was acquired through an interpersonal exchange of talking, listening, and learning. In this way, the work of epistemic reparations reveals that the very terms of the broader discussion about moral knowledge need to be expanded beyond the options of firsthand inquiry, on the one hand, and simple deference, on the other hand.

Perhaps even more importantly, however, talking, listening, and learning provides a model of a powerful form of epistemic reparations.[7] For not only can this process be epistemically generative for both those who are telling their stories and those who are appropriate listeners, it can also lead to "coconstructed" narratives that can shift and transform our relations with others along a multitude of dimensions. This, in turn, can lead to the repairing

[4] Jones (1999) argues against this view of the necessity of firsthand inquiry for moral knowledge but for reasons that are quite different from those in this chapter. I will also consider the connections between my framework and standpoint epistemology later in this discussion.

[5] While I focus on moral knowledge in this chapter since this is often taken to be the most powerful case for concluding that firsthandedness is necessary, what I say generalizes to other kinds of knowledge.

[6] See Chapter 2 for a discussion of William Peeples.

[7] As should be clear, the process of talking, listening, and learning with others is *only one* way to engage in epistemic reparations, but I devote significant space to exploring it because of its unique and impactful capacities.

of epistemic wrongs, the creation of new narratives and new identities, and, ultimately, the development of new selves.

## 1. Epistemic Disadvantages of Firsthand Knowledge

Let's begin with a case study: suppose that a 15-year-old Black juvenile, Demetrius, was initially brought to a police station as a witness so that he could view a lineup of suspects in a criminal investigation. Shortly after arriving, Demetrius was deliberately separated from his father and interrogated for 12 hours by multiple white police officers without the presence of counsel. The officers employ interrogation tactics exactly as they were trained to do, Demetrius is never physically harmed or threatened, the interrogators speak to him in a calm manner, and he is offered drinks and bathroom breaks.[8] At the end of the interrogation, Demetrius falsely confesses to having carjacked and murdered an elderly woman in Chicago.

Now suppose further that Demetrius is charged with first degree murder and a video recording of the entire interrogation is shown to the jury during his trial. As the all-white jury watches with their own eyes what happened to Demetrius on the recording, they are asked to determine whether the confession in question was unjustly extracted from the teenager. To this end, they notice how professional the interrogators seem, how relaxed Demetrius appears to be, and how he responds to the questions he is asked with relative ease. On this basis, they conclude that the confession was freely given and was in no way unfairly or unjustly obtained.

There are three points to note here. First, we can assume that watching the interrogation via video recording is firsthand in the relevant sense. The jurors are, for instance, not forming beliefs by relying on someone else's testimony but are instead doing so on the basis of their perceptual experiences of the events themselves.[9] Second, the matters that the jurors need to grapple with are distinctively moral in nature: Was Demetrius's confession coerced or otherwise extracted? Did he offer it freely? Was Demetrius treated unfairly or unjustly? Are the sorts of interrogation tactics that were used on

[8] While this case is inspired by actual events, it is fictionalized in some important ways, including details about the tactics used during the interrogation, to draw out points.

[9] I included the jurors watching a recording of the interrogation to be more realistic, and the recording itself does not impact the knowledge in question being firsthand in the relevant sense, but for those who find this feature confusing, the example can be modified so that the jurors are viewing the interrogation through a glass or screen.

Demetrius fair and just? Third, while the jurors are assessing the moral matters relevant to these questions entirely firsthand, there are significant epistemic disadvantages to them doing so.

To see this, notice that the jurors' grasp of the situation is *epistemically impoverished* in some crucial respects. For instance, *what it is like* to be a 15-year-old Black male in an interrogation room with three white police officers is a central piece of the moral picture. Upon listening to Demetrius, it is likely that the jurors would learn that he felt that he had no other way out of that room except for confessing to the carjacking and murder in question. He may have felt trapped, terrified, and threatened, even if no words from the officers themselves directly communicated this. Growing up in a community that was massively overpoliced and seeing Black neighbors shot or otherwise harmed by white police officers may have left Demetrius justifiably disposed to believe that he is in danger around those in law enforcement. This is a perspective that is the result of a host of factors about Demetrius, including his age, race, community, prior interactions, and so on, and one that is likely to be far less accessible to, say, a white 40-year-old female juror viewing the recording of the interrogation firsthand. This is especially significant against the background of the relationship between juvenile status, race, and false confessions. In their sample of wrongful convictions, for instance, Gross et al. (2005) found that 44% of juveniles who were exonerated were wrongly convicted because of false confessions, and 85% of juvenile exonerees who falsely confessed are Black.[10] Given this overrepresentation of Black juveniles within the population of exonerees who falsely confessed to crimes, there is all the more reason to conclude that Demetrius's perspective may have valuable information about the morality of his situation that is unavailable to the white, female juror.

Moreover, a firsthand grasp of this situation is likely to not only be impoverished but also *misleading*. Andrew Taslitz (2006) provides a powerful and detailed description of how a young Black male is likely to be viewed during an interrogation and subsequent trial:

> Officers start with a presumption of the guilt of a young black male based upon one-sided and limited circumstantial evidence. The kid reacts with hostility and defensiveness. These reactions, combined with his powerless speech patterns, lead police to believe he is lying. They close off alternative

[10] Gross et al. (2005, p. 550).

> theories, heightening the pressure on the kid about whose guilt they are now convinced. They make real evidence sound more inculpatory than it is, they deceive him into believing there is still more inculpatory evidence against him, they appeal to his self-interest, and they hammer away at him for hours. Young, isolated, cut off from family and friends, fearful, and rightly seeing no way out, he confesses. Falsely.
>
> Should the youth take the stand at a suppression hearing, the judge, drawing on the same racially-stigmatizing images of black youth, won't believe him. The case goes to trial, and the jury likely sees a film just of his confession . . . . the same defensiveness and linguistic barriers that made the kid seem to be a liar to the police prod the jury toward a similar conclusion. And the same stereotypes of black criminality and duplicity again favor jurors accepting the truthfulness of the confession rather than of its retraction. (2006, pp. 131–132)

As Taslitz notes, the racial biases and prejudices through which a young Black male's responses, speech patterns, and body language are viewed lend themselves to erroneous judgments at multiple layers of the criminal legal system, including by investigators, judges, and jurors.

At this point, this conclusion sounds similar to one of the central tenets of standpoint epistemology. According to José Medina, the most "celebrated thesis of standpoint theory" is that "there is a cognitive asymmetry between the standpoint of the oppressed and the standpoint of the privileged that gives an advantage to the former over the latter" (2013, p. 197). Briana Toole characterizes this "epistemic advantage thesis" as holding that "oppressed social locations confer epistemic advantages" (2023, p. 5).[11] For instance, "[m]arginalization may be epistemically advantageous in that it may place one in a position to gather more evidence (evidential superiority) or to develop certain beneficial epistemic virtues and habits (cognitive superiority)" (2023, p. 2). Applying the epistemic advantage thesis specifically to the moral domain, Nicole Dular argues that the marginalized have better access to

[11] More precisely, Toole distinguishes between two different kinds of asymmetries found in standpoint epistemology. In addition to the "epistemic advantage thesis" discussed in the text, she identifies the "epistemic privilege thesis," which maintains that marginalized standpoints "are epistemically superior" (2023, p. 5). Such standpoints, according to Toole, "must be *achieved* through the practice of *consciousness-raising*, a process that is roughly comparable to the sort of training that facilitates expertise within a domain" and they "can be achieved by the marginalized and non-marginalized alike" (2023, p. 2, original emphasis).

evidence and "are better able to interpret evidence to come to correct moral conclusions, including how they sort evidence as morally relevant or not, the significance they ascribe to the morally relevant evidence in regards to determining the moral status of a matter, and the conceptual competency they have with respect to concepts crucial for obtaining moral knowledge" (2023, pp. 1832–1833). So, according to this version of standpoint epistemology, marginalized standpoints are epistemically superior, and marginalized social locations confer epistemic advantages, some of which bear specifically on the moral domain.

It is not necessary to determine whether all of these claims of standpoint epistemology are true in every case in order for their core insights to shed some light on the issues here. We should listen to Demetrius in part because he has a standpoint that brings with it epistemically important information. At the general level, he occupies an oppressed social position as a young Black male being interrogated by multiple white police officers in Chicago, in virtue of which he has epistemic advantages relative to others about the moral status of what happened to him. He may, for instance, have *more evidence* about relevant dimensions of the situation, such as the way State power is wielded by law enforcement in his community or the lengths that detectives will go to in order to ensure cooperation from suspects. He may have greater *conceptual competency* regarding the application of a confession being "extracted," understanding the impact that overpolicing has on the psychology of young Black males and the way this shapes the experiences of being interrogated. But I want to go beyond the marginalized social positions that standpoint epistemologists insightfully highlight to focus on the epistemic benefits of Demetrius's *specific experiences of violation and injustice* and their relation to the *normative status* of what happened to him.

To see this, let's begin by considering what is involved in determining whether Demetrius's confession was *coerced*. Joel Rudinow argues that to coerce another person is to offer "*irresistible* incentives" (1978, p. 341), and Allen Wood claims that coercing someone means eliminating all of the "acceptable alternatives" (2014, pp. 21–23). Generally, coercion is said to target the decision space or the available options of the one being coerced.[12] When I say, "give me your money or I'll shoot you," there is really only one acceptable

[12] I develop a more nuanced account in Lackey (2023) according to which coercion involves "*the making of an unfair threat or offer that closes victims out of a reasonable decision-making space*" (2023, p. 124, original emphasis). For our purposes here, however, we can rely upon the simpler accounts cited above.

option here, and that is to comply with my demand for your money. Notice, however, that we cannot grasp whether an incentive is irresistible or an alternative is acceptable *without at least considering the psychology of the victim in question*. Indeed, this is especially crucial here, as psychological coercion is the central source of what are called "compliant false confessions,"[13] with classically coercive influence techniques, such as threats and promises, being the underlying cause of most present-day confessions of this sort.[14] Compliant false confessions are "given in response to police coercion, stress, or pressure to achieve some instrumental benefit—typically either to terminate and thus escape from an aversive interrogation process, to take advantage of a perceived suggestion or promise of leniency, or to avoid an anticipated harsh punishment" (Leo 2009, p. 338). One of the most distinctive features of compliant false confessions is that guilt is admitted while the confessor fully knows that he is innocent and that what he is saying is false,[15] and "psychologically oriented interrogation techniques are just as capable of eliciting [these sorts of] false confessions as are physical ones" (Leo 2009, p. 338).[16]

Perhaps most relevant for our purposes are minimization tactics, which research has shown can be powerful in leading to false confessions.[17] Minimization is a "soft-sell" approach in which the interrogator "tries to lull" the suspect into a "false sense of security by offering sympathy, tolerance, face saving excuses, and even moral justification" (Kassin and McNall 1991, p. 235). Such techniques come in three different forms: "those that minimize the moral consequences of confessing, those that minimize the psychological consequences of confessing, and those that minimize the legal consequences of confessing" (Kassin et al. 2010, p. 12). For instance, the interrogator may offer sympathy and understanding to normalize the crime, saying, for instance, "I would have done the same thing"; the interrogator might offer minimizing explanations of the crime, such as raising the possibility that the murder was spontaneous or accidental; and the interrogator might communicate promises that the suspect will be punished less severely if he or she confesses. Promises of leniency, which have been shown to be "particularly coercive in interrogations" (Joselow 2019, p. 1641), heighten the risk of false confessions by leading a suspect to believe that the

[13] Leo (2009, p. 338).
[14] Ofshe and Leo (1997a).
[15] Leo (2009, p. 338).
[16] Leo (2009).
[17] Klaver et al. (2008).

only way to reduce or escape punishment is to confess.[18] However, "[r]arely do interrogators make explicit promises of leniency—for example, that if the suspect confesses, he will not be charged."[19] Instead, police are taught to use pragmatic implication so that suspects are likely to infer leniency even when it is not explicitly promised.[20] Telling a suspect, for instance, that he will be "better off"[21] or have "nothing to worry about"[22] if he confesses can be taken as communicating that he will face less serious charges, lighter consequences, or even be able to go home for cooperating. So, whereas physically coercive techniques, such as slapping a suspect or depriving him of sleep, will be obvious to those watching a recording of an interrogation, the full force of psychologically coercive tactics on individual suspects often will not be.

What all of this shows is that since the morality of Demetrius's confession depends, in part, on assessing whether his confession was coerced, we need to pay attention to his own perspective of the situation. How did things seem to Demetrius from the inside? Was the prospect of being reunited with his father if he confessed conveyed through pragmatic implication as a promise or seen as an irresistible incentive? Was Demetrius filled with terror or feeling threatened when the police officer mentioned the possibility of a life sentence? Did he think that cooperating with law enforcement was the only option he had for leaving the interrogation room? Answers to these questions are crucial for determining whether Demetrius was coerced to confess and was thereby treated unjustly, and so listening to him is crucial not only for properly making moral judgments in this case, but failure to do so is very likely to lead to false beliefs. For instance, watching police officers calmly speak to a defendant might seem not in the slightest bit coercive to a juror who has had largely positive experiences with police officers in the past. While it would be easy for such a juror to falsely conclude that such professional interaction couldn't possibly result in a confession that wasn't freely

[18] Joselow (2019, p. 1650). Among the promises that have been made to a suspect in exchange for a confession are that a lighter sentence will be recommended (Joselow 2019, p. 1650), that lesser charges will be prosecuted (Marcus 2006, p. 623), that medical treatment will be received (Marcus 2006, p. 623), and that he will be treated better (Marcus 2006, p. 623).

[19] "If proven, such promises would result, under current law, in suppression of any ensuing confessions" (Center on Wrongful Convictions, "False and Coerced Confessions").

[20] See, for instance, Ofshe and Leo (1997a, 1997b), Kassin et al. (2010), and Bluhm Legal Clinic, "False and Coerced Confessions."

[21] Bluhm Legal Clinic, "Lavelle Burt."

[22] Nesterak (2014).

given, this mistakenly assumes that only words and actions that seem to leave no way out *for any one of us* is coercive. But as we have seen, Demetrius's subjective perspective is crucial to understanding whether he was coerced into confessing. Thus, there are significant epistemic disadvantages to firsthandedness when the jurors are assessing the moral dimensions of this situation.

While experiences like Demetrius's are far more likely to be had by those who are oppressed, they can also be had by those occupying more powerful positions in society. Consider, for instance, the similar case of Brendan Dassey, a white special education student who at 16 years old underwent four police interrogations in 48 hours without the presence of a parent or counsel, ultimately resulting in him falsely confessing to participating with his uncle in the rape, murder, and mutilation of Teresa Halbach.[23] On this basis, he was convicted of these crimes and received a life sentence, which he continues to serve in Wisconsin.[24] Brendan's interrogations were recorded and, while his attorneys and supporters argued that his confession was coerced, the United States Court of Appeals for the Seventh Circuit wrote that:

> Many . . . factors . . . point toward a finding that it was voluntary. Dassey spoke with the interrogators freely, after receiving and understanding *Miranda* warnings, and with his mother's consent. The interrogation took place in a comfortable setting, without any physical coercion or intimidation, without even raised voices, and over a relatively brief time. (*Dassey v. Dittmann*, 877 F.3d 297 (7th Cir. 2017))

The Court based their judgment that Brendan's confession was voluntary on their firsthand assessment of how his interrogation seems to them. He doesn't look like he was coerced to the judges so, therefore, they conclude that his confession was voluntarily given. But as psychologist Saul Kassin says:

> [Dassey] wasn't handcuffed, yelled at or beaten into submission. This is true. But setting the bar this low represents an incomprehensible step backward. Even the Miranda court over 52 years ago understood that a subtle psychological approach can be inherently coercive. (Kassin 2018)

[23] To be sure, Brendan may be marginalized in virtue of being intellectually disabled, but the point that is important here is that as a white male, he occupies a more powerful standpoint in society than a Black peer does.

[24] Bluhm Legal Clinic, "Brendan Dassey Case."

And indeed, the interrogators used a host of interrogation techniques that have been shown to frequently result in false confessions, such as presenting false evidence and making false threats. For instance, after Brendan said that he had been at his uncle's house and saw a bonfire with tires and a van seat but nothing suspicious, interrogators lied, telling Brendan that they had found Halbach's bones intermingled with the burned remains of the van seat and insisting "I gotta believe you did see something in that fire" (Petition for Executive Clemency for Brendan Ray Dassey 2019). They also leveled a false threat against him: "We've got people at the . . . district attorney's office . . . .saying that Brendan Dassey had something to do with it or the cover up of it which would mean Brendan Dassey could potentially be facing charges for that" (Petition for Executive Clemency for Brendan Ray Dassey 2019). Both the American Psychological Association and the nation's leading interrogation trainers have found that the use of deception is a risk factor for false confessions, with Kassin emphasizing that "misrepresenting evidence can disorient people. It can alter people's perceptions, beliefs, [and] memories . . . ." (Kassin 2018). This seems to be precisely what happened to Brendan, as immediately after his false confession, he confided to his mother, "they got to my head" (Petition for Executive Clemency for Brendan Ray Dassey 2019).

In evaluating the normative status of what happened to Brendan, the experience of the investigators getting "into" his head is an explanatorily powerful piece of the story. Focusing on only their own firsthand experience of the recording of the interrogation, the United States Court of Appeals judges noticed features like the comfortable setting and absence of physical coercion and raised voices. Even if they moved beyond the video and imagined what it was like for Brendan during his interrogation, they would very likely not get much closer to the truth, for as Kassin notes, "lay people have an easier time understanding why someone would kill themselves . . . than they do why someone would confess to a crime he did not commit" (Nesterak 2014). But if they listen to Brendan himself, they might learn that the false evidence and threats terrified and confused him and that he believed his interrogators when they assured him that as long as he "talk[ed] about it" and "fill[ed] in those gaps," they would be "in his corner," that he'd be "all right" and have "nothing to worry about," and that he'd even be "set free" (Petition for Executive Clemency for Brendan Ray Dassey 2019).

Despite the fact that Brendan's case is so similar to Demetrius's, I went through these details to highlight some important differences. For while

Demetrius and Brendan were both juveniles who falsely confessed to crimes they didn't commit and are currently wrongfully incarcerated, they did not share a social location or marginalized perspective[25] in the sense relevant for standpoint epistemology: Demetrius was a young, Black male from urban Chicago and Brendan was a young, white male from rural Wisconsin. In this way, the original case of Demetrius is important not only because of the standpoint he has through being a member of a marginalized group with a particular social location, but also because he is a survivor of a gross violation or injustice—which is something that can be true of both members of oppressed groups and of members of dominant groups—where the normative status of what happened to him crucially depends on his psychological states. In this way, and as we see with the Court of Appeals judges, assessing the sorts of situations that both Demetrius and Brendan were forced into without listening to the survivors themselves is very likely to lead to false beliefs and inferences. Of course, a white juror may have unique struggles in imagining what it is like to be a young Black male in a police station, and this may make it even more likely that she will erroneously conclude that Demetrius's confession was freely given.[26] But as was noted by Kassin, false confessions to murder defy human imagination in general, and so the same juror may also struggle to imagine Brendan Dassey, Lewis "Jim" Fogle, and Amanda Knox falsely confessing to murder, all of whom are white and represent a broad range of social positions and standpoints.[27] What we see, then, is that we need to learn directly from survivors because of an epistemic advantage they may have not only through occupying marginalized standpoints, but also in virtue of their specific violating and unjust experiences.

Of course, there are a number of different propositions that are at issue in grasping the morality of Demetrius's situation. There are questions about the way that the interrogation seems to Demetrius from the inside—such as whether he felt trapped, terrified, threatened, and so on. There are issues about the status of Demetrius confessing, such as whether he was coerced to do so or whether he freely offered his testimony. And there are questions about the moral status of Demetrius's false confession and coerced

[25] Perhaps they may now be said to share the marginalized perspective of "incarcerated person," but they did not share this at the time of their respective interrogations.

[26] Also, as mentioned earlier, young Black males in America are far more likely to be in the situation of being interrogated and falsely confessing to crimes they didn't commit in the first place, and so, in this sense, their perspective as a false confessor is more likely to occur and thus more likely to be inaccessible in practice.

[27] The cases of Fogle and Knox were discussed in earlier chapters.

confessions more generally. One might object that listening to Demetrius is important for the first, and therewith, the second, category of questions, but firsthand success is nonetheless preferable for the third one, which is the only one that is distinctively moral. In other words, while firsthandedness may be epistemically impoverished and misleading when it comes to Demetrius's experiences and whether his confession was thereby coerced, it is nonetheless preferable for those that are specifically about moral wrongness, such as "it was morally wrong to coerce Demetrius to falsely confess to murder" or "coercing someone to falsely confess to a crime is morally wrong."

By way of response, notice that questions about whether a person feels threatened, and whether a piece of speech was coerced or free, certainly have moral dimensions. Merely knowing that Demetrius felt trapped by the interrogators and was coerced into confessing to a murder he didn't commit also involves knowing that he was violated and treated unjustly. These judgments—"Demetrius's confession was coerced and thus he was violated and treated unjustly by law enforcement"—are distinctively moral and depend on knowledge that only Demetrius can reliably convey about his experiences inside the interrogation room. But even with respect to the third category, listening to others might be better in some contexts than firsthand success. Sure, a juror might be able to reason to the conclusion that coerced confessions are morally wrong on her own. She might be able to invoke the concept of epistemic agency and grasp why compromising it in order to extract testimony from another person is wrong.[28] Still, is this obviously epistemically better than listening to Demetrius when he says, "what happened to me in that room is not okay" or "treating kids the way those cops treated me is just wrong." Demetrius might have insight into the truth of these claims that provides crucial details, nuance, and explanatory depth that are simply inaccessible to a juror reasoning on her own. More generally, when agents are invited to speak for themselves, they are often in a position to tell a more comprehensive account of their experiences than would be conveyed by someone else, thereby leading to a deeper understanding on the part of the hearer. According to J. David Velleman, for instance:

> A story does more than recount events; it recounts events in a way that renders them intelligible, thus conveying not just information but also

[28] I develop an account of the epistemic wrongness of extracted false confessions in detail in Lackey (2023).

> understanding. We might therefore be tempted to describe narrative as a genre of explanation. When the police invite a suspect to "tell his story," they are asking him to explain the blood on his shirt or his absence from home on the night of the murder; and whether he is judged to have a "good story" will depend on its adequacy as an explanation. (2003, p. 1)

As Velleman notes, storytelling is intimately connected to understanding and we are often in the best position to tell our own stories. When the jurors are watching the recording of Demetrius's interrogation, for instance, there may be crucial explanatory gaps that only listening to him could shed light on. They may see Demetrius's body language shift under questioning, or see his answers change, and he may be able to say, "well, at this point, I felt like there was no way out of that interrogation room without giving the detectives what they wanted," or "I was thinking about my mother at that moment and what finally broke me is that I thought cooperating with law enforcement would spare her additional pain." These bits of information may be explanatorily essential to grasping why Demetrius falsely confessed to a crime he didn't commit, which has enormous epistemic value for making moral judgments not only about what happened to him in the interrogation room, but also about other relevant cases.[29]

In addition, listening to Demetrius may be important for grasping the concepts necessary for making correct moral judgment or acquiring moral knowledge. If my conception of coercion, for instance, does not include what happened to Demetrius in the interrogation room, then I should assign weight—perhaps even a significant amount—to his testimony that what he experienced was coercive. More generally, if my understanding of coercion excludes as coercive all purely psychological tactics, then hearing that a survivor who was repeatedly threatened with the State "going for the death penalty" felt that this was comparable to having a gun to his head is a powerful reason to revise my view.[30]

[29] Of course, we are often not in a position to speak directly to victims and survivors of gross violations and injustices, especially defendants, who frequently either accept a plea deal or are discouraged from testifying at their own trials. But this does not affect the point that I am making here that there are cases where there are distinctive epistemic benefits to relying on others for acquiring moral knowledge rather than engaging in only firsthand inquiry on our own, even if we can't always do so.

[30] We may think of what might be called "hermeneutical reparations" as involving the cultivation of hermeneutical resources that survivors lack. (See Mitova (2025b)). In the original case in Fricker (2007) of women lacking the concept of "sexual harassment," for instance, hermeneutical reparations may involve the generation, acceptance, and promotion of the concept of sexual harassment among the marginalized. But in the case here, Demetrius himself might already have an

## 2. Perspective Taking Versus Perspective Sharing

One question that may be asked is whether the imagination can fill in the relevant gaps between Demetrius and the jurors. Indeed, it is not uncommon to regard the ability to think outside of one's own perspective as a powerful or even essential moral tool. Martha Nussbaum, for instance, famously argues on behalf of the value of narrative literature in moral deliberation and judgment, claiming that literature contributes "moral perception and moral emotion" to the process of moral investigation in a way that theory cannot. Nussbaum crucially grounds this conclusion, at least in part, in literature's ability to radically expand our mental scope beyond our own experiences, writing: "We have never lived enough. Our experience is, without fiction, too confined and too parochial" (1990, p. 47). Later, she argues that "literature is an extension of life not only horizontally, bringing the reader into contact with events or locations or persons or problems he or she has not otherwise met, but also, so to speak, vertically, giving the reader experience that is deeper, sharper, and more precise than much of what takes place in life" (Nussbaum 1990, p. 48).[31] In a similar spirit, Mark Johnson holds that the moral imagination is essential to moral judgment, where this kind of imagination crucially involves empathy and perspective-taking: "moral imagination is our capacity to see and to realize in some actual or contemplated experience possibilities for enhancing the quality of experience both for ourselves and the communities of which we are a part . . . . [it] is the means by which we are able to conceive of alternative perspectives and to explore their implications for action, relationships, and communal well-being" (1993, p. 209). Given this, couldn't a juror simply imagine what it is like to be in the shoes of someone like Demetrius and thereby come to reason, in conjunction with watching the video, to an even better-grounded conclusion about the status of his confession?

While there may be benefits to imaginatively occupying the perspectives of others, there are also serious epistemic dangers when this turns out to be a replacement for listening to others about their experiences. This is especially important with respect to moral matters, where access to viewpoints

apt concept of coercion and part of hermeneutical reparations may require the generation, acceptance, and promotion of an expanded conceptual framework for understanding coercion among the non-marginalized.

[31] For an extension of Nussbaum's thesis to the general epistemic benefits of narratives, see Worth (2008).

that are generally obscured or distant from our own can be essential to accurate and well-grounded judgments, including legal ones. As noted earlier, for instance, many people report having a hard time wrapping their minds around how someone could falsely confess to something they didn't do, especially a violent crime. As law professor Steven Drizin says, "[m]ost people can't imagine any set of circumstances, other than perhaps torture, under which they would confess to a crime they did not commit. And even fewer can imagine ever falsely confessing to a murder, a crime that can lead to a death sentence or life without parole" (Drizin 2007). This is one of the central reasons why coming to know certain truths through only our firsthand resources can be epistemically impoverished and misleading. Our own limitations with respect to imagining what it is like to be someone else or to be in a wholly unfamiliar situation can lead not only to erroneous beliefs, but also to tunnel vision, which, it might be recalled from the previous chapter, involves focusing on a particular conclusion and filtering all evidence through a lens provided by that conclusion, which thereby leads to elevating the significance of information supporting this conclusion and overlooking or dismissing evidence that is inconsistent with it.[32] If a juror brings her own perspective and experiences to the viewing of Demetrius's interrogation and comes to believe in his guilt because she can't imagine someone falsely confessing to a murder he didn't commit, then Demetrius's guilt can quite easily become the conclusion through which all other evidence is filtered. For instance, the failure to follow up on other leads may be ignored, the lack of corroborating evidence may be explained away, and potentially exculpatory evidence may be dismissed.[33] Why, one might ask, didn't investigators follow up on reports that someone much older than Demetrius was seen around the location of the carjacking? Well, if it is unimaginable that someone would confess to a murder that he didn't commit, then once Demetrius's confession was secured, it is reasonable to close the investigation and focus exclusively on building the case against him. The limitations that we have with respect to another person's perspective can thus beget further limitations downstream regarding the gathering, processing, and grasping of additional evidence.

Iris Marion Young[34] makes a similar point in her powerful critique of Seyla Benhabib's notion of symmetrical reciprocity.[35] Benhabib understands

[32] Findley and Scott (2006, p. 292).
[33] I discuss this extensively in Lackey (2023).
[34] See Young (1997).
[35] Benhabib (1991).

moral respect as a relation of symmetry between the self and other, maintaining that moral reciprocity entails that the perspectives of the self and the other are reversible. To make vivid the problems with such a view, Young draws on the work of Anita Silvers[36] and discusses a case in which the state of Oregon conducted a telephone survey of its citizens to inform decisions about state funding for the health care of people with disabilities. When able-bodied people were asked to put themselves in the situation of a person in a wheelchair or a blind person, the majority of respondents said that they would rather be dead than wheelchair bound or blind because their lives would not be worth living. In fact, however, suicide among people with disabilities is low and people with disabilities often regard their lives as indeed worth living. Attempts at perspective-taking can thus lead not only to moral errors, such as a fundamental lack of moral respect of lives unlike our own, but also to distinctively epistemic ones, including false beliefs,[37] a lack of understanding, and so on. Young concludes that "with careful listening, able-bodied people can learn to understand important aspects of the lives of perspectives of people with disabilities," which "is a very different matter from imaginatively occupying their standpoint . . . " (1997, p. 344).

Of course, this danger is present not only when able-bodied persons try to take up the perspective of disabled persons. Young also raises this worry with respect to men trying to imagine what it was like to be Anita Hill during her interactions with Clarence Thomas and white persons aiming to take up the viewpoint of indigenous persons. Moreover, as we saw above, the same is true in the case of Demetrius, where it would be very easy for a 40-year-old white juror who has had largely positive experiences with law enforcement in her community to view the interrogation video and see no reason whatsoever to feel terror. In all of these cases, radically different social positions, often manifested in asymmetries of power, result in people with experiences quite unlike one another's rendering it unlikely that they would be able to successfully engage in the relevant kind of perspective-taking.

In response, Young urges what she calls *asymmetrical reciprocity* among speakers and listeners where "[c]ommunicating parties mutually recognize one another" and each participant recognizes "that others have irreducible points of view . . . . While there may be many similarities and points of contact between [people], each position and perspective transcends the others,

[36] Silvers (1995).

[37] For instance, the false belief that disabled lives are not worth living.

goes beyond their possibility to share or imagine" (1997, p. 351). Rather than trying to take up another's perspective, then, Young advises us to respect and embrace the full range of one another's differences. She continues, "[p]articipants in communicative interaction are in a relation of approach. They meet across distances of time and space and can touch, share, and overlap their interests. But each brings to the relationships a history and structured positioning that makes them different from one another, with their own shape, trajectory, and configuration of forces" (1997, p. 351).

Let us then understand *perspective taking* as involving trying to imaginatively occupy the perspectives and experiences of others[38] and *perspective sharing* as involving others sharing their firsthand perspectives and experiences with others either directly or indirectly. While perspective taking can be done without any communication of any kind with those who have the firsthand experiences in question, perspective sharing crucially requires some form of contact with them.[39] Perspective sharing thus recognizes the differences—often minor but sometimes radical—that exist between us and relies upon interpersonal exchanges of talking and listening for understanding one another.

Recent work by Joshua L. Kalla and David E. Broockman on exclusionary attitudes, which are characterized as "intergroup prejudices and opposition to policies that promote outgroups' well-being," is also illuminating here (2023, p. 185). Based on a series of field experiments of door-to-door canvassing interventions that aimed to reduce prejudice against, and increase support for, outgroups, such as transgender people or unauthorized immigrants, the authors found that "exchanging narratives that encourage individuals to consider an outgroup's perspective in interpersonal conversations can durably reduce exclusionary attitudes towards that outgroup" (2023, p. 185). Importantly, Kalla and Broockman distinguish between three different kinds of narrative strategies for considering the perspectives of outgroup members: *traditional perspective taking*, which involves imagining an experience from the perspective of an outgroup member; *analogic perspective taking*, which involves recalling a similar situation from one's own experience; and *perspective-getting*, which involves hearing about the experiences of an outgroup member from them or others.

[38] According to Galinsky et al., perspective taking is "the process of imagining the world from another's vantage point or imagining oneself in another's shoes" (2005, p. 110).

[39] Again, this contact may be direct or indirect.

After manipulating the presence of various narrative strategies, the authors consistently found that "perspective-getting effectively reduces exclusionary attitudes, whereas other strategies . . . considered have less reliable impacts" (Kalla and Broockman 2023, p. 203). Moreover, their research shows that it is the narratives that are responsible for the changes in attitudes, as removing them from the conversations eliminates the results.[40]

These results have powerful implications, leading to headlines like "These scientists can prove it's possible to reduce prejudice"[41] and "How to talk someone out of bigotry."[42] But what is of particular significance for our purposes here is that what we are calling perspective sharing seems to have greater power at coming to understand others than perspective taking does, and this is true when the decks are already stacked against doing so through intergroup prejudices and opposition to policies that promote the well-being of the outgroup members in question. In other words, listening to the stories of others, rather than imagining what it is like to be them, seems to be particularly effective at changing minds. Since much of the epistemically reparative work involved in coming to know others will involve shifts in our understanding of them—from murderer to wrongly convicted, from nothing more than a murderer to a loving mentor—there is further reason to engage in perspective sharing through listening and learning from their stories.

I should emphasize, however, that I am not claiming that we should never engage in perspective taking or that there is no value in doing so, as there is plenty of evidence showing that there is.[43] Rather, I am arguing that perspective taking should not replace or be a substitute for perspective sharing. If I have the choice between listening to Demetrius talk about his experience of falsely confessing or trying to imaginatively occupy his 15-year-old self in the interrogation room, there are significant epistemic and moral benefits to hearing directly from him. But this doesn't mean that there cannot also be cases where "putting myself in another's shoes" is helpful, perhaps because it is the only option available because he is deceased, or because the survivor doesn't want to share his story, or because it supplements what I learn from a survivor's testimony about his firsthand experiences, and so on.

[40] Kalla and Broockman (2020).

[41] Resnick (2016).

[42] Resnick (2020).

[43] Perspective taking has been connected with a host of positive effects, including social competence, closeness, cognitive complexity, interpersonal relations, intergroup relations, negotiations, group processes and outcomes, and moral decision-making and action. See, for instance, Ku et al. (2015).

## 3. Talking, Coconstructed Narratives, and Epistemic Generation

We have seen that there are epistemic limitations and dangers to relying on only one's own resources in arriving at certain judgments that are crucial for moral knowledge. I now want to turn to the distinctive epistemic benefits that emerge from processes of talking, listening, and learning, with the central one being that sharing stories might change what is even possible to know.

In the previous section, I argued that listening to Demetrius is epistemically crucial because others coming to know that he suffered violations and injustices involving coercion depends on them understanding his firsthand experiences. But what I want to show here is that telling his own story might crucially change not only what *others* know; it might also change what *Demetrius himself* knows. In a well-known article, 19th-century German playwright, Heinrich von Kleist, wrote:

> If there is something you want to know and cannot discover by meditation, then . . . I advise you to discuss it with the first acquaintance whom you happen to meet. He need not have a sharp intellect, nor do I mean that you should question him on the subject. No! Rather you yourself should begin by telling it all to him . . . . The French say: ["appetite comes with eating"] and this maxim holds true when parodied into: [*ideas come in speaking*]. (1951, p. 42)

The view that talking can itself be generative of knowledge has received a significant amount of attention in recent years. There is, for instance, wide agreement within the scientific community that there is a close relationship between talking and thinking,[44] which, in turn, has given rise to a broad range of research and educational models standardly called dialogue-intensive or talk-intensive pedagogies.[45] The core idea is that successful teaching and learning involves students actively participating in classroom discourse. Otherwise put, talking facilitates knowing. This is surely a phenomenon that many of us have experienced firsthand. I often discuss my research with a colleague and wind up coming to know the next step in my argument by the end of my spiel before he asks any questions himself. The very act of talking

[44] See, for instance, Resnick et al. (2018).

[45] See Kim and Wilkinson (2019), Snell and Lefstein (2018), and Sedova et al. (2019).

ideas through out loud can be epistemically generative even in the absence of external feedback.

Similar considerations apply to the stories we tell about our own experiences. Sharing his memories about what happened in the interrogation room can lead to Demetrius, and ultimately others, acquiring knowledge that wouldn't have otherwise been available had he not talked. According to psychologists Pasupathi et al., "the very act of narrating changes the way the teller (and listener) subsequently understands the event . . . ." (2016, p. 49) and Monisha Pasupathi maintains that "what we tell . . . influences, and may become, what we 'know' about our own past" (2001, p. 661). In a similar spirit, the character of Dr. Hoffman in Tommy Orange's *Wandering Stars* powerfully discusses the epistemic and practical value of talking our stories through:

> It's important to voice things, to sound them out, like the way we learn to spell by slowly saying words, we have to sound out our stories, and they may come out slow and clumsy, and we may misspell them, so to speak, at first, when we first go to try, which is to say we may misunderstand them. But as we frame and reframe them, our own stories, the ones we tell each other and tell ourselves about what happened to us, and what it means in the context of our lives, and the bigger life we're a part of, the better we can understand what it all means, the more sure and purposeful our steps forward will become, and the more informed our decisions will be. (2024, p. 162)

As these passages make clear, the stories we tell about our lives can change and grow and, in so doing, can affect how we understand our own experiences. The same event may be recounted with different frames, points of emphasis, normative significance, and conclusions. At 15, Demetrius may have regarded what happened to him as a standard interaction with police officers. He may have lacked a nuanced conception of coercion, believing that only physical torture can be coercive, and so the stories he told about his wrongful conviction may have been processed and framed in terms of what he could have and should have done differently. But as he talks, both he and his story may develop. He may now frame the entire experience in terms of coercion, emphasize the fact that he was a terrified child alone in an interrogation room with only adult, white police officers trained to extract a confession from him, and understand what happened to him as a gross violation or systemic injustice that resulted in life-shattering consequences.

This is related to another point: we have *agential authority* with respect to our own mental states when we are the agents of the very experiences in question. This sense of authority goes beyond access to existing mental states and captures how we are agents over time who can shift and develop and transform. For instance, unlike a recording of the interrogation, which is static, Demetrius can change his mind, come to view matters differently, develop a deeper understanding of the events in question, and so on. This allows the telling of a story that may simply be unavailable to others, such as a reporter or author who tries to take up his perspective, since it exists only through the exercise of Demetrius's agency. We can imagine Demetrius talking about his experiences in real time as follows: "I felt confused when I was first being questioned by police officers. No, actually, that doesn't seem quite right. I was terrified and it was precisely this fear that I now see set me on the path toward falsely confessing to a murder I didn't commit." The shift from understanding the experience as driven by terror rather than confusion is crucial to grasping the full normative force of the injustice Demetrius continues to suffer and it is one that only he can authoritatively make in the telling of the story of his interrogation.

While we have been focusing specifically on how talking can be epistemically generative by itself, telling and listening to stories in the context of the right to be known is distinctively interpersonal and so requires both speakers and listeners. Because of this, relevant features of the *interpersonal exchanges* are also important to consider. This is crucial, as "narratives are always evolving, both process and product of ongoing interactions" (Pasupathi et al. 2016, p. 49). For instance, according to the principle of coconstruction in psychology, "any autobiographical recollection in conversation is the product of both the speaker and the context," where "the context" crucially includes the listener. Listeners "communicate their comprehension, goals, and interests during recounting, in part through nonverbal behavior" (Pasupathi 2001, p. 652, 655). These responses from listeners can have a significant impact on stories even when they are told as narratives rather than as emerging conversationally. Herbert H. Clark emphasizes precisely this point, writing that "[n]arratives seem different from conversations, because they seem to be produced by individuals speaking on their own . . . but appearances belie reality. Narratives rely just as heavily on coordination among the participants as conversations do" (1994, pp. 1006–1007). In face-to-face dialogue, Clark notes that visibility and simultaneity are important features where participants can see one another and "can produce and receive at once and simultaneously" (1996, p. 9), resulting in the stories that are told being directly affected by the responses from listeners. Building on Clark's work, Bavelas et al. (2000) distinguish between two different kinds of relevant listener responses. Those that are *generic* are not specifically connected to what the speaker is saying in the sense that the same response would be appropriate in a wide range of narratives. For example, "one might appropriately nod while listening to a lecture, a sad story, or an exciting story" (Bavelas et al. 2000, p. 943). In contrast, *specific* listener responses are closely connected to the particular content of the narrative in question with examples including "looking sad, gasping in horror, mirroring the speaker's gesture, or supplying an appropriate phrase" (Bavelas et al. 2000, p. 943). There are a number of similarities between these two types of responses, such as that they are both appropriate, related to the narrative, show that the listener is understanding, attending, and following, and occur at effective places within the narratives.[46] And while one kind is neither preferable nor a better form of listening than the other,[47] there are also important differences between them, including that generic ones involve *listeners* who are *observers* and offer responses *to* the speakers while specific ones involve *co-tellers* who are *actors in the story* and offer responses *with* the speaker.[48] Imagine, for instance, a listener who excitedly finishes a narrator's sentence, such as by saying "and there she was!" after the speaker says, "after looking for two days for her, I walked down the road, turned the corner. . . ." Here, the listener provides a phrase that fits the narrator's point and does so in a way that permits him to "become, for the moment," a "co-narrator" who illustrates or adds to the story.[49]

Importantly, however, when listeners fail to have an appropriate response of any kind, the stories that speakers tell, and even what they understand or know themselves, can be significantly impacted. In general, when listeners are distracted, uncooperative, or dissenting, speakers include less detailed information, speak for shorter amounts of time, and are more disfluent.[50]

[46] Bavelas et al. (2000, p. 944).

[47] "It is important not to interpret our findings as showing that specific responses are in some sense preferable to generic responses or that specific responses are a better way of listening. There are simply two different kinds of responses, with different functions in conversation" (Bavelas et al. 2000, p. 950).

[48] Bavelas et al. (2000, p. 944).

[49] Bavelas et al. (2000, p. 944).

[50] See, for instance, Dickinson and Givón (1995), Pasupathi et al. (1998), and Bavelas et al. (2000).

For instance, speakers are highly sensitive to the gaze of listeners, restarting and often rephrasing a sentence when a listener looks back after looking away.[51] When listeners do not have appropriate responses at key points in a narration, speakers tell their stories worse overall, especially at the conclusion, which ends up abrupt, choppy, or told more than once.[52] Bavelas et al. maintain that part of the problem in these cases is that listeners are failing to make "their contribution to the narrative" (2000, p. 950). This point is crucial as we consider what contributions listeners ought to make when engaging in epistemically reparative work. When an exchange is face-to-face, for instance, adequate epistemically reparative work might involve not only knowing the person in the relevant sense but also having appropriate responses as a listener. This might involve conveying to him through facial expressions, gestures, and verbal responses that he is being heard and understood or, at the very least, not making him feel further unknown. Imagine, for instance, a wrongfully convicted survivor of police torture sharing his story with someone who repeatedly looks at her phone, smiles when a particularly painful detail is shared, fails to show any compassion or sadness, and provides off-topic verbal responses. Even if knowledge of the survivor is ultimately imparted through this exchange, it fails in critical respects as an act of epistemic reparations. The survivor would almost certainly feel more invisible after such an experience, and so rather than repairing the original epistemic wrong, an additional one would be perpetrated. Of course, in another context, the same features of the interpersonal exchange might not be as important. If, for example, one is listening on the phone, then eye contact and facial expressions will be irrelevant, but particular verbal responses, such as concern, sadness, or outrage, might be even more significant. Epistemically reparative work thus involves a sensitivity to the way in which one is bearing witness; more precisely, an act of epistemic reparations requires respectful recognition of and engagement with the survivor.

Moreover, attentive and engaged listeners who have appropriate responses elicit "[c]ollaboratively, agreeably coconstructed recollections,"[53] which, in turn, facilitate more detailed and elaborate stories from speakers and more detailed and long-term memories subsequently.[54] This has

[51] Goodwin (1981).
[52] Bavelas et al. (2000).
[53] Pasupathi (2001, p. 660).
[54] Dickinson and Givón (1995), Pasupathi et al. (1998), and Pasupathi (2001).

significant consequences. Listeners directly impact the stories we tell about our experiences, whether and how we remember them, how we see ourselves, and ultimately who we are. Consider the telling of our "life stories," which take autobiographical memory as the raw material and constructs our identities into coherent, ongoing narratives.[55] The responses of our listeners may result in stability in our life stories where we keep the same events, interpretations, and themes, which can trap us "in our existing identities,"[56] or they can allow us to reformulate our life stories to permit change[57] where we add or remove events, interpretations, or themes.[58] Connecting this with the framework from Chapter 2, listener responses can either lock us into flat stories or cultivate the creation of rounder ones. If Demetrius is sharing the story of his false confession, for instance, and his framing of it in terms of coercion is met with skepticism or apathy by his listeners, he might get locked into his original story that focuses on only his own actions. This might shape how he sees himself, the role of the State in the trajectory of his life, and the options that are available to him in the future, ultimately affecting who it is possible for him to be. If, on the other hand, Demetrius's listeners are deeply engaged in his narrative, nodding at appropriate moments and expressing sadness and outrage when he shares details about how his confession was coerced, this might open up radically new avenues for his sense of self and his future. He might be able to move past feelings of confusion and guilt, channel his efforts into fighting his wrongful conviction, and take on the role of educating others about juvenile false confessions. In this way, since narratives about the past can be coconstructed and remembered through conversations, "audiences play a role in shaping recollections, and in doing so they also play a role in shaping identities"[59] and lives. Part of the work of epistemic reparations thus lies in coconstructing rounder stories that can be a source of knowledge for both survivors and listeners.

This has important results for the stories—both counter and rounder—that are told as acts of epistemic reparations. Just as we grow and change and transform, and our understanding of our experiences and selves follows suit, so, too, should our stories have the option of doing so. What this means is

[55] Pasupathi (2001, p. 662).
[56] Swann (1996).
[57] McAdams (1993).
[58] Pasupathi (2001, p. 662).
[59] Pasupathi (2001, p. 663).

that we need to leave open the possibility of *editing* our stories, even after the initial reparative ones have been told.[60] If, for instance, Demetrius's original counter story focused on his wrongful conviction but framed it as stemming from being confused in the interrogation room, he should have the opportunity to revise the narrative as he comes to understand that it was actually terror that resulted in a coerced false confession and his current incarceration. Indeed, allowing edits to the stories that are told seems to be a vital component of their reparative function, as many violations and injustices not only take years to even begin to grasp, but there are also crucial connections between storytelling, understanding, and healing. As Suzanne Methot says in *Legacy: Trauma, Story, and Indigenous Healing*:

> To heal from a traumatic event, the survivor needs to create a coherent story that helps them understand that *something has happened to them*, and that this event, or series of events, is the reason why they feel the things they feel. Creating a narrative also helps the survivor see who or what is responsible for that event, which helps them understand that they were the victim and are not to blame for the original event. (2019, p. 157)

Australian author Gemma Carey, for instance, writes that "I'm a survivor of child sexual grooming. It took me 20 years to know it wasn't my fault" (2021). The story that Carey told before she came to understand that she was not in any way responsible for what her perpetrator did to her when she was 12 and 13 years old focused only on the fact that he "got [her] to say yes" and that she "welcomed him into [her] childhood bedroom" (2021). Providing space for Carey to edit her story over time opens up the door both for her right to be known to keep up with the shifts in her own life story and understanding as well as for the reparative work in question to be ongoing. Moreover, as Methot writes:

[60] I first heard the language of "editing" our stories from Beulah Mosupye and then later saw author and psychotherapist Lisa Gottlieb's TED talk in which she discusses life being "about deciding which stories to listen to and which ones need an edit" (2019). In a similar spirit, Pasupathi et al. maintain that "narratives are dynamic and fluid, changing across telling, contexts, and time. To understand how all of us tell our stories, we must reflect on how narratives that we tell, and that we listen to, are always in the process of being negotiated, contested, negated, and confirmed" (2016, p. 49). With respect to life stories in particular, Pasupathi writes, "[t]he potential to revise the life story in light of new experiences and new audiences remains an avenue for change or stability throughout adulthood" (2001, p. 662).

> As the survivor becomes more aware of the various elements of the traumatic narrative—what happened, when it happened, who was responsible, who was a bystander, and the effects the event has had on their thoughts and feelings—then they are able to see how the traumatic event has impacted their behaviours and their choices in life. As a result of this process, the survivor begins to mend the separation between sensory knowledge, memory, and their concept of self. The survivor can then build a new sense of who they are inside and who they are in relation to other people. This sets the stage for living in the present, instead of recreating the sensory memory of the past. (2019, p. 157)

Since the narratives we tell can shape who we are and who we can become, the process of creating and editing our stories not only tracks how we change and grow and transform but also provides avenues for facilitating reparative changes and growth in our identities and in our lives.

With respect to false confessions in particular, we have thus far focused only on *compliant* ones like Demetrius's, where guilt is admitted while the confessor fully knows that he is innocent and that what he is saying is false.[61] But being open to editing is perhaps even more critical when it comes to those that Leo and Ofshe (1997) call "persuaded false confessions." A *persuaded false confession* is one that occurs when "police interrogation tactics cause an innocent suspect to doubt his memory and he becomes temporarily persuaded that it is more likely than not that he committed the crime, despite having no memory of committing it" (Leo 2009, p. 339). Typically, persuaded false confessions unfold in three steps, with the first involving the interrogator causing the suspect to doubt his own innocence. This is often the result of a lengthy, accusatorial, and deceptive interrogation where the interrogator repeatedly accuses the suspect of committing the crime, attacks the suspect's denials, and presents the suspect with fabricated evidence of his guilt.[62] The second step is to provide a reason to the suspect that explains how he could have committed the crime in question without remembering it, which often involves a version of a "repressed" memory theory, such as an "alcohol- or drug-induced blackout, a 'dry' blackout, a multiple personality disorder, a momentary lapse in consciousness, . . . posttraumatic stress disorder, or, perhaps most commonly, that the suspect simply repressed

[61] Leo (2009, p. 338).
[62] Leo (2009, p. 339).

his memory of committing the crime because it was a traumatic experience for him" (Leo 2009, p. 339). The third and final step is the creation of a postadmission narrative, which is often replete with errors and offered in hypothetical, tentative, and speculative terms since the false confessor is reasoning from inference rather than knowledge.[63] In cases of persuaded false confessions, interrogators are able to alienate a suspect from her own epistemic resources regarding not only what she says, but also with respect to what she remembers and believes.

This can be powerfully seen in the case of Michael Crowe, who was 14 years old when his 12-year-old sister, Stephanie, was stabbed to death in her bedroom in Escondido, California, at some point between the evening of January 21st and the morning of January 22nd of 1998. Michael was interviewed on three separate occasions by police, beginning the day Stephanie was found murdered. During this first interrogation, he reported that he woke up at 4:30 a.m. on the 22nd with a headache and walked down the hallway adjoining Stephanie's bedroom to get a Tylenol from the kitchen. Rather than being returned to his parents after this interview, Michael and his older sister were sent to a shelter for abused and neglected children. The following day, Michael was taken back to police headquarters, where he repeated the version of events he had earlier told police and expressed his anguish over his sister's death and his separation from his family.[64] This second interrogation grew increasingly aggressive, with the police suggesting to Michael that hair that had been found in Stephanie's hand would prove to be his and outright lying to him when they declared both "that there was a mounting pile of physical and scientific evidence that would prove that he was Stephanie's killer" (Drizin and Colgan 2004, p. 135) and that they knew he was lying about walking to the kitchen because it would have been impossible to do so without seeing Stephanie's body. During the third and final interview of Michael, police continued to present evidence that was false, telling him that they knew the murderer was someone living in the house because all of the windows and doors had been closed and locked. In fact, a sliding glass door to the backyard had been left unlocked. In addition, Michael was subjected to a Computer Voice Stress Analyzer test, which is of "questionable accuracy," after which the police told him that the tests revealed that he was lying. When Michael began to "sob uncontrollably" (Drizin and

[63] Gudjonsson (2003).
[64] Drizin and Colgan (2004, p. 134).

Colgan 2004, p. 135), the police suggested to him that he might be blocking out the fact that he murdered Stephanie. They went on to propose to him that there were "two Michaels"—one who is good and another who is bad, and it was the bad Michael who killed Stephanie:

MR. CROWE: If that's true, then the other Michael has taken over because I don't know what's going on because I don't remember.
DETECTIVE WRISLEY: You know what, that's possible.
MR. CROWE: It's the most horrible thing in the world. (Drizin and Colgan 2004, p. 139)

As the interrogation continued, Michael began to accept the police's narrative that "bad Michael" had killed Stephanie and that "good Michael" had blocked out what happened. "He stated, 'I'm not sure how I did it. All I know is that I did it.'" The charges against Crowe were later dropped when a "drifter in the neighborhood that night was found with Stephanie's blood on his clothing" (Kassin et al. 2010, p. 15). Describing his experience in a 2008 interview, Crowe said, "[the police] strip away all your support systems, and once they've taken your family away from you and your friends, they start chipping away at your own beliefs and memory" (Oprah.com).

Cases of persuaded false confessions, like Crowe's, reveal the importance of leaving the door open not only for the editing, rewriting, or even wholesale recreation of narratives, but also for doing so as processes of coconstruction. Just as it took Crowe interacting with manipulative and deceptive interrogators to come to believe the false and alienating story of "bad Michael" killing his sister, so, too, it might require him being in healthy and restorative relationships to coconstruct a new, accurate narrative. This might involve others sharing information with him about the available evidence, or interrogation tactics, or what was done to him in particular, thereby facilitating the unearthing of a rounder story that is anchored in reality for Crowe to have about himself. It is a scenario like this that makes particularly vivid the need for epistemic reparations to include the "coproduction" of epistemic goods. If a victim is intentionally kept in the dark, especially by powerful forces like the State, then sometimes the only way an accurate, healthy narrative can emerge is through the process of coproduction. This is true not only at the level of individuals, but also with respect to collectives. From the impact of colonialism on the master narratives of entire cultures and peoples to the effects of State-run propaganda on a nation, being in dialogue with others, or with one another, may be ineliminable steps in the cocreation of radically new, rounder stories for groups whose master narratives have been systematically erased and silenced or are vilifying and distorting.

It is also worth returning to the earlier passage from Velleman connecting storytelling and understanding and placing it within his broader account to provide another framework for these conclusions.[65] On Velleman's view, action is "behavior aimed at intelligibility" (2009, p. 133)—in other words, when we act, we are trying to understand what we are doing and, through this, to make sense of ourselves. This notion of "sense-making" is the hallmark of agency for Velleman, as our actions are successful to the extent that they make us intelligible to ourselves. Against the background of this fuller picture, we can see that the earlier passage about storytelling is crucially connected to agency. Just as stories are vehicles for rendering events in the world intelligible to us, so, too, do they facilitate sense-making of ourselves in light of our motives and beliefs. In this way, we are like improvisational actors who, through our performances, are trying to act in ways that make sense of our characters,[66] where "reasons for acting are the elements of a possible storyline along which to make up what we are going to do" (Velleman 2009, p. 28). For Velleman, then, there is a crucial connection between stories and the construction of ourselves as agents that is potentially illuminating in the context of epistemic reparations. If stories make us intelligible to ourselves and, in so doing, facilitate the construction of agency, then those that result in or constitute gross violations and injustices can strike at the core of who we are. Flat master narratives that erase entire peoples, or those that vilify a single individual, can block or subvert who victims can become as agents. And as we have seen throughout this book, this is true of epistemic agency as well as of practical agency, which is Velleman's focus. Given this, coconstructed narratives can be a pathway for not only co-creating rounder stories of victims, but also for co-restoring the heart of what was undermined by the original wrongs: their agency.

[65] To be clear, I am not suggesting that we take on board Velleman's robust and detailed view in order to connect storytelling and agency but only that it provides one theoretical framework for shedding light on some of the issues here.

[66] "The self-narrating agent is a bit like an improvisational actor, enacting a role that he invents as he goes. The difference is that an improvisational actor usually invents and enacts a role that he is not playing in fact.... By contrast, the self-narrator is an ingenuous improviser, inventing a role that expresses his actual motives in response to real events" (Velleman 2005, p. 71).

What we see, then, is that there are distinctive epistemic benefits to listening and learning from others about their firsthand experiences. Interestingly, as was noted earlier, the moral domain is often singled out as being one that specifically requires firsthand knowledge. But Demetrius's case study reveals that it is precisely in the moral domain where relying on the testimony of others can be most important. Rather than jurors watching Demetrius's interrogation with their own eyes and forming beliefs about the morality of what happened to him on this basis, they have access to crucial information by instead listening to him.[67] This allows narratives to be coconstructed and knowledge to be mutually acquired that is simply unavailable outside of the process of talking, listening, and learning with and from others.

## 4. Epistemic Respect, Inclusion, and Proximate Sources

The epistemic benefits of talking, listening, and learning go beyond the generation of traditional epistemic goods, such as knowledge and understanding, to also include the cultivation or repair of perceptions and relations within the survivors' communities.[68] This can emerge in a number of different ways and along a variety of dimensions but here I will mention only a few.

First, listening to, rather than about, others can be a way of treating survivors with epistemic respect and dignity and, conversely, a failure to do so can be disrespectful and even violating. Viola Cordova, who was a Jicarilla and Latina philosopher and possibly the first Native American to earn a Ph.D. in philosophy, discusses a white folklorist, who was trying to defend her practice of recording the sayings of Native American elders.

> The budding folklorist follows me for days. She wants me to *understand* what she is doing. "If you think it so important that these old stories survive, then why don't you teach 'natives' how to do such transcriptions?" She apparently hadn't thought of it.
>
> Each time she finds me she has a new approach. "Don't you think it is important for those voices to be heard?"

[67] Again, in practice, jurors often will not have access to listening to defendants themselves.

[68] This will be developed in further detail in Chapter 4 when I discuss the "restoring status" sense of knowing a survivor.

> I respond: "If you write them down it isn't their voice that is speaking. It is yours." Shock. "If you speak for me, you rob me of my voice." (2007, p. 42)

Listening to the folklorist about the lives of Indigenous persons is to center her perspective and voice over those whose own experiences are at issue. This is to treat the Indigenous persons as not worthy of being listened to in their own right, as not being reliable narrators about their own lives, or as not being authors of their own stories, each of which amounts to a denigration of their dignity as epistemic agents. This is important at both the individual and collective levels. In the Summary of their Final Report, the Truth and Reconciliation Commission of Canada writes:

> [T]he importance of truth-telling in its own right should not be underestimated; it restores the human dignity of victims of violence and calls governments and citizens to account. Without truth, justice is not served, healing cannot happen, and there can be no genuine reconciliation.... (2015, p. 12)

In addition, Njabulo Ndebele famously notes that one of the most significant effects of South Africa's TRC was "... the restoration of narrative. In few countries in the contemporary world do we have a living example of people reinventing themselves through narrative" (1998, p. 27). In many cases, then, the restoration of dignity, healing, and the reinventing of self requires a sense of authorship and authority over one's story.[69]

Moreover, if we care about cultivating an inclusive epistemic community, then we should ensure that we listen to a broad range of perspectives. This is especially important when certain voices or groups have been systematically excluded from the epistemic community. As we see in the above passage from Cordova, for instance, it is not just that Indigenous voices have been drowned out over those of others; it is also that they are unable to communicate their own stories without transcription. Similarly, it is crucial that we not hear from only investigators and prosecutors about confessions, or filter such events through our own unique lenses, but that

[69] This is related to a point that will be made in Chapter 4 of how knowing someone as an act of epistemic reparations may involve, among other things, knowing him as an authority in a given domain.

we also listen to victims like Demetrius whose own voice has been relegated to the margins.

Still further, as we saw in Chapters 1 and 2, some violations and injustices are so egregious that they result in epistemic wrongs that call for epistemic reparations that involve listening to victims themselves and coming to know them through their stories. For instance, if Demetrius is wrongfully convicted by the State, and is inaccurately believed to be a murderer for decades, then part of what is needed to repair the damage that has been inflicted on him is epistemic in nature. We need to understand what happened to him and to replace the vilifying picture of him handed to us by the State with a true one. Since part of the epistemically reparative work that is necessary is bearing witness to Demetrius, that we hear *from him about him* is crucial. This is not epistemic value that can be replaced with, or increased by, any sort of first-hand experience of the events in question. Rather, the end of the epistemic work is itself bound up with its secondhand nature.

This leads to an important point about the right to be known. As I mentioned earlier, the right to know picks out a relationship between a person and a proposition, whereas the right to be known involves at least two persons—the person knowing and the person being known. A contrast between the two rights is that with the right to know, it doesn't matter *how* the knowledge is made available; just that it is. The proposition in question can be conveyed through releasing bodycam footage, speaking with perpetrators, reading reports and documents, and so on. Since there is no restriction placed on the source of the knowledge, the right to know about gross violations and injustices can, in principle, be satisfied without ever listening to a single victim or family member of these abuses. In contrast, the right to be known should center the voices and perspectives of survivors as much as possible. If a victim is not able to speak for himself, perhaps because he is in solitary confinement or has been killed, then what I call a *proximate source* can be important.[70] A proximate source in the sense relevant here is a source of knowledge sufficiently close to the victim in question who has the authority to speak on his behalf, which includes both formal and informal spokespersons.[71] If a victim has died, such as George Floyd, then the proximate source might be his family's lawyer who is functioning as a formal spokesperson. If a victim has been long deceased, such as a person who

[70] I explore in some detail in Chapter 4 how the right to be known can be understood for those victims who have died.

[71] For more on spokespersons, see Ludwig (2014), Lackey (2018c), and Salkin (2021, 2024).

was enslaved in America, and there are no recorded testimonials from her, then the proximate source might be her community members, descendants, and so on. There may even be proximate sources for entire communities or groups. In her work on informal political representation, for instance, Wendy Salkin discusses Ta-Nehisi Coates being referred to as "the neoliberal face of the black freedom struggle," the "laureate of black lives," and "a defining voice of our times" and maintains that "[w]hat he says is taken up by audiences and ascribed to other Black Americans as expressions of their own views, values, and commitments" (2021, p. 442). In this way, Salkin argues that Coates is functioning as an informal spokesperson for Black Americans. Of course, there will clearly be variety in what counts as "sufficiently close" to the victim, depending on circumstances and context, but what is crucial is that it matters not just that the person is known, but also *how* that person is known. More precisely, when we are coming to know a victim who has suffered a gross violation or injustice as an act of epistemic reparations, there are important benefits to listening either directly to him or to a proximate source.

But why? Why can't propositions about victims simply be conveyed in any way that serves the relevant practical ends best without attention paid to the source of the knowledge?[72] Much of this book has been aimed at answering this. When we are urged to center the voices of those most wronged or harmed by our social institutions, this is an appeal to provide space for the perspectives of those who have been systematically erased or distorted within it. It would inflict further epistemic wrongs on those who are unjustly invisible to render them visible only by lifting up the voices of those already in positions of power or privilege. Consider, for instance, a symposium in the *Journal of Political Philosophy* devoted to the Black Lives Matter movement that did not have a single paper authored by a philosopher of color.[73] Attention to Black lives without hearing from any Black voices not only fails to treat those directly impacted by the movement with epistemic respect and dignity, it also promotes the kind of perspectival exclusion that the symposium should have been addressing in the first place.

In addition, proximate sources often have important *epistemic insight*. Bryan Stevenson famously argues that justice requires "getting proximate" to people who are suffering because they understand the problems of injustice

[72] I am grateful to a question from Alex Guerrero that led to the inclusion of this material.
[73] For a criticism of this, see Lebron (2017).

in a direct way and thus possess a critical perspective regarding not only the ills of our society, but also their possible solutions.[74] As he says:

> In brokenness you understand something about compassion . . . . It is the broken [who] understand the way justice really needs to work. It is the broken who understand why we need mercy. It is the broken [who] can show us how we make our commitment to justice actionable. (Aspen Global Leadership Network 2016)

Stevenson is here suggesting that experiences of violation and suffering often afford one with epistemic insight. If you experience incarceration firsthand, you almost certainly will have an understanding of the carceral system that I lack. This is why it is essential that, in addition to books by social scientists, lawyers, and other scholars about mass incarceration, we need to include the voices and perspective of those directly impacted. We cannot know what incarceration is like, or the effects it has on people and communities, without listening to those who are or have been incarcerated. This is connected to the earlier discussion of standpoint epistemology where it was highlighted that an epistemic advantage can be afforded not only by a standpoint or social location of marginalization, but also by the experience of "brokenness." Moreover, as we saw above, survivors sharing stories with appropriate listener responses can result in the generation of new knowledge for both the speaker and the hearer. In this way, proximate sources often have an understanding of the relevant violations and injustices that arises because of either their lived experiences or their closeness to those with these experiences, which can then be further deepened and expanded through interpersonal exchanges of talking and listening.[75]

## 5. Deference, Learning, and Restorative Justice

As may be recalled, one of the central worries about deference to moral advice is that it would result in "truncated understanding," which is epistemically

[74] For more on understanding, see Kim (1994), Zagzebski (2001), Riggs (2003), Elgin (2006), Hills (2009), and Grimm (2012, 2014, and 2017).

[75] As with much in this context, there will be better and worse ways of fulfilling a victim's right to be known, and so there may be times when even a proximate source is not available but epistemically reparative work can still be undertaken. This is especially clear when it comes to the "restoring status" of being known, which I discuss in the next chapter.

and morally deficient because there is no grasp of the moral wrongness of the situation.[76] We can now see, however, that this is not necessarily a concern with relying on others in the moral domain, but, rather, it is a problem with the impoverished landscape in epistemology that often frames the discussion as involving only two radically different options: firsthand inquiry or wholesale deference.

Imagine a survivor testifying to a truth and reconciliation commission and one of the commissioners responds mid-testimony: "You don't need to go any further. I defer to you that you were wronged." The epistemic problem here is neither that the commissioner should have formed the belief about the survivor having been wronged entirely firsthand, nor that he should have wholly deferred to the survivor's testimony. Rather, the issue is that there needs to be an expansion of the available options for understanding how moral knowledge is acquired. Many spaces where morally significant information is conveyed are ones that involve interpersonal exchanges of talking, listening, and learning. A truth and reconciliation commission, for instance, is a space of storytelling, bearing witness, and mutual learning rather than one of either firsthand inquiry or simple deference.

Moreover, the learning involved in such spaces often goes far beyond the content of the propositions testified to. As the TRC of Canada writes. "For non-aboriginal Canadians who came to bear witness to survivors' life stories, the experience was powerful. One woman said simply, 'By listening to your story, my story can change. By listening to your story, I can change'" (2015, p. 21). What we see in this passage is that the knowledge acquired by the non-Aboriginal Canadian woman is not limited to the experiences of the survivor but, rather, can extend to her own conception of herself. This is especially powerful when interpersonal exchanges include both survivors and members of groups that have oppressed them, as the moral knowledge that

[76] See Sosa (2021). Sosa also likens the acquisition of moral knowledge to hitting a bullseye in archery or completing a crossword puzzle, both of which can be done entirely on one's own. But just as not all athletic endeavors or projects fit this model, so, too, some kinds of moral knowledge crucially require others. A basketball or hockey player's success at getting a basket or making a goal may depend on different kinds of work by teammates, such as an effective defense. Or one figure skater's ability to perform beautifully may require that her partner lift her with strength and grace. Knowledge is like this, too. Some requires a division of labor that is more analogous to a team sport. My knowing that the Pfizer COVID-19 vaccine is safe depends on a massive number of other epistemic agents, including those who conducted the initial research, ran the clinical trials, and reliably communicated the results. Others require partnerships more like the pairs skaters where the success of one crucially depends on the contribution of a specific other person. This is more like what we see in the case of Demetrius. The aim here is not to arrive at the end result of moral knowledge on one's own, but to listen to another and to learn together.

needs to be conveyed is often multifaceted. A survivor of a Residential School, for instance, may want those who are bearing witness to learn not only facts about what happened to her, but to also rethink Canadian history, their sense of themselves, the current government, and so on. In this way, it is not only important that the knowledge is secondhand in such morally complex contexts, but also that it was acquired through a *process* of talking, listening, and learning. Perhaps unsurprisingly, this conclusion supports a crucial dimension of the work of the TRC of South Africa that was highlighted in Chapter 1, according to which "[t]he process whereby the truth was reached was itself important because it was through this process that the essential norms of social relations between people were reflected" (1998, p. 114). This "social truth" or "dialogue truth" concerns the way in which truth is to be found; it is "*the truth of experience that is established through interaction, discussion and debate*" (1998, p. 113, original emphasis).[77]

We are also now well positioned to connect a number of points that have been developed throughout the previous three chapters. Returning to the criminal legal system as a paradigmatic case, even some of the most basic labels and descriptions that are used can contribute to the flat stories that are told. As Thalia González notes, "retributive justice is grounded in the use of punishment as a communicative act to an individual with a single identity, perpetrator" (2015, pp. 460–461). While we have thus far focused mostly on how this is true of those with criminal convictions, González discusses how similar considerations arise with respect to those who have been wronged. She draws attention to the "serious concerns" that come with "reliance on a simplistic victim/perpetrator dichotomy," focusing on how "a single identity

[77] While I have focused broadly on "learning," this view can also be applied to more formal educational contexts. In particular, appreciating how epistemically generative interpersonal exchanges of talking and listening can be provides a further reason for moving beyond what Paolo Freire calls a simple "banking" concept of education where teachers "deposit" knowledge into the minds of students (1990). According to Freire, "I cannot think for others, or without others . . . . Knowledge emerges only through invention and re-invention, through the restless, impatient, continuing, hopeful inquiry [people] pursue in the world, with the world, and with each other" (1990, p. 58). Even if one does not accept Freire's alternative model, according to which all knowledge is relational and produced in interpersonal interaction, and where all are simultaneously teachers and students in the classroom, what we see is that it is crucial to provide opportunities for learning that go beyond the unidirectional model of teachers lecturing from a place of expertise and students passively receiving what is given to them. In addition to the empirical literature that demonstrates, for instance, a direct link between the amount of time a student talks in class and her corresponding achievement (see, e.g., Sedova et al. (2019)), perspective sharing can lead to the generation of moral knowledge that is simply unavailable through independent inquiry. And if part of what happens in the classroom is the moral education of the future citizens of the world, then we need to ensure that we create spaces for students to talk, listen, and learn.

lens based on victimhood often further undermines social status" (2015, p. 461). Angela P. Harris makes a similar point in the context of the "story of woman as victim," which is "meant to encourage solidarity by emphasizing women's shared oppression, thus denying or minimizing difference," but which also "denies the ability of women to shape their own lives" and "may thwart their abilities" to "create their own self-definitions" (1990, p. 613). One way to understand the point being made by both González and Harris here is within the framework developed in Chapters 2 and 3. Recall that flat stories are closed and depict those in them in static, one-dimensional, and psychologically simplistic terms, while round stories are open and portray people in dynamic, multidimensional, and psychologically complex terms. As we saw, flat stories that are told about a person or group can lock them into identities, blocking agential possibilities of growth and transformation, and as González and Harris emphasize here, this can happen with flat stories of people as victims as well as of them as perpetrators. After reading a draft of Chapter 2, William Peeples notes this in the case of the person he harmed, writing "I could not help but think of Dawn, the innocent human being whose life I brutally ended. I thought about *her* 'epistemic reparations' and what is *owed* to her. She, too, has been given a 'flat story' in the sense that she's been reduced to a victim of violence . . . . My actions made her a victim, but in life she was a sister, daughter, Sunday-school teacher, and more" (personal correspondence).

It was noted in Chapter 1 that a restorative justice framework is often used to understand reparations more generally. This is illuminating, as "[r]estorative justice seeks to disrupt the limitations of socially constructed identities of victims and perpetrators" (González 2015, p. 461). Even more importantly for our purposes, González describes restorative justice as a "process of transforming harmful experiences . . . grounded in oral and affective responses that weave together personal and political narratives, particularly when addressing the complexity of multiple identities . . . . Through a process of narration and re-narration, the collective experiences of all participants, regardless of perceived or actual social status, become united into a series of new identities allowing labels of victim or perpetrator to fall aside" (2015, p. 461). Restorative justice practices thus provide space for narratives to be coconstructed by those involved, opening up not only new narrative and agential possibilities, but also new identities. As we saw earlier in this chapter, this can result from appropriate listener responses that lead to the creation of new knowledge and senses of self for both speaker and hearer.

But restorative justice also institutionalizes storytelling, especially for those who have been subordinated, which provides avenues for new political and legal identities.[78] Drawing on the work of Kay Pranis, for instance, González notes how "after each individual narrates his or her individual story" in restorative justice, "new stories are coauthored by a plurality of stakeholders in the injustice" and that this "re-narration allows for the development of new political identities" (2015, p. 469). In a similar spirit, Robert A. Neimeyer and Finn Tschudi discuss how narrative alternatives are presented through restorative justice that "(1) assist persons in finding an authorial voice, (2) invite meaningful co-authorship of life narratives by ensuring the participation of both protagonists and supporting characters, and (3) recruit a relevant audience for the performance of a new narrative that transforms the conflict" (2003, pp. 171–172). Notice that Neimeyer and Tschudi highlight the possibility of participants in restorative justice finding a voice for sharing their stories, coauthoring their life narratives together, and transforming the conflict in question itself, which parallels the process of talking, listening, and learning developed in this chapter.

To connect this more closely with epistemic reparations, particularly when a restorative justice framework is in the background, recall from Chapter 1 that there are at least three ways in which fulfilling a survivor's right to be known through the process of talking, listening, and learning provides epistemic reparations to him. First, sharing our stories can generate knowledge not only in listeners, but also in ourselves. Talking our narratives through can help us make sense out of events in our own lives, our role in their occurrence, their impact on who we are today, and the possible paths forward, leading to new knowledge and deeper understanding. As Pranis says in the context of discussing restorative justice:

> Personal narratives are a way to know and understand . . . ourselves more completely. Telling our story is a process of self reflection. In telling our story we articulate how we understand what has happened to us, why and how it has impacted us, how we see ourselves and others. Actually voicing those understandings provides an opportunity to examine the thoughts, assumptions, ideas undergirding our story . . . . Our way of constructing our story, which shapes our view of reality, becomes more transparent to us when we speak the story out loud to others. (2002, p. 5)

[78] See Pranis (2002) and González (2015).

This can be especially important in cases where flat and opposing labels and stories connect people, such as "victims" and "perpetrators." Pranis continues:

> As the story unfolds
> The labels fall away
> Tears blend
> The "other" becomes one of us
> We cannot hold the "other" separate
> We are inextricably intertwined in a combined story. (2002, p. 9)

William Peeples powerfully conveys this inextricable connectedness with the person he harmed. In expressing gratitude for the role that his story plays in this book, he writes that "centering William inevitably centers Dawn too" because "she is always with [him]" as she was the "impetus" for the transformation he has undergone over the past three decades. He continues:

> The remorse, the shame I came to feel for my actions are inextricably tied to Dawn's value and worth as a human being. When I accepted complete and unequivocal responsibility for her life, and realized the irreparable harm I'd done, that fueled my idea of "perpetual atonement," meaning I must forever try to live in a manner that seeks to atone to her, her family, the children she never got to have . . . . (personal correspondence)

William goes on to address the flat labels of "victim" and "perpetrator" directly, saying that Dawn is not "just a victim" but is the driving force for him to try to "live every single day" in a way that "honors her, and pays homage to her memory." When his death sentence was commuted to life in prison, William says that his life was spared, allowing him "to continue breathing air that Dawn no longer gets to breathe," thereby making his life "hers as well" (personal correspondence). While there are certainly other ways for this to unfold, William describes one vivid and compelling way in which his story evolved so that flat labels fell away and Dawn became part of who he is today. Moreover, as we saw in this chapter, listener responses can play a powerful role in storytelling, leading to personal narratives that are coconstructed by both speakers and audience members. As González writes in the context of discussing restorative justice, "[t]he moment of co-authorship creates a narrative in many voices, each transforming the other" (2015, p. 470).

This brings us to the second, and closely related, way in which talking, listening, and learning provides epistemic reparations to a survivor: fulfilling a victim's right to be known is to take steps to ensure that he is able to stand in right epistemic relations within his community. Indeed, according to Walker, every act of reparations aims "at an alteration in the relationship and standing of the parties" (2010, p. 530). Even more precisely, she writes that "all reparative gestures . . . are a kind of representation by exemplification of the 'right relationship' that wrongdoing has denied or broken" (2010, p. 532). Creating space for a wrongfully convicted person's story to be told, for instance, and promoting his counternarrative to the State's master narrative, is to aim to secure or restore his status among, and connections with, others. It is to provide an accurate and respectful account of who he is that undermines the inaccurate and vilifying one that has been extracted or written by those in power—such as that he is a murderer—and to seek to repair his damaged standing and relations within the community. Moreover, as we have seen, relations to others can also change through the creation of rounder versions of flat stories that have included truths all along. With respect to conflicts in particular, Pranis says, "[s]haring stories from our own personal experiences, especially stories of pain or struggle or stories reflecting our imperfections, can radically change how we see one another and therefore radically change how we relate to one another. When the way we are relating to one another is harmful, as in many conflicts, personal narrative storytelling may create new ways for the parties to see one another in a way that makes resolution of the conflict possible" (2002, p. 5). Stories told by those who have harmed others, for instance, may humanize them in ways that open up capacities for seeing them as broken or hurt rather than, say, monstrous or evil. Stories by those who have been harmed may convey the many layers or dimensions of their suffering, making possible a fuller appreciation of them as, say, courageous and wise rather than vulnerable and damaged. Along a number of normative dimensions, these new lenses for seeing one another may enable not only repaired or entirely new standings within the community but also repaired or entirely new relations. With respect to the epistemic domain specifically, parties on both sides of a conflict might come to see one another as knowers, truthtellers, credible, wise, and worthy of learning from, which, in turn, can give rise to relations of trust, sharing, listening to, relying on, and so on.

Finally, and perhaps most fundamentally, talking, listening, and learning provides epistemic reparations to a survivor by promoting the cultivation, restoration, or repair of his epistemic agency. As mentioned in Chapter 1, this involves centering the survivor from the beginning—in deciding whether to tell his story, to whom it is told, how it is told, where it is told, and so on—to the end—in determining who has access to his story, how it is shared, how it can be updated, and so on. But the very act of telling his own story—especially after demonizing or distorting ones have been told about him by others, or extracted from him through coercion, or been prevented from being told, or been taken from him—centers his epistemic agency in deep and important ways. He is able to provide testimony that is responsive to the truth rather than to the aims or desires of others; he is able to make important epistemic contributions to what is known in the relevant epistemic communities, especially about himself; he is able to shift his identity from, say, liar to truthteller, from murderer to survivor. But as we saw earlier in this chapter, talking through one's story can also open up agential possibilities of editing, envisioning new directions, and writing new chapters of our lives. Pranis explores this specifically in the restorative justice context, writing:

> In telling our story we may uncover something of ourselves or our relationships to others that we were not aware of. As we become more aware of our own internal process and its influence on our state of mind, we have more choices about how to react to events in our lives. We can then choose how the story will continue. Through telling our story, clarifying our own understanding of who we are and the choices available to us, we get a chance to rewrite the direction of the story from that point forward. (2002, p. 5)

What is particularly interesting about this passage for our purposes is that Pranis walks through all three ways in which being known through talking, listening, and learning can be epistemically reparative. First, the sharing of a story can itself be epistemically generative, leading to the uncovering of new truths about "ourselves" and "our relationships with others." Second, as we acquire this new knowledge, our relations with others can shift and transform along a multitude of normative dimensions. And then, finally, as we talk, listen, and learn, new possibilities open up about our stories, how they will unfold, and the lives we are able to live.

## 6. Conclusion

When we talk about victims of gross violations and injustices having the right to be known, traditional epistemological theories push us in the direction of understanding this as involving either wholesale deference to their testimony, on the one hand, or autonomous, firsthand inquiry, on the other. But we have seen that there is a third, powerful option available to us: knowing someone through the interpersonal process of talking, listening, and learning. This process can lead to coconstructed narratives that are epistemically generative for both those who are telling their stories and those who are appropriate listeners, leading to the repairing of epistemic wrongs, the creation of new narratives and new identities, and, ultimately, the development of new selves.

# 4
# Knowing Someone

The title of this book is *The Right to Be Known*, and yet very little has been said thus far about what it means to *know someone* as an act of epistemic reparations. In this chapter, I characterize two different ways to know a person or persons that are relevant for repairing epistemic wrongs: *bearing witness* and *restoring status*.[1] Knowing someone in a bearing witness sense minimally requires a victim's story, which needs to be appropriately anchored in reality, being given proper uptake. Knowing someone in a restoring status sense instead focuses on the perception of a victim and his relations within his relevant communities, involving, for instance, his name being "cleared," his reputation being repaired, and his appropriate status being cultivated or restored.

While this chapter takes up the question of how to understand knowing a person, and I am trained as an analytic epistemologist, I should emphasize at the outset that you will not find in the pages that follow much that looks like an analysis with purported necessary and sufficient conditions. This is at least in part because I am not interested in what it means to know a person in the same way we know other things in the world, like tables, trees, and bumblebees. Consider, for instance, Alvin I. Goldman's early causal theory of knowledge,[2] according to which I know that there is a tree in my backyard if and only if the fact that there is a tree in my backyard is causally connected in an appropriate way with my corresponding belief, such as through perception. One straightforward way of addressing the question of this chapter, then, is to simply extend this sort of causal account to persons, which Ernest Sosa does explicitly when he writes:

> Knowing someone or something, knowing some "object" in the broadest sense of this term, seems at least sometimes to require some kind of special

[1] As I have made clear elsewhere, epistemic reparations can involve knowing individual persons as well as collectives, such as Black South Africans, Canadian Residential School survivors, victims of police torture in Chicago, and so on.

[2] Goldman (1967).

*The Right to Be Known*. Jennifer Lackey, Oxford University Press. © Oxford University Press 2026.
DOI: 10.1093/9780197833988.003.0005

> causal interaction with that "object." This is plausibly a requirement for knowing a person, and for knowing an experience or a sight, say the sight of the Boston skyline two miles from the south on highway 93, or the experience of a cold shower after a hard run. (BonJour and Sosa 2003, p. 100)

While I will engage with this view directly at the end of this chapter, what I want to highlight is that, unlike with causal accounts, my aim here is to develop a framework specifically for understanding knowing a person as an act of epistemic reparations. What, that is, does it mean to know someone in a way that fulfills his right to be known in the face of a gross violation or injustice? Causal interaction may be neither necessary nor sufficient for this.[3]

But perhaps even more importantly, this sort of starting point seems to involve the wrong approach for this altogether. Knowing persons in the sense that is central for epistemic reparations will be radically heterogenous in form, content, and elements. It may involve everything from one-on-one conversations and truth and reconciliation commissions to memorials and museums; from updating beliefs and attitudes to coconstructing rounder narratives; from written testimony and documentaries to art, poetry, and music; from overtly empathetic engagement to quiet resolve; and so on. Given this, although I will for the sake of clarity briefly connect the framework developed here with a traditional account of testimonial knowledge, what will be the most original and, I think, most illuminating is not identifying the lowest common denominator that all epistemic reparations share but, rather, exploring some of the paradigmatic ways fulfilling a victim's right to be known might be done. The ultimate goal is to shed light on the most powerful features of such cases so that each of us might roll up our sleeves and take part in the collective work of repairing some of the most devastating epistemic wrongs of the past and the present.

## 1. Bearing Witness

"Bearing witness" is often understood in terms of the sharing of a story or experience or providing testimony or evidence. In a review of its impact on survivors of abuse and trauma participating in official processes, such as national and international commissions or tribunals, Wyles et al. characterize

[3] Indeed, this is what I ultimately argue later in this chapter.

bearing witness as "a means for trauma survivors to give voice to lived experience" (2023, p. 3078). But rarely do we hear about a survivor bearing witness in private; rather, it is most often used when there is a current or anticipated audience. For instance, engraved in stone in the entrance to the United States Holocaust Memorial Museum are Elie Wiesel's words, "For the dead and the living, we must bear witness" (1993). While Wiesel is here noting the deep importance of telling the stories of the violations and injustices inflicted during the Holocaust on both those who are still alive and those who are no longer with us, he is also clear that it is to "further the cause of remembrance,"[4] which crucially involves listeners and viewers. This central role for an audience is echoed in the description of Martin Puryear's sculpture, which was installed in 1997 in the courtyard of the Ronald Reagan Building and International Trade Center in Washington D.C.: "the sculpture's poetic title . . . *Bearing Witness* suggests an observer, perhaps even the collective consciousness."[5] Indeed, in many contexts, the focus of bearing witness has shifted to the actions of the audience, such as their listening and acknowledging. With respect to caregiving, for instance, Rahel Naef holds that "[b]earing witness is being present and attentive to the truth of another's experiences" (Naef 2006, p. 146) and in discussing Allissa Richardson's book, *Bearing Witness While Black*, Ted B. Kissell writes that "'[b]earing witness' is a term used by psychologists, who note that listening to and watching others recount their traumatic experiences can be key to recovery and healing" (2020). I will be understanding bearing witness as encompassing both aspects of the process—the sharing of a story or experience and the audience's uptake. However, when I talk specifically about knowing a victim or survivor in a bearing witness sense, I will typically focus on what is needed from the one who is doing the listening and learning.

With this in mind, let's consider a paradigmatic case of knowing someone in the bearing witness sense: I have a face-to-face conversation with Demetrius where I have appropriate listener responses—such as physical and verbal expressions of engagement and care—I fully believe what he truly tells me, and I experience fitting emotions of sadness and outrage at his recounting the horrors and injustices inflicted upon him by the State. I center the cultivation, restoration, and repair of his epistemic agency[6] and

[4] Wiesel (1993).

[5] General Services Administration (n.d.).

[6] As mentioned in earlier chapters, this includes whether he tells his story, what is told, to whom it is told, how it is told, where it is told, who has access to it, how is it shared, how it can it be updated, and so on.

ensure that he feels truly seen, heard, and understood especially regarding the ways in which the gross injustice of his wrongful conviction has rendered him both invisible in some ways and hypervisible in others. As we saw in the previous chapter, all of this may help Demetrius understand these injustices better himself—my listening may invite him to revise his life story and my responses may help his coconstructed narrative grow and deepen, opening up the possibility of new chapters that have yet to be told.

There are many dimensions of this scenario that may each be partially epistemically reparative for Demetrius. Providing space for Demetrius to tell his story may, by itself, make him feel seen and heard in deeply transformative ways. In *Dust Tracks on a Road*, Zora Neale Hurston powerfully captures the absence of this when she says "[t]here is no agony like bearing an untold story inside you" (2010, p. 176). In contrast, the opening pages of the present book highlight the flipside of this when Lucas Baba Sikwepere likens his having the opportunity to tell his story to the TRC to "get[ting his] sight back." Both passages make clear that the very act of sharing one's story with others can have profoundly reparative effects. Similar thoughts are found in the report submitted by the National Centre for Truth and Reconciliation on survivor perspectives on the Indian Residential Schools Settlement Agreement, where one of the main positive outcomes identified was the "public recognition of the harm done by the residential school system and its legacy (truth)" (National Centre for Truth and Reconciliation 2020). The TRC hearings in particular were highlighted as being "the first opportunity" that some survivors had "for family members to witness one another's truths.... One survivor recounted... her parents not believing her experience of abuse and underscored that the TRC allowed her to finally tell her story and to be believed" (National Centre for Truth and Reconciliation 2020). In addition, "[t]he process of honourary witnesses, where non-Indigenous leaders came forth from all sectors of Canadian society to bear witness to the truth of Survivors and afterwards share what they learned with their very diverse circles of influence, was highlighted as a critical piece of truth-telling" (National Centre for Truth and Reconciliation 2020). In general, the sharing of stories, as well as the listening and learning, at the TRC of Canada were said to have had a profound impact on survivors, breaking cycles of silence, promoting healing, and facilitating reconciliation.

While the cases involving both Demetrius and the TRC of Canada are paradigmatic instances of knowing survivors through bearing witness, there are also many scenarios that call for epistemic reparations that deviate from these in crucial respects. Perhaps incarceration makes a face-to-face conversation impossible, or lingering doubt renders full belief difficult, or emotional overload makes fitting emotions challenging, or there are no uncensored avenues for promoting a truthful and rounder story. Should these sorts of barriers and constraints relevant to fulfilling the right to be known of survivors lead to despair at our inability to truly right these wrongs? Indeed, even in the absence of these specific kinds of limitations, it is not even clear in the central cases of this book what would be appropriately reparative in the face of the effects of systemic injustices like colonialism, racism, or an unjust criminal legal system. What, that is, could possibly sufficiently make up for the effects of, say, deep, widespread, and pernicious intergenerational invisibility, vilification, and distortion of an entire group of people or even decades of hypervisibility and demonization of a single person?

What this points to is that epistemic wrongs that result from or constitute gross violations and injustices typically involve *ongoing harm*. The vilification of Black men in the American criminal legal system, for instance, is often traced to the history of slavery, convict leasing, and Jim Crow, revealing the deep and continuous intergenerational epistemic effects that gross violations and injustices often bring in their wake. There will, then, almost certainly never be a "one and done" act that rights the initial epistemic wrong resulting from or constituting a gross violation or injustice, even when the conditions are ideal for engaging in it. Rather than leading to despair, inertia, and inaction, however, this points to the need for shifting our understanding of the demands of epistemic reparations, both theoretically and practically, as being similarly ongoing. More precisely, moving away from a strictly *act-based account* of reparations, where there are discrete acts on each side of the wrong and repair, to a *process-based account*, where there are ongoing processes on each side of the wrong and repair, is illuminating along a number of dimensions.

First, it makes clear that the work of epistemic reparations does not fit into a "one-and-done" transactional model precisely because the wrongs themselves often don't fit into such a model. If I let my friend use my car and she unlawfully sells it, then seeking restitution in a civil case may ask the court, in part, to restore me to where I was before my car was sold. Requiring that I be paid the fair market value of the car when it was borrowed is a straightforward one-time transaction that aims to make me whole. The epistemic wrongs at issue in this book are not like this. Even limiting our focus to a single individual, there is, for instance, no single act that could restore

Demetrius epistemically to where he was before his wrongful conviction narrative occupied center stage in the public's consciousness for decades.

Second, shifting over to seeing our engagement in the epistemic work of reparations as an ongoing process similarly alters our expectations about what each single act needs to accomplish. If what we do is only one of many acts in a process, each of which is partially epistemically reparative to varying degrees, then even very small acts of listening and learning along the way can contribute to the process. This is theoretically important, as it captures that individual acts of wrongdoing and reparations are each only *part* of the normative story. But it is also practically important, as it punctures the inertia that may follow from the hopelessness of expecting epistemic reparations to be "one and done."

Finally, this process-based model leads to a greater appreciation of the need for *collective action* when it comes to engaging in epistemic reparations.[7] While no single act of knowing will make up for, say, Demetrius's wrongful conviction, we each can take part in the process of doing so, which needs to be both ongoing and collective. This is because the epistemic wrong is both ongoing and collective, encompassing many layers of impact that follow from the State creating and promoting an official story of him being a murderer, the media fueling it through danger narratives of young Black men in America, and the public's acceptance of these systems and accounts.

With all of this in mind, let's look at some ways of bearing witness that differ from the opening case of knowing Demetrius but might still be important acts in the process of engaging in epistemic reparations. Consider my friend, Keith LaMar, who is currently in solitary confinement on Ohio's death row, wrongfully convicted of murdering five incarcerated people during the 1993 Lucasville Prison Uprising.[8] Along with a group of collaborators, Keith became the first artist in history to release an album while on death row.[9] Many of the songs on *Freedom First* tell the story of Keith's wrongful conviction, current incarceration, death row sentence, anticipated execution, and fight for truth and justice. Given that Keith is in solitary confinement at the "supermax" Ohio State Penitentiary, knowing him through a face-to-face conversation as described above is not possible for most people. Nevertheless, just about anyone can bear witness to the gross violations and

[7] I explore the role that we each play in the process of engaging in epistemic reparations in Chapter 5.

[8] Justice for Keith LaMar.

[9] Justice for Keith LaMar, *Freedom First*.

injustices inflicted on Keith by streaming or downloading *Freedom First* and listening to Keith tell his own story through his spoken word poetry. For such a listener, there may be no direct, in-person interaction with Keith, and so the features of the interpersonal exchange in the central case above will not be present: Keith will not be able to see or hear the listener's responses, there won't be a coconstructed narrative that emerges in that moment, and a new sense of self or of future possibilities won't emerge for Keith on this basis. So, in what sense is a listener—perhaps in her car driving down Lake Shore Drive in Chicago or drinking tea in a café in Barcelona—bearing witness to Keith, who is currently sitting in a cell in solitary confinement in Youngstown, Ohio?[10]

In both the central case of listening to Demetrius's story in a face-to-face conversation and listening to Keith's song while driving down Lake Shore Drive, I believe what they tell me, I feel sadness and outrage, and I replace the false and flat public narratives of them with truthful and rounder ones. Yet despite these similarities, not even all of these shared features are themselves necessary for knowing Demetrius and Keith in a bearing witness, epistemically reparative sense. Consider my feelings of sadness and outrage. Some philosophers have argued that there are "apt" or "fitting" affective responses to events in the world, including the injustices experienced by others. Amia Srinivasan, for instance, writes:

> Imagine a person who does everything, as it were, by the ethical book—forming all the correct moral beliefs and acting in accordance with all her moral duties—but who is left entirely cold by injustice, feeling nothing in response to those moral wrongs of which she is perfectly aware. I don't want to say that such a person has done anything wrong. But I do think it is natural to say that there is *something missing in her*.... (2018, p. 132)

While appropriate emotional responses—both internal and external—to hearing stories of gross violations and injustices are indeed often very important, they do not seem to be *necessary* either in general or for bearing witness more specifically. Suppose, for instance, that I listen to *Freedom First* on a loop for a week. After the 200th time, I may not have an internal or external

[10] Although there can be limited contact with Keith while he is incarcerated, I will be focusing on listeners who have no direct connection with him except through *Freedom First*. In this way, I intend what I say about Keith to also apply to cases of listening to the stories of those with whom there can be no direct, in-person contact, such as the deceased.

emotional response at the time of the listening, but I still seem able to bear witness to Keith's struggles in an epistemically reparative way. Moreover, this isn't simply because I keep hearing the same story told by the same person over and over. Consider a civil rights attorney working for months through deposition transcripts involving police violence in connection with a class action lawsuit. Each narrative that she reads may involve bearing witness to a survivor, but she may not be experiencing internal or external emotions every single time. Indeed, in contexts or professions where people frequently listen to many stories of traumatic experiences, it can sometimes be helpful or even necessary to regulate emotional responses to avoid secondary or vicarious trauma. In a qualitative study on the impact of listening to other people's traumatic experiences, for instance, Livanou et al. discuss how "the emotionally composed or 'uninvolved'" can provide greater support to survivors. One of the counselors interviewed in the study emphasizes the importance of emotional boundaries: "[y]ou can see that they are metaphorically swimming in their trauma and it's about not jumping in with them and trying to save them whilst drowning in it. It's about throwing them a rope to pull them out, but you are not going to do any good if you drown in that sea with them" (Livanou et al. 2024, p. 6). Emotional regulation is one of the ways of avoiding "drowning" in other people's trauma, and there are two dimensions to this that are especially relevant here: "attentional deployment," which "may be used to select which aspect of a situation a person focuses on," and "cognitive change," which involves "selecting which of the many possible meanings . . . will be attached to a situation" (Gross 1998, p. 282). The civil rights attorney, for instance, may actively choose to focus on the aspects of the depositions that will provide the strongest case for the lawsuit, and she may attach to them the hope of obtaining justice for the survivors, which may result in a very different emotional reaction than expected, such as excitement. Despite this, she may be bearing witness in an even more epistemically reparative way than someone who, upon hearing a survivor's story of police violence, has a fleeting moment of, say, sadness or outrage, and then quickly moves on. She may be engaging with all of the stories with respect and care, recognizing each survivor as a full person deserving of justice, and making a commitment to each that he will not be forgotten. Of course, this is to deny neither that many or even most cases of knowing a survivor will involve appropriate affective attitudes in order to be epistemically reparative, nor that some affective responses—such as complete indifference—are fundamentally incompatible with epistemic reparations. But given the broad range of violations and ways of listening, it is crucial that we not get locked into features of the paradigmatic cases that obscure or miss out on other valuable ways of bearing witness.

What about belief? Can I bear witness in an epistemically reparative way without believing what a survivor is telling me? Imagine a visitor from Norway meeting Demetrius for the first time in an unfamiliar context. While she is an engaged and compassionate listener, she doesn't know much about the criminal legal system in the United States and so she is initially cautious about believing what she hears because some of it is hard to wrap her mind around. She may be thinking, "wait, how can the police lie to someone during an interrogation" or "how could a 15-year-old be interviewed without an adult present supporting him" or "how could a child be given a *de facto* life sentence?" As she continues to listen, she gradually comes to believe more and more of Demetrius's story, ultimately coming to fully see the depth and breadth of the violations inflicted on him by the State. In such a case, it doesn't seem right to say that only mid-way through the conversation, when she shifts from a state of suspending judgment to belief, does the bearing witness begin. Indeed, there may even be epistemically reparative value in the evolution of the listener's attitudes. Demetrius may feel more seen when, despite her initial incredulity that a country like the United States could treat children the way he describes, she comes to accept that these violations were in fact inflicted on him. In other words, the fact that she finds it so hard to believe what he is telling her may, in a sense, be affirming of the egregiousness of the injustices.

Of course, the visitor from Norway ultimately does come to believe Demetrius, even in the very same context and conversation in which she initially doubted him. But what, it might be asked, if a listener never comes to believe the survivor's story? Related to our discussion in Chapter 1, there are many aspects of our stories that may be insignificant to their core reparative work. Perhaps a listener may wonder, for instance, if an event really lasted the number of hours stated, or there were as many people involved, or that it occurred in that location. Not accepting every detail of a story does not necessarily interfere with fulfilling a survivor's right to be known. Some of the central epistemic wrongs inflicted on Demetrius involve him being vilified as a murderer and invisible not only as a victim of a coerced false confession and wrongful conviction, but also as a multidimensional person. Bearing witness to Demetrius in ways that are reparative of these specific wrongs is not incompatible with questioning whether, say, his interrogation took place on a Tuesday.

This is related to a slightly different but equally important issue. Human memory is complicated and fallible and we can easily get details wrong. Indeed, studies show that we often forget events, distort details, and even remember things that never actually happened.[11] We also filter experiences through beliefs and attitudes, bringing "scripts" and "schemas" to our interactions in the world that influence how we experience and remember events.[12] This allows us to "fill in" information about incomplete memories, with one recent study revealing "a bias to recall coherent, completed events, even if this resulted in memories that were inaccurate records of what had been presented" (Raykov et al. 2023, p. 3472). Autobiographical memory in particular is often "a *constructive* and *reconstructive* process used to condense everyday memories of events and activities, extracting those features that embrace and maintain meaning in one's self-knowledge system" (Barclay and DeCooke 1988, p. 92). So, how do we reconcile the fallibility and sometimes even unreliability of human memory with the right to be known developed here?

Since knowledge has an essential connection to truth, a person's story has to have an anchor in reality in order for him *to be known* as an act of epistemic reparations. If a person shares with me a story that purports to be about his life but is in fact entirely fictional, then I cannot know him in an epistemically reparative sense because I cannot in fact know him at all.[13] Of course, I may listen to him in ways that mirror what I do when I am actually bearing witness to a survivor's violation, but I cannot know a person through a wholly false narrative. Given this, I cannot engage in epistemically reparative work for a violation that did not occur or satisfy a right to know that does not exist. Marya Schechtman's narrative self-constitution view, which holds that a person creates his identity through forming an autobiographical narrative, is helpful here. According to Schechtman, " . . . individuals constitute themselves as persons by coming to think of themselves as persisting subjects who have had experience in the past and will continue to have experience in the future, taking certain experiences as theirs. Some, but not all,

[11] See Johnson et al. (1993), Loftus and Pickrell (1995), Schacter (1999, 2022), Strickland and Keil (2011), and Raykov et al. (2023).

[12] See Bransford and Johnson (1972), Dooling and Christiaansen (1977), Schank and Abelson (1977), Alba and Hasher (1983), and Schacter et al. (2007).

[13] This is one of the important ways in which knowing someone may be different from simply acknowledging him. Acknowledging someone is sometimes understood in terms of validating a person's feelings or experiences without judgment and, thus, without a sensitivity to the way the world actually is. Knowing someone, in contrast, has to have a connection with the truth.

individuals weave stories of their lives, and it is their doing so which makes them persons" (1996, p. 94). Crucially, however, Schechtman includes a "reality constraint," which requires that a narrative not be "deeply out of touch with reality" (1996, p. 120). The motivation for this constraint, she writes, "should be clear. To be a person in the sense at issue here is to be able to engage in certain kinds of activities and interactions with others, and living the life of a person requires living in the same world as other persons" (1996, p. 119). In a similar spirit, knowing survivors through their stories requires that they not be profoundly out of touch with reality, particularly with respect to being the victim of a gross violation or injustice. More precisely, *there needs to in fact be a gross violation or injustice suffered and the deep nature of it has to be anchored in reality, even if some details of the narrative are not.* Schechtman's argument on behalf of this reality constraint is even more compelling in the case of knowing someone as an act of reparations. Repairing epistemic wrongs involves engaging in certain kinds of activities and interactions with others, which requires occupying the same world as the survivors who have suffered the wrongs in question. Floating freely from these wrongs makes the reparative work in question targetless at best and additionally harmful at worst.

It may be helpful for some readers for me to briefly translate some of this framework into the language of traditional epistemology. Coming to know a survivor, whether through a story told directly by him or about him, is largely a form of testimonial knowledge. In much of my earlier writing, I emphasize how acquiring knowledge through another person's testimony requires work on the part of both the speaker and the hearer.[14] Very generally, in order for me to know something on the basis of your testimony, your testimony needs to be appropriately connected to the truth and I need to be a proper recipient of it. These conditions can, in turn, be fleshed out in different ways, such as through externalist constraints of, say, reliability or internalist ones of, say, evidence. So, for instance, in order for me to know something on the basis of your testimony, an externalist version might say that the testimony needs to be reliably produced and conveyed and the hearer needs to reliably receive it, while an internalist version might say that both the offering and uptake of the testimony in question need to be adequately grounded in evidence. Applying this to the present discussion, the "anchoring in reality" or "occupying the same world" constraint mirrors the traditional justification or warrant

[14] See, for instance, Lackey (2008).

condition on the speaker in testimonial exchanges. In particular, in order to fulfill a victim's right to be known, the deep nature or heart of the story about the gross violation or injustice has to be appropriately connected to the truth, such as through being reliably told or adequately grounded in evidence.

On the side of the hearer, knowing someone in the bearing witness sense as an act of epistemic reparations requires, at a minimum, proper uptake of the victim's story. Proper uptake involves some appropriate reparative shift in the epistemic states of the hearer, including ultimately believing on the basis of the "anchored in reality story" that the victim suffered the gross violation or injustice in question. While details about even the central wrongs suffered in someone's story may not always be entirely accurate, precise, or accepted, a hearer may still come to know the victim in the bearing witness sense—she may learn that he was in fact wronged in deep and pernicious ways, even if not exactly in the way that he says, come to know that he is so much more than the public narrative about him says he is, contribute to the restoration of his epistemic agency, and so on. In this way, she still knows him in an epistemically reparative way, as she is replacing the unjust flat story about him with a rounder one.

While knowledge involves something like true belief that is justified, and so fulfilling a victim's right to be known involves an appropriate reparative shift in the epistemic states of the hearer based on the speaker's anchored-in-reality story, knowing someone as an act of epistemic reparations is not merely a run-of-the-mill testimonial exchange. This brings us to a feature of bearing witness that has distinctive normative power in this context—providing what I call *value-reflecting attention*. There is a great deal of work in psychology and cognitive science on how attention is a "limited resource," with Scalf et al. writing, "[f]or over a century, psychologists have understood that the primary problem with attention is that we do not have enough of it . . . ." (2013, p. 1). But what is standardly meant here is that we "cannot process and respond to all the information in the environment that may be relevant to our current task . . . nor can we completely inhibit distracting information" (Scalf et al. 2013, p. 1). For instance, high perceptual load[15] in the environment can lead to "inattentional blindness"[16] in which easily visible stimuli fail to be noticed and "inattentional deafness"[17] where

[15] Perceptual load is "the amount of information involved in the processing of the task stimuli" (Macdonald and Lavie 2011, p. 1780).

[16] See Macdonald and Lavie (2008) and Lavie et al. (2014).

[17] See Macdonald and Lavie (2008, 2011).

an auditory stimulus fails to be detected while "engaged in a high visual load task" (Murphy and Greene 2016, p. 2). There is, however, also the kind of attention that is concerned less with the information and distractions in our immediate perceptual environment and more with the choices we make that reflect our values and commitments. In his book on the relationship between attention and consciousness, Sebastian Watzl identifies a number of different forms of attention, including "voluntary attention," which is "roughly controlled by the subject's intentions or goals, whereas involuntary attention occurs without such intentional or voluntary control" and "endogenous attention," which is "internally controlled, while exogenous attention is controlled by [an external] stimulus" (2017, p. 26).[18] Both of these distinctions move beyond the attention that is tied to our immediate perceptual environment. I can, for instance, have the internal intention to "sit with" Keith and voluntarily choose to turn my attention to thinking about him in solitary confinement while largely ignoring the sights and sounds of the city square that I am currently sitting in.

Nevertheless, there still seems to be something missing in these discussions that is of importance here. When I give attention to my daughter over yard work, for instance, or to the incarcerated students in the Northwestern Prison Education Program over running an errand, my actions manifest what I care about and what I believe ought to receive my limited time and energy. This *value-reflecting sense of attention* often has a great deal of normative significance. There are people, projects, and issues that are owed my attention, including not only those involving personal connections, but also those that arise out of broader social expectations.[19] I should, for instance, give some of my attention to my children, students, and work, but also to the local recycling efforts, to current politics in the United States, and to staying updated on what is happening in Ukraine and Gaza. In each of these cases, I would be subject to criticism for not having given any of my attention to the person, project, or issue in question. But then there is space where there is considerable latitude in where I direct my attention, and the choices I make

[18] These are the forms of attention Watzl discusses that are closest to what is relevant to the topic under consideration here, but he also identifies a number of others.

[19] There are also discussions about attention rights, such as whether "attention should be legally protected, either by introducing novel rights or by extending the scope of pre-existing rights" (Kärki and Kurki 2023, p. 1). While the right to attention is distinct from the right to be known, especially when the former is understood in purely legal terms, there are some ways in which they can shed light on one another.

here reflect who and what I value.[20] Since attention in this value-reflecting sense is also a limited resource, appropriately listening to Keith and his story, whether it is in face-to-face conversation or through *Freedom First*, shows that I *value him* and that I recognize and care about the injustices he has faced. I could, after all, be listening to other music or a podcast or nothing at all. In the opening song of *Freedom First*, Keith says, "[t]he music you are about to listen to comes out of the realm of the impossible, something that, in reality, should not have been doable. Whether or not I am successful in stopping these people from killing me, you are right now listening to my last will and testament, the embodiment of everything I've endured, learned, and conquered."[21] Importantly, Keith notes that even if the album does not result in supporting the overturning of his wrongful conviction and saving his life, there is value in listening to his story—that is, in bearing witness to "everything [he has] endured, learned, and conquered." Moreover, in that moment of listening, I am making Keith the focus of my life and, in this sense, our lives intersect in a meaningful way. This is similar to saying "I'm thinking about you" or "I'm holding you in my thoughts" in response to news of a loss or illness. The act of turning my attention to you and your suffering in my thoughts shows that I value you and am making space in my own life for yours.

According to the Meriam-Webster dictionary, one of the definitions of "to bear witness" is "to show that something exists or is true."[22] As noted earlier, human psychology is complicated and fallible, and details both big and small may be wrong or distorted. So, bearing witness cannot literally make the false true. But for those stories of gross injustice that already carry a deep truth, such as Demetrius's and Keith's, giving my attention to them in the value-reflecting sense is to acknowledge through my actions that their violations and suffering exist and are real. As Daniel Philpott writes in the context of discussing truth commissions, "... acknowledgment is knowledge—victims' suffering comes to light" (Philpott 2008, p. 129). When there is no acknowledgment of this sort, survivors are denied not only what they often need or

[20] This is connected to the latitude found in the imperfect epistemic duty of knowing someone that will be discussed in Chapter 5. I should also note that even within the domain of attention that is owed, there are choices to be made that reflect values. While I have a duty to give my daughter attention, for instance, telling her that I will give her my "undivided attention" when I visit her in college conveys to her the significance that I place on our time together, which may go beyond what I, strictly speaking, owe to her.

[21] Justice for Keith LaMar, *Lyrics: LIVE from Death Row and Freedom First Songs*.

[22] "Bear witness," *Merriam-Webster Online Dictionary*.

desire, but also what they are owed. In her work on trauma, Methot draws on the work of Lakota scholar Maria Yellow Horse Brave Heart, who "has written about the concept of 'disenfranchised grief,' which she defines as 'the sense that you cannot grieve; that no one hears or is listening to your grief'" (2019, p. 235).[23] To disenfranchise someone is to deprive him of a right or privilege, and so the concept of disenfranchised grief fits well within the framework of the right to be known. When the grief that often accompanies gross violations and injustices is not listened to, survivors are being deprived of their right to be heard. Bearing witness to a survivor's story, then, is to show through your appropriate actions of listening, acknowledging, recognizing, believing, feeling, or sharing that his violations, suffering, and grief exist—that is to say, that he is known.

Knowing someone in a bearing witness sense thus minimally involves a victim's story, which needs to be anchored in reality, being given proper uptake. Proper uptake, in turn, requires giving value-reflecting attention to the story, centering the cultivation, restoration, or repair of the victim's epistemic agency,[24] and ultimately believing on the basis of the true story that he suffered the gross violation or injustice in question. From here, there are many additional layers and dimensions of knowing someone in the bearing witness sense, such as having appropriate affective attitudes, making him feel seen or heard, promoting rounder stories of him, and so on. While these features may not be required in all cases, they can nonetheless deepen knowing someone in important respects and can further the broader aim of providing epistemic reparations to victims of gross violations and injustices.

## 2. Restoring Status

The second sense of knowing someone that is relevant here is what we might call the *restoring status sense*, which is a fundamentally social notion that involves epistemic effects between the survivor and his social standing or relations with others. What is of significance with this sense of knowing is that the counterstories and rounder stories being told as acts of epistemic reparations are having an epistemic impact within the relevant communities

[23] For more on the concept of "disenfranchised grief," see Doka (1989, 1999), Corr (1999), and Heart (2003).

[24] As noted in Chapter 1, a survivor is not known in an epistemically reparative sense if epistemic agency isn't cultivated or restored in some sense.

so that the wrongs suffered by the victim in question are at least partially repaired and he is at least partially restored to the epistemic status he should have had. The victim comes to be known, for instance, as trustworthy, credible, authoritative, multidimensional, agential, and so on.

To make this vivid, consider all of the forces at work to create and share Keith's narrative—in order to write, record, and release *Freedom First*, Keith worked with an entire team of musicians, who now, in partnership with a host of supporters both near and far, perform concerts literally across the globe. These concerts are not only attended by the local community members in which they are performed, but they are also often covered by journalists, who then add to and spread the rounder story of Keith's life.[25] Along the way, we learn that Keith is innocent of the crimes that put him on death row, that he is brilliant and beautiful, that he suffers ongoing injustices while in solitary confinement every day, that his scheduled execution is haunting, that he is a profoundly talented artist, and that he is guided by truth and justice. Each element of this movement to spread Keith's story is a part of coming to know him in a status-restoring sense.

To develop this in more detail, recall from Chapter 2 the discussion of cognitive biases and salience perspectives and their relation to flat stories. Cognitive biases, for instance, are unconscious, systematic errors in an individual's thinking and reasoning that can influence their *decisions and judgments*.[26] Similarly, harmful salience perspectives involve aspects of the identity of a person that do not reflect his personhood being more prominent *in the minds* of others.[27] While it is indeed true that what takes place in the minds of others is relevant to the epistemic wrongs discussed in this book, this is only one dimension. Returning to the case of William Peeples, it is not just—or even necessary—that people *believe* the flat story that he is only a murderer, but that this is the official story or public narrative of him. Even if, say, the Illinois Prisoner Review Board did not believe only this about him, if they said it, shared it, and made decisions based on it, they would be unjustly creating and promoting a flat narrative about him. To make this clear, let's distinguish between *agent knowing*, which involves particular cognitive agents knowing a fact, from *social knowing*, which involves

[25] See, for instance, Zornosa (2022).
[26] See, for instance, Tversky and Kahneman (1973), Kahneman et al. (1982), and Da Silva et al. (2023).
[27] See Whiteley (2022).

the publicly available, accepted, or dominant view of a fact.[28] Social knowing is to be distinguished from *group* or *collective* knowing, which can be understood as an instance of agent knowing. For instance, a group or collective may, as a cognitive agent, know a particular fact, such as Philip Morris knowing that smoking is harmful to the health of its consumers.[29] In contrast, social knowing does not pick out a cognitive state of an agent—whether an individual person or group. Instead, it highlights what is known in the public domain, which can come apart from the individual knowing of both persons and groups. Even if few individual persons or groups in William's life know him as only a murderer, for instance, the systemic forces outlined in Chapter 2 may nonetheless promote this social knowledge of him. Moreover, social knowing can, but need not, be connected to misknowing, as the publicly dominant picture of a person may in fact involve a very robust, multidimensional set of facts, such as the social knowing of Martin Luther King Jr.

With this in mind, a failure to be known in the sense relevant for epistemic reparations might involve individual knowing, social knowing, or both. This is crucial, for as we engage in epistemically reparative work, we typically do not have direct voluntary control over what we believe, remember, and forget—I cannot, for instance, simply take up the belief that I am six feet tall or scrub my mind of a difficult memory at will. But in my social interactions, including in the rounder stories that are told and shared about others, I can reprioritize what is central to a person's identity through *social forgetting*, which involves centering and augmenting some facts about a person and relegating others to the margins. It is specifically *social* forgetting, rather than forgetting simpliciter, because nothing about this activity requires the literal loss of information that is stored in a person's memory. The opposite of social forgetting in this respect is *social remembering*.

Consider, for instance, Monika Lewinsky, who is widely known for one moment in her over 50 years of life—her relationship with President Bill Clinton in the 1990s. In a 2019 piece for *Vanity Fair*, "Monika Lewinsky on the Decade We Reclaimed Our Stories—and Ourselves," Lewinsky reflects on the night before the publication in 2014 of her first public words[30] since Clinton's impeachment, writing "[t]omorrow, I would begin the Sisyphean

[28] While there are similarities between social knowing as I am understanding it here and the notion found in Alexander Bird's (2010), I do not intend to take on Bird's account in all of its detail.
[29] For more on how to understand group or collective knowledge, see Lackey (2021b). For more on group agency, see List and Pettit (2011).
[30] See Lewinsky (2014).

task of attempting to reclaim the narrative I'd unintentionally lost to the politicians, media, and culture in the late 1990s" (2019). Since those first published words, Lewinsky has been a champion of "women's acts of reclamation," discussing lost or stolen narratives (such as Chanel Miller's), narratives of justice (such as Christine Blasey Ford's), and narratives that recast those under 21 (such as Greta Thunberg's).[31] In a January 2025 interview with *Vanity Fair* about her new podcast, *Reclaiming*, the interviewer notes the years of shame that Lewinsky suffered over "the scandal that defined her public narrative," with Lewinsky saying, "[m]y life is full of things other than just my past" (Walsh 2025). Despite all of her work as a writer, advocate, and podcaster in the past decade, it may be psychologically impossible for some people to hear the name "Monika Lewinsky" and not immediately think of Bill Clinton or the image of Lewinsky in a beret or her testimony about her blue dress.[32] Indeed, I was talking to a fellow academic recently who was persuaded about the wrongs inflicted by some flat stories but noted specifically that while Lewinsky is an extremely courageous and admirable person, her relationship with Bill Clinton continues to occupy center stage in his cognitive framework. In other words, while he has accumulated many additional facts about Lewinsky and knows her as more than "that woman,"[33] the ordering of the corresponding beliefs in his mind persists in centering the one fact that led to her being a household name.

While there may be efforts that can be taken to alter this ordering within an individual's cognitive architecture,[34] what I want to emphasize here is the importance of social knowing for the purposes of restoring status as well as for the broader framework developed here. If we grant that the widespread and unrelenting bullying Lewinsky suffered rose to the level of a gross violation and injustice—she herself talks about how the "shame, the scorn, and the fear" that had been thrown at her made her mother afraid that she "would literally be humiliated to death"[35] and that public shaming "can be

[31] See Lewinsky (2019).

[32] I mention these details because Lewinsky writes in her 2014 piece that it is time to "burn the beret and bury the blue dress" (2014).

[33] See Bennett (2021).

[34] One way of doing this was discussed earlier in relation to the availability heuristic where I suggested that if, say, photos of incarcerated people playing with their children or reading books were shared as often as those of them in handcuffs are now, images of them as parents and scholars would not only more easily come to the public's minds, but would also likely impact judgments about how common it is for justice-impacted people to live these kinds of lives. More generally, exposing oneself to some images and narratives over others can impact the availability and ordering of content within one's cognitive framework.

[35] Lewinsky (2014).

violence"[36]—then she is owed epistemic reparations in the form of a rounder story. But how is this done when the centering images, labels, or facts about a person continue to dominate everything else? Suppose I am talking about Lewinsky's new podcast and how powerful and thoughtful a recent episode was and another colleague says, "hey is that the same Lewinsky who was Clinton's mistress?" Such a label not only flattens Lewinsky's life story to a single moment in time, it also introduces a memorable description of her into a space that unjustifiably threatens to crowd out all of her success at becoming someone new. It denies the fullness of Lewinsky as a person, augments a fact about her life that she deeply regrets,[37] and pushes years of transformation and growth to the margins. Even if we are not able to forget about her connection to Clinton at will, however, we can take concrete steps to facilitate social forgetting. In response to the above interaction, for instance, I can shift the focus back to the podcast episode, highlight Lewinsky's writing and advocacy, and ignore or very briefly acknowledge my colleague's comment. Notice, for instance, that the interviewer above talks about the scandal that defined Lewinsky's "public narrative" and in Lewinsky's TED talk she advocates for an end of "public shaming as a blood sport."[38] It is not only what is inside of people's heads that matters; it is also what is in the public domain in their comments and headlines and articles and news stories. So, while we may not be able to immediately change the centrality of a belief in our cognitive architecture, we can change it in our social architecture. Otherwise put, even if an individual struggles to know Lewinsky as more than Clinton's mistress, we can socially know her as so much more and thus take steps to restore her public status. And that is precisely what Lewinsky herself has spent the last decade doing, writing in her original 2014 article, "I am determined to have a different ending to my story. I've decided, finally, to stick my head above the parapet so that I can take back my narrative and give a purpose to my past."

It is important to highlight two points here. First, in order for epistemic reparations to be called for, there has to be an original gross violation or injustice that gives rise to a distinctively epistemic wrong. In the case of the need for social forgetting as a part of epistemically reparative rounder stories, the original gross injustice often involves too much social remembering that

[36] Kreps (2021).
[37] Lewinsky (2014).
[38] Lewinsky (2015).

can then lead to invisibility along some dimensions and vilification and distortion along others.[39] As we saw earlier, many aspects of the United States result in people who have been convicted of a crime having this one act in their lives systemically magnified and locked into social memory with all other aspects of their identities ignored, erased, or forgotten. In the case of Lewinsky, the scale, depth, and kind of public shaming she experienced—with everyone from members of the White House and the criminal legal system to the media and late-night comedians—resulted in one relationship in her life coming to define her and swamping everything else she did prior to it and afterward. The second point is that the normativity of social forgetting and social remembering is highly contextual. For instance, while I largely focused here on cases in which too much social remembering calls for epistemically reparative work that involves social forgetting, there are likewise cases of too much social forgetting that require social remembering. Consider, again, the case of Limpho Hani from Chapter 1. When a white South African judge told her and her children to "move on" after her husband was murdered by Janusz Walus in cold blood in front of their daughter, it is arguable that this is a case in which the State is not only forcing a certain kind of narrative on Hani, but also where they are engaged in, and demanding, social forgetting. The call to "move on" sounds very much like an imperative to cease focusing on and talking about the act of violence perpetrated against Hani and her family. Given that there is no sense in which the State, via a white judge in a position of privilege and power, is entitled to make such a demand, epistemically reparative work is required in the form of social remembering. More precisely, Hani is owed a space in which she and her family can freely remember, focus on, and talk about the grave injustices inflicted on them through her husband's assassination. This would be a case in which the original gross violations of her husband being murdered and the resulting State-fueled social forgetting led to Hani's grief and rage being rendered invisible, thereby demanding social remembering as part of the required epistemically reparative work.

To be clear, bearing witness and restoring status often go hand in hand. Let's return to the central case of Demetrius. If I am a member of a community in which the false narrative that he murdered an elderly woman in Chicago has been told and promoted, then the very act of listening to him

[39] In order for social remembering to rise to the level of being a gross violation or injustice, it would most likely be systemic or widespread, as we see in the cases discussed above and below.

and believing the reparative counternarrative of his life involves me knowing him in both senses—I am bearing witness through my value-reflecting attention that makes him feel seen and heard and I take a step toward restoring his status by replacing the vilifying story of him told by the State with the accurate and respectful one told by him. Providing avenues for Demetrius's story to be made rounder through further development, and spaces for it to be shared by him and others, can then expand this epistemically reparative work in terms of both depth and breadth. This can involve many different people and pathways, such as educators who cultivate Demetrius's skills as a storyteller, editors open to publishing the work of incarcerated writers, readers open to revising their beliefs, journalists who replace flat narratives with rounder ones, and so on.

While I focus on a case where there are individuals on both the sharing and listening sides of the epistemically reparative work, this can be, and often is, done with collectives. Consider, again, the report submitted by the National Centre for Truth and Reconciliation on survivor perspectives on the Indian Residential Schools Settlement Agreement. One of the main positive outcomes identified was that "[t]he report of the TRC [Truth and Reconciliation Commission] and commentary on the TRC, in the media and in academic articles, validated their experiences. This was seen as a beginning of a new chapter in the lives of the Survivors and the relationship between Canada and Indigenous peoples" (National Centre for Truth and Reconciliation 2020). Notice, first, that this passage makes clear that the TRC, its report, and the commentary on the TRC in the media and in academic articles provided *validation for their experiences*. This highlights the bearing witness sense of knowing—as individual persons, as survivors of the Residential Schools, and as Indigenous persons, participants in the TRC were listened to and believed. This then gave rise to the restoring status sense of knowing in which their stories were shared and promoted in publicly recognized venues, which then opened up new possibilities both for survivors and for their relations with others in Canada. The report notes, for instance, that "[t]he TRC provided an opportunity for the truth to be told, both in terms of the big picture of Canadian history and government policy and the lived experiences of individual Survivors" (National Centre for Truth and Reconciliation 2020). This is crucial, as it might be recalled from Chapter 1 that one of the criticisms of the current UN report on the rights of victims of gross violations and injustices is that they can seemingly be fulfilled without ever listening to the story of a single survivor. This, in turn, leaves open the door that the historical record of mass atrocities and related events could be told wholly from the perspective of perpetrators, entirely leaving out the voices of those targeted and impacted by the violations in question. This passage from the TRC's report makes clear the importance of epistemic reparations involving bearing witness to the "lived experiences of individual Survivors" as well as restoring their status within the "big picture of Canadian history and government policy."

Knowing someone in the restoring status sense thus involves stories—either those that were never told or those that counter or round out those that should never have been told as they were—having epistemic effects within the relevant communities that create or repair the standing of the victim in relation to the epistemic wrongs in question. The two senses of knowing someone outlined in this chapter combine epistemic versions of the ends of reparations more broadly mentioned by Roht-Arriaza in Chapter 1, where she noted that they are both backward-looking in aiming to "recompense for loss and to restore the good name of those defamed" and forward-looking in aiming to "reintegrate the marginalized and isolated into society so that they can contribute to the future rebuilding of the [society]" (2004, p. 122). Bearing witness through accepting and promoting a rounder, healthier narrative of a person may aim to recompense for the loss resulting from the vilifying, flat story told about him, but it may also be restoring his good name so that he can be reintegrated into the epistemic community and can play a substantive role in the historical record.

## 3. Epistemic Reparations for the Deceased

There is a difference between being known and feeling or knowing that you are known, or being seen and feeling like you are seen. Given this, one question that might be asked is whether true or proper epistemic reparations require that the victim's story be given proper uptake or that he also be made aware that his story has been given proper uptake. On the view that responds affirmatively to this question, if Keith is never made aware of my knowing him through *Freedom First*, it wouldn't just be that my act of listening to his album is merely a step in the ongoing process of providing epistemic reparations but, rather, that this act itself is importantly deficient. Otherwise put, this view holds that to succeed in satisfying a person's right to be known as even an act in an ongoing process of doing so necessarily involves the victim knowing or feeling that he is known.

While this book opens with Lucas Baba Sikwepere likening being able to tell his story at the South African Truth and Reconciliation Commission to feeling like he got his sight back after blindness, and Chapter 3 focuses on the distinctive benefits of talking, listening, and learning in interpersonal exchanges, these represent powerful examples of epistemic reparations rather than involving necessary features that all epistemic reparations must have. To see this, one way to cut up the theoretical pie would be to say that bearing witness requires some sort of direct, interpersonal exchange between the victim and an audience, leading to the victim not only being known but also knowing or feeling that he is. This would leave open the possibility of restoring status capturing the sense in which epistemic reparations might involve knowing or seeing a victim without him correspondingly knowing or feeling this.

And yet this doesn't seem quite right. Alone in my apartment in Amsterdam, listening to Keith's *Freedom First* album, I seem to be bearing witness to his struggle—his wrongful conviction and incarceration, his scheduled execution, and the colossal injustice of it all. Something similar seems to be the case when, in his absence, we read a victim's memoir or autobiography, view his artwork, or engage with his poetry, even if we never discuss these works with the author or artist himself. This is why Elie Wiesel's words engraved in the entrance to the United States Holocaust Memorial Museum, "[f]or the dead and the living, we must bear witness," make sense to us. In the very act of giving Keith value-reflecting attention, and properly taking up his story through his words, I am bearing witness to the violence inflicted on him by the State. In this way, we can *both* bear witness and restore status even when the victim cannot—such as Keith due to being in solitary confinement—or can no longer—such as Anne Frank due to death—know or feel that we are.

At the same time, and as the above view presses, we might wonder whether something deeply important is missing in the cases of Keith and Anne Frank, something that is fundamental to true or proper epistemic reparations. There is no doubt that it can be tragic when people miss out on meaningful interpersonal engagement with their stories or work. Even when we are not talking about reparations, there is something heartbreaking about, say, Herman Melville dying not knowing that *Moby Dick* would become a masterpiece or that he would be regarded as the literary genius that he is today. But this doesn't mean that this interpersonal engagement—the knowing or feeling that one is known—is necessary or even always more effective as acts of epistemic reparations than cases where it is absent.

Compare two cases: (1) one person listens to *Freedom First* with interpersonal engagement so that Keith is made to feel seen or known; (2) a million people listen to *Freedom First* with no interpersonal engagement so Keith is not made to feel seen or known. Is (1) clearly better than (2) or, for that matter, is (2) clearly better than (1)? I would suggest that we respond negatively to both questions. (1) and (2) are different, and each provides something powerful for epistemic reparations. Recall from Chapter 1 that there are at least three ways that knowing someone is potentially epistemically reparative for a victim: first, sharing stories can generate knowledge not only in listeners, but also in the storytellers themselves; second, knowing victims can take steps to ensure that they are able to stand in right epistemic relations within their communities; and, third, being known promotes the cultivation, restoration, or repair of a victim's epistemic agency. As should be clear, while generating new knowledge through coconstructed narratives may be limited to (1), (2) may be more effective at creating or restoring right relations within communities as well as certain kinds of epistemic agency in victims. A million people coming to know Keith as wrongfully convicted, for instance, may repair his epistemic relations throughout his home community in Ohio or within the criminal legal system, and promote his epistemic agency through him being the author of his own story. What we see here is the interaction of bearing witness and restoring status, both of which are occurring in the absence of Keith ever knowing that he is being known in these ways or with this reach.

This way of understanding Keith being known not only sheds light on how to understand epistemic reparations for the dead, like Anne Frank, but also further clarifies the difference between epistemic and psychological reparations. Epistemic agency can be promoted through centering a victim's voice in the public narrative of his life even if he is not made to feel less distressed, more seen, agentially empowered, and so on. Epistemic relations of, say, acknowledgment, respect, trust, credibility, and authority can be cultivated despite a survivor not coming to feel more respected or trustworthy. This is one of the reasons why we need epistemic reparations in addition to those that are psychological; not only can they come apart, but they do different sorts of reparative work.

Nevertheless, it is important to not overstate their separation, as they often do come hand in hand. Consider, again, the opening passage from

Sikwepere, who believes that being unable to tell his story is what has been making him "sick all the time." Sharing his experiences at the South African TRC not only seems to be a move toward greater wellness, it also makes him feel like he can see again, which sounds epistemic as well as psychological. Notice that seeing involves both epistemic agency and a causal connection with the world that goes beyond a person's mental life. To see that there is a room full of people at the TRC, for instance, requires appropriate responsiveness to the perceptual evidence in the environment. Moreover, this general sort of experience of multiple kinds of reparations being connected to one another does not seem uncommon. The very act of being able to author one's own story, especially after it was originally stolen, is likely to not only be a step toward restoring epistemic agency but also toward feeling, say, less sadness or anger or despair or loneliness. Sharing one's story at a TRC may not only partially repair one's epistemic relations of trust and credibility within a community, but also one's moral and political status.

And yet a natural question that might be raised is *how precisely* to understand epistemically reparative work for those who are deceased, not only for someone like Anne Frank where we can read her own words, but also for victims like George Floyd and Breonna Taylor, who do not have posthumously published diaries. While there is not work on this specific issue, there are discussions about whether we can wrong the dead, whether they have rights, and whether we have moral or legal obligations to them.[40] Moreover, there are certainly common public reactions to the treatment of those who are deceased that support affirmative answers to these questions. In 2019, for instance, the man who murdered 17-year-old Bianca Devins shared graphic photos of her body online, which quickly spread across the internet. A BBC article about Bianca's murder wrote that "this kind of public violence" revictimizes "Biana herself," with Dr. James Densley, a professor of criminal justice, saying, "We have this term for people to rest in peace . . . . Well, really, she can't, because she's living in this sort of perpetual infamy online every time her image is shared" (Cooper 2019).

There is, however, far less attention paid in the literature to the question of whether we can repair wrongs or restore status to the dead, and there is even less on the question of whether the dead can be epistemically wronged. One reason why some might be inclined to answer both questions negatively is

[40] Can we, for instance, morally or legally wrong the dead—and not just their living descendants—by digging up their remains for scientific purposes? See, for instance, Scarre (2003).

because many views draw very close connections between rights, interests, harms, and wrongs. According to Joel Feinberg, who has developed a rich and detailed interest-based theory of harms, an interest is something that a person has a "stake" in (1984, pp. 33–34) and "the sorts of beings who *can* have rights are precisely those who have (or can have) interests" (1974, p. 51). Harm is then understood as a "setback" to a person's interests, but crucially "only setbacks of interests that are wrongs, and wrongs that are setbacks to interests, are to count as harms in the appropriate sense" (Feinberg 1984, p. 36). So, rights, interests, harms, and wrongs are all inextricably connected on this view. But this then faces what is sometimes called the Epicurean "problem of the subject," which challenges how there can be harms or wrongs without a subject. More precisely, if the dead do not have interests, then, it is concluded, they can be the subject of neither harms/wrongs nor reparations.[41]

These conclusions have been resisted in at least three different ways. According to Geoffrey Scarre, for instance:

> Most people care not just what subjective experiences they have but also about their objective standing with others. They dislike the thought of being insulted or despised not only to their faces but also behind their back.... So even if the dead feel no joy or pain and have no functions to be impaired, it does not follow that they cannot be wronged. (2003, p. 240)

According to Scarre, then, if you can wrong a living person by destroying her standing with others without her knowledge, then you can likewise wrong a dead person. Indeed, we can even imagine that there are no perceptible signs for the living person of the damage done to her status—people do not treat her differently to her face, do not exclude her from participation in activities, and so on. Still, she seems to have been wronged. But how precisely? Feinberg himself addresses this as follows:

> The ante-mortem person was harmed in being the subject of interests that were going to be defeated whether he knew it or not.... It does not become

[41] For instance, Ernest Partridge claims that "[n]othing happens to the dead.... Accordingly, after death, with the removal of a subject of harms and bearer of interests, it would seem that there can be neither 'harm to' nor 'interests of' the descendent" (1981, p. 253). A similar but interestingly different view is developed by Stephen Winter, who writes that "... possessing the kind of interests necessary for claim-bearing requires an entity to have the capacity to experience things as significant" (2010, p. 186).

> retroactively true that as a subject of doomed interests he is in a harmed state: rather it was true all along. . . . Exactly when did the harmed state of the ante-mortem person . . . begin? I think the best answer is: "at the point, well before his death, when the person had invested so much in some postdated outcome that it became one of his interests." (1984, pp. 89–90)

Feinberg thus concludes that "the subject of harm in death is the living person ante-mortem, whose interests are squelched" (1984, p. 93). In a similar spirit, T. M. Wilkinson writes that:

> The antemortem person has interests that can be satisfied or dissatisfied after death: for instance, interests in reputation. On this picture, before death the person has an interest in her reputation after death. If her reputation is ruined after death, then it is the same ante-mortem person who, unbeknownst to her, is harmed. (2002, p. 34).

In addition to reputation, Wilkinson argues that the dead have other interests, such as in privacy, bodily integrity, the suffering of their "nearest and dearest," and the desecration of their remains. He motivates his view with an analogy with memory: if I remember my grandmother, who is dead, I am remembering the living woman in the past, not the grandmother as she is now. In this way, we can understand wronging someone after her death in the same way that we understand remembering someone after her death: in both cases, it is the living person who is the subject. Indeed, Wilkinson notes that it is "perhaps slightly misleading to say that the dead have interests, since it is the living who have interests in what happens after their deaths" (2002, p. 34). Scarre develops a similar account, arguing that the "evaluation of a life, or a phase of it, not uncommonly turns on the posthumous fate of its key projects or interests" (2003, p. 241). He asks us to imagine an author who devotes many of his last years of life to writing his masterpiece, which would have been received with universal acclaim, but all copies of it are destroyed the day after his death. Here, Scarre says, "the author is harmed or benefited during his lifetime by events that happen after it" (2003, p. 241).[42]

[42] This also explains why people are often concerned with or value their "legacy." Ronald Dworkin says something similar: "It makes sense to say that people who are now dead or permanently unconscious still have interests. We mean that their lives will have been more successful if the interests they formed while alive and conscious flourish when they are unconscious or dead" (2006, p. 79).

In addition to views like these that identify the locus of the wrong as the living subject, there are others who argue that even after death, there can be a current subject of posthumous wrongs, at least in some cases. In discussing postmortem privacy, which is understood as "the right of a person to preserve and control what becomes of his reputation and dignity after death,"[43] J. C. Buitelaar argues that posthumous social network profiles can function in the same way as narratives of living people do, creating digital legacies that include rights to informational self-determination. In particular, he writes:

> From the point of view of the narrative technique, it can be argued that a self-conscious individual imposes a linguistic unity on the events that he has experienced in his autobiography. In general, the individual attributes agential capacity to the personality that he deals with in his autobiography. These normative, informational activities thus permit a self-governing individual to constitute himself as a person and articulate his life stories in autobiographical narratives. Social network profiles, which in various forms can subsist after death, can very well serve the same goal. Indeed, autobiographies are in many ways similar to the public personae as they are composed in the form of social network profiles. Assuming . . . that posthumous personae are similar in their discursive and textual ontologies to living claimants . . . it is a reasonable proposition to argue that attributing claims to a posthumous public persona is identical to attributing moral claims to a vital person. (Buitelaar 2017, p. 140)

According to this view, then, social network profiles can function as posthumous personae that can be the subject of claims of wrongs and, presumably, of reparations. Of course, given that Buitelaar is specifically interested in postmortem privacy in a digital age, the focus on social network profiles would have to be expanded to the narratives of our lives more generally in order to have broader applicability. But his account can nonetheless serve as a model of a view that accepts that there needs to be a subject of posthumous wrongs but rejects that such a subject is the antemortem person.

In contrast to both of these views of posthumous wrongs, there are also loss- or deprivation-based accounts. Barbara Baum Levenbook, for instance, holds that a person is harmed if she loses or is deprived of something and this loss or deprivation is bad for her.[44] According to Levenbook,

[43] Buitelaar (2017, p. 129).
[44] Levenbook (1984, p. 412).

these conditions are "not the only necessary conditions of harm, nor are they jointly sufficient" (1984, p. 413). She argues, for instance, that a further condition is that the loss in question must be "worse than barely bad for someone" (1984, p. 413). But her central aim is to provide a framework for understanding posthumous harms and wrongs without needing to posit a subject with interests. On this view, then, the loss of a positive reputation, privacy, or bodily integrity harms or wrongs a person because it is a deprivation that is bad for him, and this is true whether he is alive or not.

So, we can explain how the dead can be morally wronged by maintaining that the subject of the wrong is the antemortem person, the postmortem person, or by denying that a subject is needed in the first place.[45] My purpose here is not to endorse one of these views over another but, rather, to make clear that there are ways to understand how the dead can be wronged so that we can make some progress toward grasping posthumous epistemic wrongs and reparations. As may be recalled, the three epistemic wrongs highlighted in Chapter 1 that are deserving of epistemic reparations are invisibility, vilification, and systematic distortion. But notice that false, demonizing, and distorting narratives can inflict grave injustices against a living person regardless of whether he is aware of them. As Scarre notes above, we care about what people believe and say about us both in our presence and in our absence and this is true regardless of whether our absence is due to our death, especially if we imagine, as we did above, that there are no causal effects of the narratives in question. In his discussion of posthumous rehabilitation, for instance, Nelson P. Lande writes:

> One's good name can be distorted, and in addition, in can be destroyed. It is distorted if it is rendered either incomplete or inaccurate, i.e., if truths are severed from it or if lies are attached to it. It is destroyed if all memory of the person and his achievements is obliterated. (1990, p. 279)

[45] As noted above, there is a fourth option that we are not considering; namely, for wrongs to the dead to be understood in terms of wrongs to their living relatives. The European Court of Human Rights, for instance, maintains "that dealing appropriately with the dead out of respect for the feelings of the deceased's relatives falls within the scope of Article 8 of the Convention" (*M.L. v. Slovakia*), where Article 8 of the European Convention on Human Rights holds that "[e]veryone has the right to respect for his private and family life, his home and his correspondence" (Council of Europe). I do not deny that wronging the dead can involve wronging their living relatives, nor that reparations for the dead can involve reparations for their living relatives. My view is that this does not exhaust the way to understand posthumous wrongs and reparations.

According to Lande, a "name" is a person's reputation or public image, which involves a "cluster of beliefs . . . held in a given community" about him. A person has a right to possess a "good name" so long as he has "done nothing deemed discreditable" by this community (1990, p. 269), and this right can be violated through the "undeserved transformation" of his positive good name into a bad name. But crucially, this is true for both the living and the dead, and we can make sense on all three models discussed above of how stories that endure or are told posthumously about a person can inflict epistemic wrongs. Obviously, the living person cares about his good name, which can be damaged after his lifetime, a posthumous persona can have his good name undermined, and the underserved transformation of a positive good name is a loss that is bad for the person.

On the view developed here, then, a person is owed epistemic reparations in the case of such epistemic violations whether he is alive or not. This is why a *New York Times* headline like the following from 1988 makes sense to us: "50 Years After His Execution, Soviet Panel Clears Bukharin" (Taubman 1988). The article goes on to discuss how a Communist Party commission reviewed the "purge trials of the 1930s" and announced that "Nikolai I. Bukharin, among the most prominent victims of Stalin's terror, was wrongly convicted and executed" (Taubman 1988). In particular, the commission found that Bukharin was a victim of "gross violations of Socialist legality" that included falsifying evidence and "admissions of guilt wrung from the accused through unlawful methods" (Taubman 1988). The article concludes that "the decision to clear Bukharin, coupled with the recent publication of some of his principal political writings, restores to good standing a figure whose political legacy has a direct bearing on Mikhail S. Gorbachev's efforts to change the Soviet Union" (Taubman 1988). Notice the language used by the *New York Times* of *clearing* Bukharin and *restoring him to good standing*, which is a call both for a counterstory and for knowing Bukharin in the restoring status sense developed above. In particular, it matters not only that the report *exists*, but also that it be made publicly available so that his good name can be restored within the community.

Recall that in Chapter 2, I argued that engaging in epistemic reparations through promoting counter and rounder stories helps with both the epistemic wrongs of invisibility and hypervisibility, unlike legislation focusing on being forgotten and clean slates, which addresses only the latter. This is relevant here as well. As Lande says:

> rehabilitation may be in order not only to restore one's *good* name, but also to restore, or establish, one's good *name*. Suppose, for instance, that one has earned a place in history .... Then he is wronged not only if he is prevented from occupying that place, but also if insufficient measures are taken by those in a position ... to take them, to ensure the perpetuation of the memory of the person and his achievements. (1990, p. 279)

Stories involving both the living and the dead matter not only when they are false, flat, or distorted but also when they are absent. Sometimes, the cruelest forms of epistemic wronging involve failing to even notice that someone isn't at the table rather than vilifying the person who is already in a seat. And so crucially acts of epistemic reparations need to involve ensuring that the stories that haven't been told, or the chapters and characters that are missing, are also present. This is important both for providing redress for the epistemic wrongs in question and for supporting a historical record that is accurate and inclusive of all of the relevant perspectives. Consider, for instance, part of Prime Minister Justin Trudeau's apology on behalf of the Government of Canada to former students and family members of the Residential Schools of Newfoundland and Labrador:

> To all of you—we are sorry.
>
> To the students who experienced the indignity of this abuse, neglect, hardship, and discrimination by the individuals, institutions, and system entrusted with your care, we are sorry for the harm that was done to you.
>
> Sadly, not all former students are here with us today, having passed away without being able to hear this apology.
>
> We are sorry for not apologizing sooner. For not righting this wrong before now. (2017)

While Trudeau acknowledges that those who have passed away are not able to "hear this apology," he also clearly intends for it to not only apply to them but for it to also have some normative force, even posthumously. Notice, for instance, that he doesn't say that Canada is sorry that they are unable to apologize to those who have died but, rather, that they did not do so "sooner" and thus did not right "this wrong before now."

This is connected to another important point that cuts across both notions of knowing someone: epistemic reparations might involve not only knowing certain facts about a person but also knowing him as a particular kind of person. For instance, Veli Mitova (2025a) argues that one of the central epistemic wrongs of colonialism involves the deprivation of epistemic authority to those who have been colonized, such as regarding traditional healers in South Africa as practicing witchcraft rather than a legitimate form of treatment.[46] Epistemic reparations in such a case would thus involve not only bearing witness to the wrongs perpetrated against traditional healers through colonialism, but also, as Mitova argues, ensuring that their status as epistemic authorities is restored within the community. Otherwise put, a critical part of knowing them is knowing them *as epistemic authorities* in both the bearing witness and restoring senses. This is true of other dimensions of a person's identity. All of the epistemic wrongs in question involve a violation of a person's epistemic agency, and so at a minimum epistemically reparative work requires knowing survivors as epistemic agents, but may also necessitate knowing them as political participants, or as credible persons deserving of respect, and so on. Moreover, such work may include both overt actions—seeing, listening, creating spaces for stories to be told, sharing them, and so on—and, importantly, stepping back or to the side so that survivors can exercise their epistemic agency without some of the barriers created by others. Indeed, this can be a fundamental part of the restoring status sense of knowing someone—contributing to the conditions for victims to take up places within the communities that they should have occupied were it not for the epistemic wrongs in question.

## 4. Causal Accounts of Knowing Someone

One question that may be asked is whether bearing witness and restoring status as developed in this chapter really capture what it means to know a person. Perhaps surprisingly, there is very little work in philosophy on how to understand knowing a person rather than a proposition, but there are a few authors who have explored this question. Recall, for instance, Sosa's view mentioned at the start of this chapter:

[46] See, also, Townsend and Townsend (2020) for a similar argument specifically about authority in Indigenous communities.

> Knowing someone or something, knowing some "object" in the broadest sense of this term, seems at least sometimes to require some kind of special causal interaction with that "object." This is plausibly a requirement for knowing a person, and for knowing an experience or a sight, say the sight of the Boston skyline two miles from the south on highway 93, or the experience of a cold shower after a hard run. (BonJour and Sosa 2003, p. 100)

To be clear, Sosa is offering only a necessary condition for knowing a person; namely, having a special kind of causal interaction with him. Matthew Benton develops this condition further, arguing that I know someone interpersonally only if I have had reciprocal causal contact in which I treat him second-personally and he treats me second-personally.[47] Like Sosa, Benton focuses on causal contact but fleshes out what kind of interaction is required. In particular, he maintains that in order for me to know someone, I need to treat him as a subject and he needs to treat me as a subject. To make this sort of second-personal stance clear, Benton asks us to imagine two colleagues, Juan and Julia, who attend the same large committee meetings over many years. During this time, they come to know many facts about one another, but it is always through overhearing other conversations and never by addressing one another directly in conversation. According to Benton, "Juan and Julia do not know each other personally" (2017, p. 821).

Although there may be a sense of knowing a person that such causal accounts capture, it is clear that they will not help us understand the right to be known relevant for epistemic reparations. We can bear witness to Keith's injustice, and restore his status in the community, while never having direct causal contact with him. Indeed, as argued above, we can engage in epistemic reparations involving the right to be known in both senses for those who are dead, such as with George Floyd or Breonna Taylor. It is even clearer that *reciprocal* causal contact in which I treat someone second-personally and he treats me second-personally is not necessary for knowing someone in either of the senses relevant to epistemic reparations. Again, while Keith sits in solitary confinement in Ohio and you listen to *Freedom First* in Barcelona, there is no sense whatsoever in which there is reciprocal causal contact, and yet my view holds that you can know him via his music and spoken word poetry.

[47] More precisely: "Encounter: S knows [interpersonally] R only if (i) S has had reciprocal causal contact with R, in which (ii) S treats R second-personally, and (iii) R treats S second-personally" (2017, p. 822).

Taking a step back, it is not clear what the precise value is of knowing someone on the causal accounts.[48] If I read Keith's autobiography from cover to cover eight times, listen to his album on a loop for a year, and attend multiple *Freedom First* concerts—but never have reciprocal causal contact with him—in what sense is my knowing him inferior to the person with whom I have a five-minute conversation on the subway—but where there is such contact? To be sure, reciprocal causal contact may be necessary for *having a relationship* with someone, and there may be a sense of knowing someone that implies a relationship. However, knowing someone is not the same as having a relationship with him, and so there should be no strain in grasping how you could know Keith in the absence of causal contact with him, reciprocal or otherwise.

Even when the focus is on knowing a person *well*, there are instances of knowing someone in powerful ways that do not satisfy the conditions of the account. According to Bonnie M. Talbert, for instance, knowing someone well minimally requires the following:

1. We have had a significant number of second person face-to-face interactions with A, at least some of which have been relatively recent.
2. The contexts of those interactions were such as to permit A to reveal important aspects of her/himself, and A has done so.
3. A has not deceived us about him/herself in important respects.
4. We have succeeded in accurately perceiving what A has revealed—i.e. we are not "blinded" by our own biases or other impairments. (2015, p. 194)

Again, I can satisfy these conditions with someone with whom I ride the subway each morning for 10 minutes, so long as she shares some important aspects of herself with me. Perhaps over the course of our regular brief encounters, she tells me about her father's battle with cancer or the challenges of being a single mom. Do I know this woman better than I know Keith? Indeed, there are many cases where someone might be known "well" in the absence of such causal contact: after writing two comprehensive biographies of Herman Melville, Hershel Parker knows Herman Melville well—indeed,

[48] This is not to say that there are not uniquely valuable effects that may arise from reciprocal causal contact, as we saw in the last chapter and as I will mention below. Rather, it is to say that it is unclear what is distinctively valuable about the causal contact itself.

far better than I know the woman on the subway despite the fact that the requisite second person face-to-face interactions is present in the latter but not the former case. Similar considerations apply to reading someone's daily blog posts for five years or their lengthy Facebook updates for 10 years. Neither knowing someone, nor knowing him well, seems to require second-personal causal contact.

This is not to say, of course, that there aren't uniquely valuable features of different ways of knowing a person. Face-to-face interaction, for instance, enables listeners to respond through facial expressions, body language, and physical gestures that might allow for the emergence of coconstructed narratives that are simply not possible through other forms of communication. The power of being in the same physical space and experiencing immediate compassion or understanding—perhaps through a listener holding a speaker's hand or sharing tears while providing substantive responses—may be transformative. All of these examples have valuable effects that specifically depend on in-person engagement, such as coconstructed narratives that arise from in-real-time facial expressions from listeners. But this doesn't mean that there aren't potentially distinctive advantages to other forms of knowing a person. Interacting via Zoom or on the phone may enable some survivors who would find in-person contact overwhelming to share more freely, thereby leading to the creation of entirely new coconstructed stories through verbal listener responses. There are also benefits specific to written communication. Studies show, for instance, that texting in relationships is regarded as "more constant and private,"[49] allows users to "assert autonomy,"[50] and provides advantages for "socially anxious mobile phone users."[51] People may also have different voices in their writing, allowing them to express thoughts or emotions that would be difficult or awkward to share in person. And there are different forms of writing—autobiographies may facilitate more deeply round stories, biographies may take advantage of the skills and expertise of professional writers, and social media may maximize accessibility and reach. In addition, documentaries, music, and poetry may in various ways evoke powerful emotions and connections, and collective storytelling—such as truth and reconciliation spaces—may create opportunities for reciprocal growth and empathy. Some of these involve reciprocal causal contact of

[49] Pettigrew (2009).
[50] Pettigrew (2009).
[51] Reid and Reid (2010).

various kinds—such as in-person conversation and texting—while others do not—such as a biography written about someone who died a century ago.

What all of this shows, however, is that there is a broad spectrum of ways to know someone, with causal accounts capturing only one kind. Indeed, even within the domain of reciprocal causal contact, there is tremendous variation in what is epistemically possible. Since the nature, scope, and impact of the epistemic wrongs that result in not knowing someone are many and various, it should be unsurprising that the corresponding epistemically reparative work is similarly diverse with uniquely valuable results.

## 5. Conclusion

Fulfilling the right to be known possessed by survivors of gross violations and injustices involves understanding what it means to know a person as an act of epistemic reparations. We have seen that broadly speaking, there are two central kinds of knowledge for this purpose. Bearing witness focuses on the survivor's story being appropriately anchored in reality and given proper uptake through value-reflecting attention, while restoring status involves this story creating or repairing perceptions of him and his relations within the relevant communities that take steps toward righting the epistemic wrongs in question. We have also seen that there are numerous avenues to knowing people in either of these ways, such as through face-to-face interaction, reading their stories, listening to their poetry, playing their music, sharing their posts, supporting or collaborating on their projects, and having their voices shape historical records, memorials, and policies. In practice, the right to be known can be fulfilled by local, state, and federal governments creating and promoting public places of storytelling and record keeping after gross violations and injustices through truth and reconciliation commissions, town halls, restorative justice circles, monuments, museums, archives, educational materials, and other community gatherings and documents. But just as importantly, each of us has a role to play in ensuring that the stories that have been ignored, erased, extracted, vilifying, or distorting are told, heard, and shared. It is only through true collective action, where both groups and individuals do their part, that we can fulfill the promise of epistemic reparations to those in our communities whose experiences demand them.

# 5
# Duties to Know Someone

We have seen that survivors of gross violations and injustices can be epistemically wronged in ways that demand epistemic reparations, including the right to be known. We have also seen what is involved in knowing someone in epistemically reparative ways. But rights have corresponding duties and so a central question that has not yet been addressed is who has the *duty* to engage in the reparative work at issue. Taking the right to be known as the central case, I develop a view in this chapter according to which the relevant duties are on a spectrum: at one end lie what I call perfect epistemic duties, which those who bear responsibility for the epistemic wrongs in question, such as perpetrators, must fulfill; at the other end lie imperfect epistemic duties, which we all need to fulfill regardless of whether we are responsible for the relevant epistemic wrongs, but there is latitude in how we do so. In between lie duties that have normative force of greater specificity than standard imperfect epistemic duties but less so than their perfect counterparts. Here questions of complicity and special relationships to persons, issues, spaces, and social structures determine the normative force of the duty to know someone. What emerges is a framework that supports understanding epistemic duties to know survivors of gross violations and injustices as an ongoing, collective process in which each of us has a crucial role to play.

## 1. Perfect and Imperfect Epistemic Duties

The distinction between perfect and imperfect duties occupies an important space in ethics regarding what is required to live a moral life. Perfect duties are those that must be done; they do not admit of exceptions in favor of inclination. If I make a promise to take you to the doctor on Tuesday, for instance, I have the perfect duty to do so; I cannot, without incurring moral blame, simply fail to show up because I prefer to enjoy the sunshine at the last minute. In contrast, at the heart of the notion of an imperfect duty—paradigmatically including charity, mercy, gratitude, beneficence, and the

*The Right to Be Known*. Jennifer Lackey, Oxford University Press. © Oxford University Press 2026.
DOI: 10.1093/9780197833988.003.0006

like on the moral side—is the idea that *discretion* and *latitude* are allowed in their fulfillment.[1] Charity, for instance, might require that I donate to the poor, but it doesn't specify to whom or how much. I may fulfill this duty by sending $200 to Oxfam every month or by sending $500 to Habitat for Humanity twice per year. Again, contrast this with the classic perfect duty of promise-keeping, where there is no discretion or latitude regarding how I satisfy it. If I promise to visit Rose in the hospital on Tuesday, then I have a duty to do just this. It won't do to instead visit George in the hospital on Tuesday, or to visit Rose at home on Thursday.[2] Indeed, this leads some to understand imperfect duties as being disjunctive in nature: unlike my duty to keep my promise, which has the form of the duty to do act X, my duty to donate to the poor has the form of the duty to do act <X or Y or Z>.[3] But regardless of whether imperfect duties admit of such a disjunctive explanation, the key point is that there is latitude in their satisfaction or, as Richard Robinson puts it, "practical limits to their pursuit," which are determined by circumstances and inclination (2019, p. 119). Regarding charity, the "limit of circumstance requires that the giver not impoverish herself by the charitable action" and the inclination limit is "established by the giver's character . . . . For example, one might have an inclination toward one particular charitable action, but not another" (Robinson 2019, p. 119). So, while I am blameworthy if I fail to keep my promise to visit Rose in the hospital on Tuesday, I am blameworthy for failing to engage in any charitable giving within my means but not for specifically failing to donate, say, $200 to Oxfam every month. As Michael Stocker says:

> By calling something a perfect duty, I mean to say of it that it must be done, that it is right to do and wrong not to do. By calling something an imperfect duty I . . . mean that like a perfect duty it is right to do, but unlike a perfect duty it is not wrong not to do. Rather it is wrong not to do it or some other act or acts. (1967, pp. 507–508)

[1] See, for instance, Schroeder (2013).

[2] Of course, latitude might be built directly into the *content* of a promise. I might, for instance, promise Rose that someone in my family will visit her in the hospital this week, which might be fulfilled by my visiting her on Monday, or my daughter visiting her on Tuesday, and so on. But this is a separate point from latitude being tied to the fulfillment of the duty itself.

[3] See, for instance, Price (1974). See Stocker (1967) for an argument that virtually all duties are infinitely disjunctive, and hence this cannot adequately capture imperfect ones.

While we are wrong, then, to not satisfy our specific perfect duties, we are not wrong for not fulfilling our imperfect duties in a specific way, but only for not doing so in any way that is determined by our circumstances and inclination.

Despite this, there are circumstances in which even paradigmatically imperfect duties can require specific acts. Suppose that I know that if my neighbor does not receive $50 within the next 15 minutes, he will die. Further, suppose that this is an amount that would be a very minor sacrifice on my part, and I am the only person who is in a position to assist him. During that 15-minute interval, it would be odd to say that I have the duty to donate $50 to my neighbor *or* to Oxfam *or* to Habitat for Humanity. The urgent, high-stakes needs of my neighbor combined with my relation to him seem to generate a very particular obligation on my part.

This sort of distinction is familiar to many, made famous by Peter Singer's discussion of the duty to *Rescue* and the duty to provide *Aid*.[4] Suppose that you're walking past a shallow pond and you see a child drowning whom you could easily rescue, though it would mean ruining your expensive outfit. Surely, you have the duty to rescue the child in such a case since doing so would prevent a significant harm without sacrificing anything of even roughly comparable moral value. Now compare this with the duty you have to aid a child across the globe who would avoid starvation if you write a check for the same amount you spent on the ruined outfit in *Rescue*. Despite the fact that both involve preventing significant harm at minimal cost, the duties involved are standardly regarded as importantly different.[5] As S. Andrew Schroeder writes, "although both *Aid* and *Rescue* call for beneficence, the duty in *Rescue* is perfect, since it allows no latitude, while the duty in *Aid* is imperfect. We'd then say that the duty of beneficence, usually imperfect, becomes perfect in rescue cases" (2013, p. 560). Indeed, Schroeder identifies criteria that any account of imperfect duties should satisfy, with the ability to capture this difference between *Aid* and *Rescue* as central to one of them:

> LATITUDE. An account of imperfect duties should specify the duty in *Aid* (and relevantly similar cases) so as to make it in some respect less onerous than the duty in *Rescue* (and relevantly similar cases), allowing agents some kind of discretion. (2013, p. 560)

[4] For the original discussion of these two kinds of cases, see Singer (1972).
[5] Of course, Singer himself denies this.

In addition to LATITUDE, it is commonly noted that it is not only possible to do more than is required with imperfect duties, but that doing so is morally valuable. Schroeder writes:

> you can be more gracious, merciful, charitable, or beneficent than morality demands. You can't, on the other hand, keep more of your promises than morality requires, nor can you repay more than what you owe. You can, of course, do more for a friend than you've promised and you can give more money to a creditor than you agreed to, but the surplus in each case is no longer regarded as an instance of promise-keeping or debt-repayment. Rather, it is typically described as beneficence or gratitude. (2013, pp. 560–561)

This leads to the second criterion that Schroeder claims any plausible account of imperfect duties should accommodate:

> IMPERFECTION. An account of imperfect duties should say what distinguishes imperfect from perfect duties, in a way that explains why it is frequently possible to do more than what an imperfect duty requires and why such excess frequently has moral value.

Of course, while clearly different, LATITUDE and IMPERFECTION are nonetheless related to one another, for it is the latitude involved in the satisfaction of imperfect duties that opens up moral space for agents to do more than is required.[6]

I have elsewhere argued that just as there can be both perfect and imperfect moral duties, so, too, there can be both perfect and imperfect *epistemic duties*, and I take the *duty to object* as a paradigmatic case.[7] For instance, while not ignoring direct, compelling counterevidence to your belief is an epistemic duty that must be fulfilled, there is latitude in how you fulfill the epistemic duty to object to what you take to be false or unwarranted that is constrained by practical limits determined by your circumstances and

[6] The third criterion that Schroeder claims any account of imperfect duties should satisfy is below, though it won't figure directly into my discussion:

> SPECIFICATION. An account of imperfect duties should precisely identify what is required, what an agent must do (Schroeder 2013, p. 559).

[7] See Lackey (2018b). Stapleford (2013) also argues on behalf of imperfect epistemic duties but he does so with respect to the intrapersonal duty we have to proportion our beliefs to the evidence.

inclination. Given the many other commitments in your life, you do not need to spend all of the hours in the day objecting on your Facebook feed, on Fox News, on the subway, and so on. In addition, there may be some objections that you should not make—perhaps because you are not well positioned to receive uptake in some contexts—and others that you may be especially drawn to making—perhaps because the issue in question is one about which you have particular expertise. But crucially, just as you ought to engage in some charitable giving as a member of the moral community, with latitude in how you do so specifically, so, too, you should engage in some objecting to false or unwarranted claims as a member of the epistemic community, with latitude in how you do so specifically.

The duty to object also shares the second feature said to be true of imperfect duties; it is possible to do more than what the duty to object requires, where such excess has both moral and epistemic value. Consider charity first: a graduate student might donate to Oxfam 50% of her annual stipend, leaving herself able to live only a very modest lifestyle. Clearly, this goes beyond what the imperfect duty of charity calls for, but also does so in a way that has moral value. A person who is already struggling to survive need not give so generously to others, yet doing so is nonetheless deserving of praise and admiration. Now suppose this same graduate student also frequently speaks out in a very public way against, say, sexual violence against women, both in general and in particular cases. She does this at great expense to herself in terms of time and exposure, and she does so when members of the profession in positions of far greater power and security, such as tenured faculty members, remain silent. These actions go beyond what the duty to object calls for, especially when one is a student without secure employment, and also in a way that can have both moral and epistemic value. We can imagine, for instance, that the student's objections lead to policy changes at her home institutions, to false narratives about sexual assault being replaced with accurate ones, and to victims coming forward and feeling supported. In this way, both LATITUDE and IMPERFECTION, which are features that are distinctive of imperfect duties, apply to the duty to object.

We can also envisage *Aid* and *Rescue* versions of the epistemic duty to object. Suppose that you're a scientist at a conference on innovative cancer treatment, and a fellow participant speaks hopefully about a protocol that you've already tried for the past three years and found to be not only systematically ineffective, but also often harmful. As a cancer researcher, you have the general duty to object to epistemically problematic assertions about cancer treatment, which may be satisfied by doing so in academic journals, at conferences, among colleagues in your lab, and so on. But here your imperfect duty seems to become a perfect one to weigh in about this specific protocol. Saving this scientist from heading down a fruitless and potentially destructive path in her research is the epistemic analogue of rescuing the drowning child. Indeed, we might even extend the language in the original scenarios as follows: we have the general duty to provide *epistemic aid* to others, but sometimes we are in contexts in which we need to engage in *epistemic rescues*. We can imagine many other cases like this: I know that I am the only person who is aware that your theory about the defendant is based on misleading evidence, or that your source that tsunamis aren't expected during your vacation in Thailand is unreliable, or that your view of our colleague's work is sexist. We might say, then, that there is an *imperfect epistemic duty* to object in epistemic aid cases but a *perfect epistemic duty* to do so in epistemic rescue cases.

While wading into the discussions in ethics about what explains the difference between *Aid* and *Rescue* will take us too far afield for our purposes, it will be helpful in our understanding of imperfect epistemic duties to at least briefly mention what might account for this. One of the most obvious differences between the cases is the proximity that one bears to the person in need. Singer himself argues that "[i]t makes no moral difference whether the person I can help is a neighbor's child ten yards from me or a Bengali whose name I shall never know, ten thousand miles away" (1972, pp. 231–232).[8] But we may think that proximity is connected to other important differences. For instance, Violette Igneski maintains that it is really an asymmetry in the moral determinacy of the situation that is doing the explanatory work in *Aid* and *Rescue*. She writes:

> Whenever we may think that distance makes a difference it is really the determinacy of the situation that explains this difference. Thus when the victim is near the agent, we think the agent has an obligation to aid this person not because they are close to each other but because their closeness makes it more likely that there is a specific act that the agent at the scene can do to end the peril (and thus it is a morally determinate situation). When the agent and victim are distant, it is much less likely that there is some

[8] Kamm argues that geographical proximity can make a moral difference because "as the costs involved in acting go up, a duty to aid a distant person may be defeated whereas a duty to aid a near person would not be" (2004, p. 70).

> specific act that is morally required of this specific agent—and so it is not the fact that they are distant from each other that explains why the agent is not bound to do something in this particular situation but that the situation is not morally determinate. (Igneski 2001, p. 612)

If Igneski is right here about the significance of moral determinacy in explaining the difference between *Aid* and *Rescue*, there is certainly an epistemic analogue. There is a specific objection that the cancer researcher in the above scenario can raise to prevent the epistemic peril of her colleague, whereas the general duty to object to what is epistemically improper is far more indeterminate. Of course, it isn't clear how much talk of determinacy adds to saying that there is latitude in the fulfillment of the duty in *Aid* that is not present in *Rescue*, but what I want to emphasize here is the epistemic version of the claim.

Another proposal is that we have *special relationships* with some people that give rise to distinct obligations. For instance, I have duties to my own children that I don't have to others, the President of Northwestern has obligations to the students on his campus that he doesn't have to those at Stanford, and Emmanuel Macron has duties to the citizens of France that he doesn't have to Americans. Similar considerations might apply with respect to our neighbors or other members of our community, even those who are temporary. This might explain why proximity matters—it is not literally the proximity that generates obligations, but the special relationships that can be brought about by proximity that do. Once I am standing next to a child who is drowning and am the only person who can save her, I bear a special relationship to her—perhaps by being members of the same community or the same high-stakes event—that demands action on my part.

Whether this explanation works in the moral case is an open question, but the epistemic analogue is quite powerful, at least in a range of cases. The imperfect epistemic duty to object might become perfect when it is generated by special relationships. For instance, professional roles bring about various obligations, many of which involve objecting both to what is false and morally problematic. Consider the various responsibilities associated with doctors, prosecutors, university administrators, research scientists, police chiefs, and so on. Each brings about both general and specific obligations. A university administrator might have the imperfect duty to object to policies that are harmful to universities in general but a perfect duty to speak out against such problems at her home institution. A doctor might have the imperfect duty to challenge discredited medical treatments but a perfect duty to do so when her own colleague or patient is relying on them. Moreover, as with the case of the child drowning, sometimes perfect duties are generated by relationships grounded in proximity. If I know that I am the only one privy to the fact that the gun in your hand is loaded, I might have the perfect duty to object when you say that it is not. Relying on our earlier language, such special relationships might help distinguish cases of *epistemic rescue* from cases of mere *epistemic aid*.

## 2. Perfect and Imperfect Epistemic Duties to Know

At this point, we have explored the central differences between perfect and imperfect duties in ethics, and we have seen that such a distinction can be applied to the epistemic realm, with the duty to object as a paradigmatic example. I now want to extend this framework to help us better understand the epistemic duties we have to know survivors of gross violations and injustices.

Let's begin with perfect duties. Just as I might have the perfect epistemic duty to correct an error in my own research or to inquire into a question for which I bear responsibility, perpetrators of a given violation, and those who have directly benefited from it, have the perfect epistemic duty to engage in the specific epistemically reparative work associated with it. As should be clear from previous chapters, both perpetrators and survivors, on the view developed here, can be individuals—such as the interrogator who extracted the false confession and Demetrius—or collectives—such as the City of Chicago and survivors of police torture. It was earlier noted that special relationships with some people can give rise to distinct obligations, some of which are generated by our actions. A perpetrator bears a special relationship to his victim that generates the perfect duty to make amends—one that those who were not involved in the wrongdoing in question do not have. This at least partially explains why the duty for him to know his victim as an act of epistemic reparations is a perfect one.

Moving down the spectrum, there may also be varying degrees of complicity or accountability in the perpetration of an injustice that can lead to corresponding degrees of normative pressure to know. Just as descendants may inherit wealth or property, for instance, they may also inherit an erased, vilifying, or distorting history, and so epistemic wrongs can be intergenerational. In *Taking Responsibility for the Past: Reparation and Historical Injustice*, Janna Thompson writes:

> when a nation is dispossessed, this is not only a great evil to existing members; it harms their successors, robbing them of the inheritance to which they are entitled, and by so doing disrupts their ability to carry on their common life. Nothing but the return of their national territory counts as appropriate reparation for this wrong. (2002, p. 61)

Thompson is here talking about the inheritance of land, but we can extend her thoughts to the realm of the epistemic. Descendants of Black Americans, for instance, inherit not just the material consequences of slavery and Jim Crow, but also the epistemic ones. They are given a history replete with erasure, vilification, and distortion, one where Black Americans are entirely absent from some narratives, criminalized and presented as dangerous and violent in others, systematically misrepresented as fundamentally matriarchal or angry in still others, and so on. But even at the individual level, the intergenerational impact of the failure to be known can be powerful. Without knowing Demetrius, for instance, his descendants are handed a public story in which their loved one is a murderer. No matter how many times he personally tells them the truth, the public would still have a vilifying and demonizing picture of him that would be preserved in the history of their family and community.

In the same way that victims of gross violations and injustices inherit an erased, demonizing, or distorting history, so, too, are the benefits and corresponding accountability that come from them intergenerational. As Ta-Nehisi Coates writes:

> One cannot escape the question [of reparations] by hand-waving at the past, disavowing the acts of one's ancestors, nor by citing a recent date of ancestral immigration. The last slaveholder has been dead for a very long time. The last soldier to endure Valley Forge has been dead much longer. To proudly claim the veteran and disown the slaveholder is patriotism à la carte. A nation outlives its generations. (Coates 2016)[9]

[9] Later in the same article, Coates quotes Yale President Timonthy Dwight saying in 1810, "We inherit our ample patrimony with all its incumbrances; and are bound to pay the debts of our ancestors. *This* debt, particularly, we are bound to discharge: and, when the righteous Judge of the Universe comes to reckon with his servants, he will rigidly exact the payment at our hands. To give them liberty, and stop here, is to entail upon them a curse."

Those who profit from the oppression and abuse of others pass down the privilege, power, and benefits that result from the relevant institutions and acts to their descendants. For instance, Black Americans descend from a history of slavery, Jim Crow, convict leasing, and mass incarceration, but so, too, do white Americans inherit a legacy of white supremacy. We cannot embrace and celebrate some parts of our past while disavowing and distancing ourselves from our role in others. As Coates says, America needs to reckon with the full scope of its history, and white Americans need to acknowledge and address their roles within this inherited past.

Just as Thompson maintains that reparations require the return of national territory to a nation that is dispossessed, so, too, do epistemic reparations require the return of epistemic goods—knowledge, relations within the epistemic community, epistemic agency, stories, and so on—to those who have been epistemically wronged through gross violations.[10] But how do we determine who has the epistemic duty to engage in this reparative work via complicity or accountability? Many of the standard accounts understand complicity in terms of a causal contribution plus some other feature that appropriately connects it with the agent in question, such as intention, foreseeability, ability to do otherwise, control, and so on. Jeff McMahon, for instance, maintains that the extent of a person's responsibility for a wrongful harm is determined in part by the degree of his causal contribution to the harm, whether it is foreseeable, and, if so, whether he contributes to its occurrence intentionally, recklessly, or negligently.[11] One problem with all accounts that include a causal contribution condition, however, is that there are cases where individuals are tied to collective harms in ways that are normatively important despite not making any clear causal contribution to them. Christopher Kutz, for instance, discusses the Allied firebombing of Dresden, where, because of the magnitude of the firebombing and the negligible contribution of each participant, "no bomber makes an individual difference" to the outcome. This leads Kutz to hold that a person is accountable for the wrongful harms of others when he intentionally participates in the wrong they do or harm they cause, regardless of his causal contribution.[12] But even this weaker understanding of complicity is unable to accommodate wrongful

[10] This is reminiscent of what we saw Amanda Knox say in Chapter 2: "Once you become a figure in a story, your story doesn't belong to you anymore. And that is the sort of shocking experience that I've had that I noticed other people having all the time . . . and so it seems like the only thing to do is to try to give people their stories back" (Burbank 2021).

[11] McMahon (2009).

[12] Kutz (2000, p. 122).

harms that are the result of less organized acts, like climate change, because "individual polluters are not intentional participants in a collective act of pollution" (Kutz 2000, pp. 166–167). Because of this, Brian Lawson argues that a person is accountable for what others do when he knowingly contributes to a harmful outcome that results from their collective contributions.[13] In other words, he is accountable for the harm or wrong they do together, independently of the actual difference he makes as an individual.

While Lawson's account is best suited for understanding the sorts of duties to know survivors of gross violations and injustices that complicity requires, there is one crucial modification needed. In particular, it matters not only whether someone knowingly contributes to a harmful outcome but also whether he *should know* that he is contributing to a harmful outcome. Recall Charles Mills's concept of white ignorance, for instance, which is a state of *non-knowing* that is caused and sustained by white racial domination and its ramifications. Indeed, as we saw in Chapter 2, white ignorance can be both dispositional and propositional, involving the absence of belief or the presence of false beliefs as well as "the cultivation of epistemological practices and dispositions to ignore important information," (Bain 2023, p. 20) such as "self-deception, bad faith, evasion and misrepresentation" (Mills 2007, p. 17). In a similar spirit, Peggy McIntosh understands willful ignorance as comprising patterns of assumptions and privileges that license those in privileged positions to "be ignorant, oblivious, arrogant, and destructive" (1989, p. 11) and, following this view, Vivian M. May notes that "there are many things those in dominant groups are taught not to know, encouraged not to see, and the privileged are rewarded for this state of not-knowing" (2006, p. 113). White and willful ignorance should not be ways of avoiding complicity in racism because they involve non-knowingly contributing to racism, especially when the ignorance is cultivated. Indeed, despite what Lawson's account says, he seems to agree with a general conclusion of this sort, as he maintains that his view "allows us to assign responsibility to individuals who participate in harms produced by groups whose members do not necessarily take themselves to be contributing to a goal as such, but who nevertheless ought to recognize that they are producing cumulative harm" (2013, pp. 234–235).

We are now in a position to draw upon several of the insights found in these views to understand complicity. While McMahon's account faces

[13] Lawson (2013).

problems with the causal constraint, his formulation of responsibility coming in degrees[14] is important, as responsibility is frequently a matter of "more or less" rather than "yes or no." So, let's say that a person is accountable for the epistemic wrongs of others *to the extent* that he knows, *or should know*, that he is contributing to an epistemically wrongful/harmful outcome that results from their collective contributions. As with the right to be known and the epistemic duty to do the knowing, both individuals and collectives can be complicit in the actions of others. At the individual level, for instance, even if the prosecutor in Demetrius's case is not the person who extracted the false confession from him, she should know that there is reasonable doubt regarding his guilt and thus that she is contributing to the unjust vilification of him. At the collective level, many authors have documented white Americans' complicity in racism, with Coates writing that "the crime with which reparations activists charge the [United States] implicates more than just a few towns or corporations. The crime indicts the American people themselves, at every level, and in nearly every configuration."[15] With respect to the perpetration of epistemic wrongs specifically, Mills writes that "white normativity manifests itself in a white refusal to recognize the long history of structural discrimination that has left whites with the differential resources they have today. . . . What makes such denial possible, of course, is the management of memory" (2007, p. 28). Mills argues that America has selectively engaged in collective amnesia so as to forget or deny its history and role in the nation's racist practices, laws, values, history, and structure. Since the "should know" component of the account makes clear that this sort of cultivated non-knowing does not result in a lack of complicity for the epistemic wrongs perpetrated by selective forgetting, there is significant normative pressure on white Americans to know victims and survivors of racism in the United States.

More generally, at one end of the spectrum of this view are perfect epistemic duties to know, which perpetrators and direct beneficiaries of gross violations and injustices that result in invisibility, vilification, and systematic distortion have; along the spectrum are varying degrees of perfect duties grounded in complicity, shading into the other end of the spectrum, where imperfect

[14] As a reminder, McMahon maintains that the extent of a person's responsibility for a wrongful harm is determined in part by the degree of her causal contribution to the harm, whether it is foreseeable, and, if so, whether she contributes to its occurrence intentionally, recklessly, or negligently (McMahon 2009).

[15] See Coates (2016).

epistemic duties to know lie. Here is the space that non-perpetrators occupy, where the duty to know victims of gross violations and injustices has the first feature earlier identified for imperfect duties: latitude in its fulfillment. Like the imperfect duty of charitable giving in the moral realm—where you ought to engage in some charitable giving as a member of the moral community, with discretion permitted in how you do so specifically—the imperfect epistemic duty here requires that you know some relevant survivors, with latitude in how you do so specifically that is determined by circumstances and inclination.[16] To illustrate this, just as I may satisfy my imperfect duty of engaging in charitable giving by donating $5000 annually to Farm Sanctuary or $3000 twice per year to the Innocence Project, I may satisfy my imperfect epistemic duty to know victims of gross violations and injustices by restoring status to people who have been wrongfully convicted, or by bearing witness to survivors of sexual violence, or by supporting the telling of rounder stories of Residential School survivors. This is crucial, as there are countless victims of gross violations and injustices who should be known as acts of epistemic reparations, and yet it is simply not possible for each of us to do all of this epistemic work on our own. Moreover, even if we were to spend nearly all of the hours in our days bearing witness to survivors, this would involve neglecting all of our other important goals and values.

This worry is a version of a familiar one facing utilitarianism, often leading to the *over-demandingness constraint* on moral theories according to which there is a "limit to how great a sacrifice morality . . . can legitimately demand of agents" (Murphy 1993, p. 268). While bringing about goodness is important, the idea underlying this constraint is that morality should not demand actions that are "incompatible with the motivations necessary for fully valuable personal projects and relationships" (Murphy 1993, p. 270). Similar considerations arise in the epistemic realm where there is a limit to how great a sacrifice epistemology can legitimately demand of agents and where our obligations—including the duty to know survivors—should be sensitive to, and compatible with, the broad range of goals and values important to human flourishing. For instance, in the same way that it is too much to expect me to donate nearly all of my income to the poor, despite

[16] Of course, this doesn't mean that there are not some persons whom every member of the social world ought to know. Perhaps Ida B. Wells, Martin Luther King Jr., and Nelson Mandela fall into this category. Similarly, perhaps there are some facts or persons about which every member of a particular community ought to know. For instance, perhaps every American who is socially connected ought to know about the murder of George Floyd.

the fact that this would bring about much good, it is also too much to demand that I spend most of my waking hours knowing victims, even if this were to bring about much epistemic repair. To be sure, each of us needs to do our share. We each need to listen, bear witness to some who have been horribly wronged, and do what we can to restore their status in our epistemic communities. And, collectively, we need to do everything in our power to ensure that no victim of atrocities is left invisible, vilified or demonized, or systematically distorted. But since there is a seemingly endless number of gross violations and injustices across the globe, each one of us cannot be epistemically obligated to know every victim involved in each of them. The framework of imperfect epistemic duties provides space for there to be the duty to know victims of gross violations and injustices, while not succumbing to worries of normative over-demandingness here.

To make this clearer, recall that the practical limits of the pursuit of imperfect duties are determined by circumstances and inclination. In the case of charity, the limit of circumstances involves not impoverishing oneself by the charitable action, and the inclination limit is established by one's character. Similar considerations apply in the case of knowing victims. One should not disable oneself cognitively by the knowing, a constraint that is determined by capacities that will vary significantly based on circumstances. For instance, those who are already deeply immersed in violations and injustices—either as victims themselves or as providers of care for those who have been victimized—may have less cognitive capacity for knowing others before it becomes disabling and thus will have less normative work to do to fulfill this imperfect epistemic duty. In contrast, those who occupy spaces or positions of relative privilege and safety may have more cognitive capacity and thus greater normative demands to engage in the epistemically reparative work of knowing. Similarly, the inclination limit to knowing victims will also be sensitive to circumstances, which explains why victims themselves do not have a particular epistemic duty to know the wrongdoer who wronged them, or even wrongdoers like them. Consider, for instance, a woman who has been sexually assaulted. Even if the perpetrator is himself a victim of a gross injustice, the sexual assault survivor has neither a perfect nor an imperfect duty to know him: it is not perfect, as she is not responsible for the injustice he experienced, and it is not imperfect, as she can bear witness to or restore the status of many different other victims of injustice, just as she can make a variety of acceptable choices about how she would like to distribute her annual giving. Indeed, she has no epistemic duty of any kind within this framework to know people who have committed acts of violence. Given this, she can be driven by her inclination to focus her attention on, for instance, knowing other survivors of sexual assault and fully satisfy her imperfect epistemic duty.

So, the duty to know survivors of gross violations and injustices has the first feature essential to imperfect duties: there is latitude in its fulfillment. It also shares the second feature: it is possible to do more than what the duty to know requires, where such excess has both moral and epistemic value. Recall the example involving charity, where a graduate student goes beyond what the imperfect duty calls for by donating 50% of her annual stipend to Oxfam. A person who is already living modestly need not give so generously to others, yet her doing so is nonetheless morally admirable. Now suppose that this same graduate student also frequently bears witness to and restores the status of survivors of sexual violence, both in general and in particular cases, and she does so at great cost to herself in terms of time and emotional investment. She devotes value-reflecting attention to their stories, has appropriate listener responses, engages in the coconstruction of more authentic, rounder stories of them, and helps promote their narratives in ways that center their epistemic agency. These actions go beyond what the duty to know calls for, but also do so in ways that have moral and epistemic benefits both for survivors of sexual violence and the broader community, as new knowledge is being generated in all of them, relations of acknowledgment, respect, trust, credibility, and authority are being cultivated, and the moral and epistemic agency of the survivors is being created, restored, and repaired. Thus, both LATITUDE and IMPERFECTION apply to the epistemic duty to know.

## 3. Duties and the Epistemic

One worry that might be raised about the framework developed here is that even if we do have duties to know survivors of gross violations and injustices, why should we regard them as *epistemic* duties? Moreover, if they are not epistemic duties, then it may be further asked in what sense the reparations in question are epistemic.

My response will have a number of different layers. To begin, there are two different ways we might understand what it means for there to be an epistemic duty. On the one hand, we might have in mind that there is a duty to do something epistemic in nature. According to this view, the mere fact that there is a duty to know someone—with knowledge obviously being epistemic in nature—would show that there are epistemic duties, and so on this conception, we clearly have epistemic duties to know survivors of gross violations and injustices. On the other hand, we might have in mind that the source of the normativity in question is itself epistemic. On this view, the very normative pressure to know someone flows from the epistemic. I will also defend this stronger sense in which there are epistemic duties to know, but to do so, it will be helpful to have a deeper understanding of how the standard view of epistemic duties will resist this claim.

According to the standard view, epistemic duties concern only beliefs, and thus their domain strictly concerns believing, disbelieving, or withholding belief. I call this the *doxastic thesis*. For instance, Chase Wrenn says that "[e]pistemic duties are doxastic duties that are grounded in purely epistemic considerations, such as what evidence one has" (2007, p. 117). Given this, the typical strategy for arguing that there are no epistemic duties is to show that there are no propositions that we ought to believe. Wrenn makes this point clear when, in summarizing arguments against epistemic duties put forth by William Alston and Alvin Plantinga, he writes:

> if it is truly one's duty to X, one must have voluntary control over whether or not one X-es. People do not have voluntary control over whether or not they believe something. Therefore, it is never one's duty (not) to believe something. Epistemic duties pertain to what one believes, and so there are no epistemic duties. (2007, p. 116)

In a similar spirit, Mark Nelson states the plan for his paper, "We Have No Positive Epistemic Duties," as follows: "I think that we have negative epistemic duties, but no positive epistemic duties. There are things that we ought not to believe, but there is nothing that we ought to believe, on purely epistemic grounds" (2010, p. 83).

The thesis that epistemic duties concern only what we ought to believe is so widely accepted that it is frequently presented without any direct argument on its behalf. A central assumption at work here is that the realm of action is governed by moral duties, and so any normative pressure to *do* something is ultimately moral rather than epistemic. Support for this can be found in the classic characterization of evidentialism from Earl Conee and Richard Feldman, according to which a belief is justified for someone insofar as it fits the evidence he has for the belief at that time.[17] Evidentialism is a paradigmatic instance of what Sarah Moss calls "time-slice epistemology," where the core thesis of such a view is that "what is rationally permissible or obligatory for you at some time is entirely determined by what mental states you are in at that time" (2015, p. 172). Moreover, according to Moss, there is an important connection between time-slice epistemology and the view that "all fundamental norms of rationality are temporally local" (2015, p. 172). This is clearly true of the evidentialism of Conee and Feldman, which endorses a *temporally local* version of epistemic duties where one's epistemic obligations are exhausted by temporally local facts.

But this view is challenged by even some of the most ordinary epistemic demands. Consider the following: suppose that a racist claims to have epistemically justified racist beliefs on the grounds that the very limited amount of cherry-picked information he is exposed to supports them. This is because he actively insulates himself from conflicting evidence, surrounds himself with like-minded racists, carefully curates his news consumption so that it reflects his already existing views, and so on. Surely, the racist's beliefs here are not only false but also *unjustified*. What cases like this self-insulating racist show is that you cannot get off the epistemic hook by simply failing to expose yourself to counterevidence you should have.[18] This would have the consequence that the person whose racism is so pernicious that he won't even put himself in situations where his beliefs might be challenged ends up epistemically in the clear precisely because of this insulation. Here is another example: a police detective has enough evidence to justifiably believe that the innocent suspect in question is guilty of the murder, but only because he fails to follow up on leads that he knows might challenge his theory. Again, this is overtly epistemically problematic behavior.

What these cases show is that we should be concerned with not only counterevidence that one in fact possesses, but also its normative counterpart—counterevidence that one *ought to have*. This flies in the face of time-slice epistemology by virtue of making epistemic justification a matter, not only of one's mental states at a given time, but also of the mental states one should have at a time. The epistemic duties in question here go beyond

[17] More precisely: "EJ Doxastic attitude *D* toward proposition *p* is epistemically justified for *S* at *t* if and only if having *D* toward *p* fits the evidence *S* has at *t*" (Conee and Feldman 1985, p. 15).

[18] This is, of course, related to the earlier discussion of white and willful ignorance.

the evidence that is represented in the hearer's present psychology and are thus temporally non-local.[19]

Now, it might be objected that the evidentialist can accommodate these sorts of cases by arguing that the subjects in fact have relevant evidence that can capture the epistemic deficiencies in question. In particular, they have *evidence that there is evidence* that should have been gathered, and this provides them with the appropriate counterevidence in question. For instance, it might be said that the reason the racist is still on the epistemic hook in the above case is that he has evidence that there is evidence that he should have acquired; namely, despite the fact that he holds racist beliefs, he knows that there is counterevidence that he is ignoring. In this way, he has evidence that he should have more evidence concerning his views about the members of underrepresented groups.[20]

But this response does not work when people make life choices that severely restrict the evidence in their possession and, thus, aren't aware of all of the relevant consequences that follow from their choices. When white supremacists are surrounded by only sources that support their preferred racist views, they might be so insulated that they are unaware that there is in fact specific evidence that they have failed to gather. Of course, in a broad sense they might be aware that there is evidence "out there" that conflicts with their beliefs. But surely this isn't sufficient for their having evidence that there is evidence that they should have, since this is arguably true of each one of us. I know right now that there is evidence "out there" that conflicts with many of my beliefs, yet this by itself doesn't prevent them from being justified. If it did, there would be very little knowledge of any kind. The problem with the racist beliefs of the white supremacists is that there is evidence they *should* gather, regardless of whether they are aware that it exists. When the white supremacist says, "I had no idea that there was evidence that challenged my beliefs of white supremacy," this might mean that he lacked the higher-order evidence, but it does not render his beliefs free from epistemic criticism. This is why evidence that one should have cannot be fully captured by evidence that one in fact has, even when higher-order evidence of the sort considered here is factored in.

What all of this shows is that even at the most basic level of appropriate sensitivity to evidence, epistemic duties go beyond what we believe to

[19] See also Goldberg (2017).
[20] I'm grateful to Kevin McCain for pressing this objection.

include *what we do*. Normative demands here don't concern just a failure to believe in accordance with the evidence; they also extend to a failure to collect, or expose ourselves to, evidence that we ought to have. The police detective who comfortably sits with his belief in the guilt of his suspect is not disregarding evidence that he has, but rather, is failing to follow up on leads. This involves actions, not beliefs. He ought to inquire into other possibilities, interview potential witnesses, pursue other suspects, consult with experts, and so on. The doxastic thesis of the standard view of epistemic duties should thus be rejected.

The second dimension of the standard view of epistemic duties that I want to discuss is what I call the *intrapersonal thesis*, according to which epistemic duties concern only one's own beliefs, and thus their domain is importantly intrapersonal. According to this standard view, if, for instance, there is an epistemic duty to believe in accordance with the evidence or to exercise my epistemic agency, then this applies only to me and my beliefs. Otherwise put, I have the duty to manage my own epistemic life, not that of others. This point is supported, in part, by the doxastic thesis. If epistemic duties concern only beliefs, then it seems to follow fairly naturally that my epistemic duties do not extend to others. This is especially clear if duties require voluntary control, as I rarely have direct or even indirect voluntary control over what others believe.

But as was the case with the doxastic thesis, there are good reasons to reject this. To see this, notice first that it is undeniable that we have obligations to others and to our communities. This is so obvious in the moral case that it hardly needs to be noted. As we saw in the earlier discussion of *Rescue*, if I am walking past a very shallow pond where a toddler is drowning, and I would barely need to get my shoes wet in order to save her, I clearly have a moral obligation to do so. Failure to intervene would render me subject to moral criticism—indeed, people would rightly regard me as morally callous or depraved for walking past a dying child and withholding assistance when providing help would be extremely easy. But now consider: If I know that through very little effort on my part, I could save you from a false belief, why do I not similarly have an epistemic duty to intervene? Why should I care about others only when wrongness or harm are at issue, but not, say, truth or knowledge? Otherwise put, whatever we take to be of epistemic value—truth, knowledge, understanding, evidence, epistemic agency, intellectual virtues, epistemic relationships, and so on—there is simply no reason why we would have obligations to promote these ends only in ourselves. If it is valuable for me to believe truly, then it is also valuable for you to believe truly. If I have obligations to ensure this end in myself, why would I not, at least sometimes, have duties to assist others in this end?[21]

One may argue that while caring about, say, the truth or grounding of my own beliefs is epistemic, any responsibility that I have regarding the beliefs of others is moral. But, why? If there is a distinctively epistemic ought governing me and my beliefs that is not ultimately reducible to the moral, it is unmotivated to say that an ought that is identical in all respects except that it concerns another person becomes moral by this very fact. Thus, I'm going to put forward what I call the *parity thesis*: If it is an epistemic duty to promote an aim in myself, then a duty that is identical except that it regards others is also epistemic. Accordingly, if it is an epistemic duty to promote true beliefs in myself or to believe in accordance with the evidence or to exercise my epistemic agency, then if I have the duty to promote true beliefs in others or to assist them in believing in accordance with the evidence or to cultivate their epistemic agency, it is also epistemic. Of course, one who believes that, in general, all epistemic oughts are ultimately moral oughts does not violate the parity thesis; rather, one who believes that epistemic oughts are ultimately moral oughts only when others are at issue does.

A related point that is frequently assumed, often tacitly so, is that if having a true belief or knowledge matters, say, practically or morally, then this shows that the duty at work cannot be epistemic. For instance, consider, again, a police detective who falsely believes that his suspect is guilty of murder. If I have evidence that would put pressure on the detective's false belief, it seems that I have a duty to share this with him. What is the nature of the duty? Clearly, a suspect being wrongfully accused or convicted of a crime is a serious moral wrong that causes a great deal of harm, and so there is undoubtedly moral pressure to do so. But surely this doesn't rule out there *also* being an epistemic duty to share the evidence. It matters not only that the detective pursues the right suspect, but also that he has true beliefs and knowledge about the situation. The moral value of avoiding perpetrating a moral wrong or harm does not need to swamp or rule out the epistemic value of him having a true belief or knowledge about the murder. Consider the intrapersonal case: if I am the police detective in question, I have moral duties to pursue the right suspect and also epistemic duties to have true beliefs about the matter. We would

[21] Until recently, there was very little work in the epistemological literature devoted specifically to understanding our epistemic duties *to others*. A rare exception was Jason Kawall's (2002). I also take up this issue directly in Lackey (2020b), on which the material in this section relies.

not say that the pressure to believe in accordance with the evidence in the intrapersonal case is moral when the stakes are high. In other words, my epistemic duties do not become moral ones simply because their truth value bears on moral matters or has practical urgency.[22] As the parity thesis makes clear, we should say the same thing in the interpersonal case. Given this, it is not an objection to the claim that there are interpersonal epistemic duties to point out that in many of the most compelling cases, there are moral and practical stakes involved that can explain the intuition that we should intervene. Yes, there are moral and practical stakes in such cases, as there are with most of our own beliefs. But none of this shows that there are no epistemic duties in either the intrapersonal or interpersonal cases.

This is crucial to recognize since the framework developed in this book involves epistemic reparations that are owed because of gross violations and injustices, and so there will almost always be moral pressure to engage in the work in question. For instance, survivors of apartheid-era violence have the right to be known at least in part because they have been morally wronged by the government. Indeed, most would probably understand South Africa's Truth and Reconciliation Commission—which facilitated a great deal of knowing of victims—as importantly grounded in moral and political normativity rather than in anything epistemic. Nevertheless, different layers of normativity can clearly live side by side with one another. In other words, the fact that there is a moral duty to do something does not squeeze out the possibility that this same action can also be epistemically obligatory. While South Africa's TRC indeed promoted reconciliation and forgiveness, it also facilitated, at the same time, the sharing and recording of knowledge.

Once we see that epistemic duties include actions in addition to beliefs, and that they concern others as well as ourselves, we have an epistemological framework for thinking through epistemic reparations. When victims of gross violations and injustices have been epistemically wronged through invisibility, vilification and demonization, or systematic distortion, they have the epistemic right to be known for who they truly are. This, in turn, brings with it the duty for others to know them as an act of epistemic reparations, which requires *doing things*. For instance, knowing victims involves seeking out their stories, bearing witness to them with value-reflecting attention,

[22] This is, of course, a different claim than the central thesis of pragmatic encroachment, according to which practical stakes can bear on whether someone has knowledge. See, for instance, Fantl and McGrath (2002).

having appropriate listener responses, inquiring, remembering, and so on. It also demands that we go beyond the evidence currently in our possession to acquire evidence that we should have. It is, for instance, expected that a person who is not in highly unusual circumstances will know about Nelson Mandela or that an average American knows about the murder of George Floyd. These are relatively current examples, but there is a seemingly endless list of such facts, including many about other people. For instance, we should know that Black Americans are the victims of racism, that there was a genocide in Rwanda, and so on. As social creatures, then, we ought to know about the world we live in, including the gross violations and injustices inflicted upon members of our communities.

## 4. Epistemic Reparations Versus Epistemic Repair

While the first instance of the term "epistemic reparations" is found in Lackey (2021a) and is further developed in Lackey (2022), there are other concepts in the literature concerning what we might think of as "epistemic repair"[23] more broadly. Since the differences between them are both theoretically and practically significant, drawing them out may also shed additional light on what is unique about the work of epistemic reparations.[24]

George Hull (2022), for instance, introduces the concept of "epistemic redress," which he understands as addressing both epistemic and non-epistemic wrongs and as having both doxastic and non-doxastic forms. Doxastic epistemic redress includes redress through either the formation of beliefs whose content is specific in advance (predetermined doxastic epistemic redress) or the formation of beliefs whose content is not specific in advance (open-ended doxastic epistemic redress).[25] Non-doxastic epistemic redress includes making redress by refraining from forming a belief, deciding to remain agnostic on some matter, or assuming or supposing

[23] As I will discuss below, Almassi (2018) focuses on the need for epistemic amelioration in the face of epistemic injustice and then provides an account of "epistemic repair" as a promising step toward this goal. I will later engage with Almassi's specific view but I want to note here that I am using epistemic repair in a loose and intuitive way to pick out epistemic work that makes up for or corrects epistemic wrongs without taking on board any specific view of it.

[24] I should note that I am discussing these concepts near the end of this book, rather than much earlier, since it is only against the backdrop of a full development of my view of epistemic reparations that I can make clear how it is significantly different from accounts of related phenomena in the literature.

[25] Hull (2022, pp. 10–16).

something.[26] As should be clear, Hull's concept is both far more expansive, and yet also significantly narrower, than that of epistemic reparations. Regarding the former, the starting point of this book is the UN's framework for understanding the *rights* of victims of *gross violations and injustices*, whereas Hull focuses on what is *normatively owed* to victims of *wrongs more broadly*, where this could involve even a one-off offensive or hurtful belief. For instance, one of the central cases he discusses is where a woman comes home in the morning looking tired and is met by a questioning look from her husband, who is eating breakfast at the kitchen table. According to Hull, the wrong in this case is the *belief* that she committed a transgression last night. This seems to be a paradigmatic case of what Rima Basu and Mark Schroeder (2018) call "doxastic wronging," where one person wrongs another in virtue of what he believes about her. Basu and Schroeder characterize doxastic wrongs as having three features: (1) being directed, (2) committed by beliefs, and (3) being wrong in virtue of what is believed rather than merely because of relevant consequences. They provide an example very similar to Hull's, where your spouse smells wine that a colloquium speaker spilled on your sleeve and believes that you have fallen off of your sobriety wagon, despite the fact that you have not had alcohol in eight months. Both examples involve beliefs that are hurtful or offensive, especially given the nature of the interpersonal relationships in question, but it should be clear that they are not candidates for epistemic reparations. They do not, for instance, arise from or constitute a gross violation or injustice, at least not as described. As noted earlier, "reparations" is a politically and legally weighty notion, with central cases involving governments or institutions engaging in them through various forms of legislation and policies that target deep, systemic injustices. While I extend this notion to involve distinctively epistemic wrongs and to also be applicable to individual cases, the weightiness of the normativity remains because of the focus on the rights held by survivors of gross violations and injustices. So even if some sort of redress is called for in cases of simple doxastic wronging, the question of epistemic reparations does not arise.

At the same time, the concept of epistemic redress is far narrower than epistemic reparations. On Hull's view, the person who is the subject of the doxastic wronging is owed epistemic redress by the perpetrator either in the form of believing that, say, the transgression in question didn't occur, or

[26] Hull (2022, pp. 7–10).

through refraining from forming such a belief, deciding to remain agnostic on what occurred, or assuming that the transgression did not take place. While he calls the former doxastic redress and the latter non-doxastic, all but one focus on states directly connected to believing, such as not believing that something is true or withholding judgment about it. Even the last one of "assuming" involves an attitude narrowly targeting the content of the belief in question. But as we have seen, providing epistemic reparations is an ongoing process involving a multitude of dimensions both of the wrongs perpetrated and of the corresponding duties to know. Among others, the distinctively epistemic wrongs may involve various forms and combinations of invisibility, vilification and demonization, or systematic distortion, including being the subject of false or flat stories. The corresponding duties are both perfect and imperfect and may include centering the epistemic agency of survivors, promoting counter and rounder stories about them, listening, bearing witness, having appropriate responses, and facilitating the restoration of relationships and status. All of this, in turn, brings along epistemic pressure to do things that go far beyond what is found in the traditional doxastic and intrapersonal theses, such as seeking out reparative stories, asking questions, paying attention, listening, memorializing, and so on. Thus, the framework of epistemic reparations is far more expansive than that of epistemic redress.

Similar considerations apply to two other related notions. Ben Almassi (2018) discusses the explosion of work on various forms of epistemic injustice and argues on behalf of the need for "epistemic amelioration" in the form of "epistemic repair," which he understands as involving the following practices in sequential order: perpetrator (and community) acknowledgment of injustice; perpetrator amends in accordance with victim subjectivity; and victim forgiveness and renewed trustful collaboration. Following this view, Seunghyun Song argues that "morally responsible agents are liable to make epistemic amends for past epistemic injustices" (2020, p. 165) and she characterizes such moral liability in terms of the moral agent directly causing the epistemic harm; the moral agent being autonomous; and the moral agent being epistemically competent in that he has access to the relevant epistemic resources. As a paradigmatic example, Song discusses the state-led denial of Japan's military sexual slavery, concluding that the Japanese government is a liable agent who must make epistemic amends for the past epistemic injustice of the denial. She then develops Almassi's notion of acknowledgment as involving the liable agent's recognition of "1) what the injustice entailed for the victims, 2) that the injustice should have not occurred, followed by his or her 3) genuine commitment to not repeat the injustice" (2020, p. 167).

We saw above that Hull's concept of epistemic redress is both more expansive and yet more targeted than that of epistemic reparations, and this is also true of the accounts developed by Almassi and Song. Both focus very broadly on epistemic injustice as the wrong in need of being addressed, which subsumes even a one-off instance of a speaker receiving slightly less credibility than the evidence warrants because of a prejudice on the part of the hearer. Yet despite this they both also develop accounts of repair or amends that are much narrower in scope than the framework found in this book. While Song attends primarily to a perpetrator's acknowledgment of wrongdoing, Almassi focuses on relational repair where victims are able to trust that they will not be subject to epistemic injustice—that they will be believed, given the credibility they deserve, not dismissed, and so on. Again, these are far more circumscribed than the work demanded of epistemic reparations.

What is important to highlight, then, is that there are many different kinds of epistemic wrongs and injustices and most or even all of them might normatively require epistemic repair in a broad sense but only a subset of these will be candidates for epistemic reparations. Even with respect to the phenomenon of not knowing a person, there is considerable variation in how this might arise or unfold. Online interaction, for instance, is poised for telling flat stories about both ourselves and one another, with character limits, hashtags, and short attention spans. Many of these flat stories inflict epistemic wrongs and, it may be argued, normatively demand epistemic repair in the form of rounder stories. As I have emphasized throughout this book, however, epistemic reparations are not required for every act of epistemic injustice but, rather, only for those epistemic wrongs that arise from or themselves constitute gross violations and injustices.[27] In this sense, they have real political and legal purchase to them and can be pursued through various forms of legislation and policies that target deep, pernicious systemic injustices perpetrated by governments or institutions. And so while there are concepts in the literature that focus on making up for past epistemic wrongs, none involve what I regard as epistemic reparations.

[27] As my discussion throughout this book makes clear, the media, including in its online form, often plays a crucial role in the epistemic wrongs that do demand epistemic reparations. My point here is simply that many flat stories on the internet do not rise to this level.

## 5. Conclusion

While there remains much work to be done here, I've shown that there is room for expansion within the traditional epistemological picture to accommodate the right to be known, the duty to know, and epistemic reparations. Appreciating that epistemic duties can be imperfect in nature, that they can govern actions, that we can be obligated to go beyond the evidence we currently have in our possession, and that we have epistemic duties to others, we see that we have the theoretical resources for understanding how we all are obligated to bear witness to and restore the status of victims of gross violations and injustices. While no one group or person is responsible for righting all of the epistemic wrongs in the world, each of us needs to roll up our sleeves and do our part in engaging in the business of providing epistemic reparations through knowing victims of gross violations and injustices. For it is only through true collective action that we will be able to make meaningful progress in the ongoing process of addressing the deepest, most violating epistemic wrongs that have been inflicted on those in the past and the present.

# Conclusion

On any given day, the scale, scope, and depth of the pain, violations, suffering, and injustice that exist—both locally and globally, past and present—can feel soul crushing. When this is combined with the recognition that each of us is just one person, living in our small corner of the universe, going about our daily lives, a sense of futility or hopelessness can begin to creep in. What could I possibly do in between, say, grocery shopping and laundry, that could make even a dent in the colossal wrongs of the world?

A central goal of this book is to provide not only a theoretical framework for understanding how to answer this question, but also a practical guide. We cannot sit idly by in the face of such injustices while pointing the finger at others who are the "real" perpetrators of, say, the invisibility of Residential School survivors in Canada, or the flat stories of those who are incarcerated in America, or the systematic distortion of victims of apartheid in South Africa. Even if we are not directly responsible for inflicting such epistemic wrongs, each of us, through complicity, special relationships, or imperfect duties, has work that we need to do. But this should not provoke despair. Whether you are reading these words from a prison cell or a dorm room, an office or a café, a community center or the subway, there are steps you can take *right now* to know the unknown as acts of epistemic reparations. Listen to someone's story or coconstruct another's; read an autobiography or visit a memorial; post a rounder story on Instagram or watch a documentary; listen to Keith's album or share it on TikTok.

To get you started in the process, I will share with you links to some counter, rounder, or otherwise reparative stories of victims of gross violations and injustices. Each of these stories is either from or about someone discussed in this book or the result of the work of the Buffett Institute for Global Affairs Epistemic Reparations Working Group:[1]

[1] This list is included as an invitation to the reader to get started on the work of epistemic reparations and is not intended to be complete in any way.

*The Right to Be Known*. Jennifer Lackey, Oxford University Press. © Oxford University Press 2026.
DOI: 10.1093/9780197833988.003.0007

- Jeffery Campbell: https://youtu.be/-O5Kq9lZBVw?si=y60zVuZ3iMtRKIUD
- Oliver Crawford: https://www.youtube.com/watch?v=3sfcKlxhIQs&t=10s
- Demetrius Cunningham: https://sites.northwestern.edu/npep/2025/05/29/beyond-the-walls-music-as-connection-and-escape/
- Anthony Ehlers: https://chicagoreader.com/news/on-prisons/ehlers-solitary-is-torture/
- Keith LaMar: https://www.keithlamar.org/live-album
- Hugo Ocon: https://www.youtube.com/watch?v=6nX-Ik8qrWg
- Michael Ortega: https://www.youtube.com/watch?v=0-rERMJ8a0Q
- *Northwestern Insider*: https://www.northwesterninsider.com
- William Peeples: https://magazine.northwestern.edu/features/prison-education-unlocks-potential/when-you-know-better-you-do-better
- Erika Ray: https://sites.northwestern.edu/npep/2023/08/22/logan-student-erika-ray-publishes-first-poetry-collection-42-and-freedom/
- James Soto: https://www.chicagotribune.com/2025/05/04/jimmy-soto-wrongful-conviction/

You can bear witness to, and restore the status of, these survivors of gross violations and injustices by reading, watching, or listening to their stories. You can give them value-reflecting attention, you can have appropriate affective attitudes toward them, you can see them as multidimensional agents with open doors to their futures, you can know them for who they truly are. You can then deepen or extend the reach of the epistemic reparations by sharing their stories across a number of different platforms, such as via social media, listservs, or even word of mouth.

Moreover, your efforts do not need to be limited to only stories that are already being told. At this very moment in time, there are stories that are erased, exploited, coopted, falsified, vilifying, distorting, or otherwise stolen. Maybe this is even happening to the narrative of your own life. But no matter where you are in the world, you can be part of the process of restoring, co-producing, or creating new ones. Document someone's experiences or write down your own; paint a self-portrait or grab your cell phone the next time the State tries to demonize your neighbor; create a TikTok of a forgotten survivor or a rounder post of one who has been flattened.

Most importantly, do something. Right some wrong. Know someone.

# References


Ackerman, Joshua M., Jenessa R. Shapiro, Steven L. Neuberg, Douglas T. Kenrick, D. Vaughn Becker, Vladas Griskevicius, Jon K. Maner, and Mark Schaller. 2006. "They All Look the Same to Me (Unless They're Angry): From Out-Group Homogeneity to Out-Group Heterogeneity." *Psychological Science* 17: 836–840.

Adamson, Bryan. 2016. "Thugs, Crooks, and Rebellious Negroes: Racist and Racialized Media Coverage of Michael Brown and the Ferguson Demonstrations." *Harvard Journal on Racial and Ethnic Justice* 32: 189–278.

Alba, Joseph W. and Lynn Hasher. 1983. "Is Memory Schematic?" *Psychological Bulletin* 93: 203–231.

Alexander, Michelle. 2012. *The New Jim Crow: Mass Incarceration in the Age of Colorblindness.* New York, NY: The New Press.

Almassi, Ben. 2018. "Epistemic Injustice and Its Amelioration: Toward Restorative Epistemic Justice." *Social Philosophy Today* 34: 95–113.

Almassi, Ben. 2020. *Reparative Environmental Justice in a World of Wounds.* Lanham, MD: Lexington Books.

Alper, Mariel, Matthew R. Durose, and Joshua Markman. 2018. *2018 Update on Prisoner Recidivism: A 9-Year Follow-up Period (2005–2014).* Washington, DC: Bureau of Justice Statistics. NCJ No. 250975. https://bjs.ojp.gov/library/publications/2018-update-prisoner-recidivism-9-year-follow-period-2005-2014.

Amsterdam, Anthony G. and Jerome Bruner. 2000. *Minding the Law.* Cambridge, MA: Harvard University Press.

Arendt, Hannah. 1994. "Organized Guilt and Universal Responsibility," in Jerome Kohn (ed.), *Essays in Understanding 1930–1954.* New York, NY: Harcourt Brace & Company.

Arnold, Miriam, Mascha Goldschmitt, and Thomas Rigotti. 2023. "Dealing with Information Overload: A Comprehensive Review." *Frontiers in Psychology* 14. doi: 10.3389/fpsyg.2023.1122200.

Aspen Global Leadership Network. 2016. "Death Row Attorney Bryan Stevenson on 4 Ways to Fight Against Injustice." Blog Post, https://www.aspeninstitute.org/blog-posts/death-row-attorney-bryan-stevenson-4-ways-fight-injustice/.

Associated Press. 2019a. "25 Years After Rwanda Genocide, Survivors Forgive Killers." *Crux*, https://cruxnow.com/church-in-africa/2019/04/25-years-after-rwanda-genocide-survivors-forgive-killers.

Associated Press. 2019b. "Michigan State Reaches $500M Settlement for 332 Victims of Larry Nassar." *Chicago Tribune*, https://www.chicagotribune.com/sports/college/ct-spt-michigan-state-larry-nassar-settlement-20180516-story.html.

Auxier, Brooke. 2020. "Most Americans Support Right to Have Some Personal Info Removed from Online Searches." Pew Research Center, https://www.pewresearch.org/short-reads/2020/01/27/most-americans-support-right-to-have-some-personal-info-removed-from-online-searches/.

Bailey, Olivia. 2022. "Empathy and the Value of Humane Understanding." *Philosophy and Phenomenological Research* 104: 50–65.

Bain, Zara. 2023. "Mills's Account of White Ignorance: Structural or Non-Structural?" *Theory and Research in Education* 21: 18–32.

Baines, Erin, Kamari M. Clarke, and Mark A. Drumbl. 2021. Submission of *Amicus Curiae* Observations on the Merits of the Legal Questions Presented in the "Order Inviting

Expressions of Interest as Amici Curiae in Judicial Proceedings (Pursuant to Rule 103 of the Rules of Procedure and Evidence)" of October 25, 2021, *Prosecutor v. Dominic Ongwen*, ICC-02/04-01/15A (filed December 23, 2021).

Baldwin, James. 1993 [1961]. *Nobody Knows My Name: More Notes of a Native Son*. New York, NY: Vintage International.

Barclay, Craig R. and Peggy A. DeCooke. 1988. "Ordinary Everyday Memories: Some of the Things of Which Selves Are Made," in Ulric Neisser and Eugene Winograd (eds.), *Remembering Reconsidered: Ecological and Traditional Approaches to the Study of Memory*. New York, NY: Cambridge University Press; 91–125.

Barkley, Charles. 1993. "I Am Not a Role Model." Nike Television Commercial, https://www.youtube.com/watch?v=R8vh2MwXZ6o.

Basu, Rima and Mark Schroeder. 2018. "Doxastic Wronging," in Brian Kim and Matthew McGrath (eds.), *Pragmatic Encroachment in Epistemology*. New York, NY: Routledge; 181–205.

Batson, Daniel C., Marina P. Polycarpou, Eddie Harmon-Jones, Heidi J. Imhoff, Erin C. Mitchener, Lori L. Bednar, Tricia R. Klein, and Lori Highberger. 1997. "Empathy and Attitudes: Can Feeling for a Member of a Stigmatized Group Improve Feelings Toward the Group?" *Journal of Personality and Social Psychology* 72: 105–118.

Bauman, Zygmunt. 2003. "The Uniqueness and Normality of the Holocaust," in Neil Levi and Michael Rothberg (eds.), *The Holocaust: Theoretical Readings*. Edinburgh: Edinburgh University Press; 82–88.

Bavelas, Janet B., Linda Coates, and Trudy Johnson. 2000. "Listeners as Co-Narrators." *Journal of Personality and Social Psychology* 79: 941–952.

BBC Sport. 2018. "Simone Biles: Larry Nassar Abused Me, Says Four-Time Olympic Champion." https://www.bbc.com/sport/gymnastics/42697952.

"Bear Witness." *Merriam-Webster Online Dictionary*. Merriam-Webster. Accessed January 3, 2026, https://www.merriam-webster.com/dictionary/bear%20witness.

Bedford, Leslie. 2001. "Storytelling: The Real Work of Museums." *Curator: The Museum Journal* 44: 27–34.

Benhabib, Seyla. 1991. *Situating the Self*. New York, NY: Routledge.

Bennett, Jessica. 2021. "Monica Lewinsky Is (Reluctantly) Revisiting 'That Woman.'" *The New York Times*, https://www.nytimes.com/2021/09/01/arts/television/monica-lewinsky-impeachment-american-crime-story.html.

Benton, Matthew. 2017. "Epistemology Personalized." *The Philosophical Quarterly* 67: 813–834.

Berenstain, Nora. 2016. "Epistemic Exploitation." *Ergo* 3: 569–590.

Bilz, Kenworthey. 2010. "We Don't Want to Hear It: Psychology, Literature, and the Narrative Model of Judging." *University of Illinois Law Review* 2010: 429–487.

Bird, Alexander. 2010. "Social Knowing: The Social Sense of 'Scientific Knowledge.'" *Philosophical Perspectives* 24: 23–56.

Bishop, Jeanne. 2015. *Change of Heart: Justice, Mercy, and Making Peace with My Sister's Killer*. Louisville, KY: Westminster John Know Press.

Bluhm Legal Clinic, Center on Wrongful Convictions, Northwestern Pritzker School of Law. n.d. "False and Coerced Confessions." Accessed January 3, 2026, https://www.law.northwestern.edu/legalclinic/wrongfulconvictions/issues/falseconfessions/.

Bluhm Legal Clinic, Center on Wrongful Convictions, Northwestern Pritzker School of Law. n.d. "Lavelle Burt." Accessed January 3, 2026, https://www.law.northwestern.edu/legalclinic/wrongfulconvictions/exonerations/il/lavelle-burt.html

Bluhm Legal Clinic, Wrongful Convictions of Youth, Northwestern Pritzker School of Law. n.d. "Brendan Dassey Case." Accessed January 3, 2026, https://www.law.northwestern.edu/legalclinic/wrongfulconvictionsyouth/making-a-murderer/.

Bogert, Carroll and LynNell Hancock. 2020. "How the Media Created a 'Superpredator' Myth That Harmed a Generation of Black Youth: Twenty-Five Years Ago This Month, the Word 'Superpredator' Spread in the Media Like Wildfire, Shaping Criminal Justice Policy for

Decades." *NBC News*, https://www.nbcnews.com/news/us-news/analysis-how-media-created-superpredator-myth-harmed-generation-black-youth-n1248101.

BonJour, Lawrence and Ernest Sosa. 2003. *Epistemic Justification: Internalism vs. Externalism, Foundations vs. Virtues*. Oxford: Wiley-Blackwell.

Boult, Cameron. 2024. "The Relational Foundations of Epistemic Normativity." *Philosophical Issues*. https://doi.org/10.1111/phis.12270.

Boutet, Isabelle, Jean-Christophe Goulet-Pelletier, Safae Maslouhi, Daniel Fiset, and Caroline Blais. 2022. "Criminality Labelling Influences Reactions to Others' Pain." *Heliyon* 8: 1–9.

Bransford, John D. and Marcia K. Johnson. 1972. "Contextual Prerequisites for Understanding: Some Investigations of Comprehension and Recall." *Journal of Verbal Learning and Verbal Behavior* 11: 717–726.

Brookman, Fiona. 2015. "The Shifting Narratives of Violent Offenders," in Lois Presser and Sveinung Sandberg (eds.), *Narrative Criminology: Understanding Stories of Crime*. New York, NY: New York University Press; 207–234.

Brooks, Samantha K. and Neil Greenberg. 2021. "Psychological Impact of Being Wrongfully Accused of Criminal Offences: A Systematic Literature Review." *Medicine, Science and the Law* 61: 44–54.

Brown-Iannuzzi, Jazmin L., Kelly M. Hoffman, B. Keith Payne, and Sophie Trawalter. 2014. "The Invisible Man: Interpersonal Goals Moderate Inattentional Blindness to African Americans." *Journal of Experimental Psychology* 143: 33–37.

Brown-Iannuzzi, Jazmin L., Sophie Trawalter, Jaclyn A. Lisnek, Kelly M. Hoffman, and B. Keith Payne. 2024. "The Invisible Man: A Replication Study Investigating Whether Interpersonal Goals Moderate White Women's Inattentional Blindness to African American Men." *Group Processes & Intergroup Relations* 27: 583–596.

Bruner, Jerome. 1987. "Life as Narrative." *Social Research* 54: 11–32.

Buckley, Madeline. 2025. "A Life Taken and Won Back: The Extraordinary Journey of Jimmy Soto." *Chicago Tribune*, https://www.chicagotribune.com/2025/05/04/jimmy-soto-wrongful-conviction/.

Buergenthal, Thomas. 1995. "The United Nations Truth Commission for El Salvador," in Neil J. Kritz (ed.), *Transitional Justice: How Emerging Democracies Reckon with Former Regimes Volume I*. Washington, DC: United States Institute of Peace.

Buitelaar, J. C. 2017. "Post-Mortem Privacy and Informational Self-Determination." *Ethics and Information Technology* 19: 129–142.

Burbank, Megan. 2021. "Miscarriage Is Common, Yet Shrouded in Stigma and Shame. Amanda Knox Wants to Change That." *The Seattle Times*, https://www.seattletimes.com/life/miscarriage-is-common-yet-shrouded-in-stigma-and-shame-amanda-knox-wants-to-change-that/.

Burger-Caplan, Joshua I. 2017. "Time of Desperation: An Examination of Criminal Defendants' Experiences of Allocuting at Sentencing." *Columbia Journal of Law and Social Problems* 51: 39–77.

Burns, Robert P. 1999. *A Theory of the Trial*. Princeton, NJ: Princeton University Press.

Carey, Gemma. 2021. "I'm a Survivor of Child Sexual Grooming: It Took Me 20 Years to Know It Wasn't My Fault." *The Guardian*, https://www.theguardian.com/commentisfree/2021/jan/29/im-a-survivor-of-child-sexual-grooming-it-took-me-20-years-to-know-it-wasnt-my-fault.

CBS News. 2018. "Ethan Couch Release Is 'Grave Injustice' for Victims, MADD President Says." https://www.cbsnews.com/news/ethan-couch-affluenza-teenrelease-outrage/.

CBS News. 2021. "Residential School Survivors on the Scars of Abuse." *The National*, https://www.youtube.com/watch?v=6OuTuTG5liQ.

Chan, Celine. 2009. "The Right to Allocution: A Defendant's Word on Its Face or Under Oath?" *Brooklyn Law Review* 75: 579–625.

Chatterjee, Partha. 1997. *Our Modernity*. Rotterdam/Dakar: SEPHIS/CODESRIA.

Chicago Torture Justice Center. n.d. "History of Chicago's Reparations Movement." Accessed January 3, 2026, https://www.chicagotorturejustice.org/history.

Chicago Torture Justice Memorials. n.d. "The Reparations Ordinance." Accessed January 3, 2026, https://chicagotorture.org/reparations/ordinance/.

Clark, Herbert H. 1994. "Discourse in Production," in Morton Ann Gernsbacher (ed.), *Handbook of Psycholinguistics*. San Diego, CA: Academic Press; 985–1021.

Clark, Herbert H. 1996. *Using Language*. Cambridge: Cambridge University Press.

Clean Slate Initiative. n.d. *Clean Slate Initiative*. Accessed January 3, 2026, https://www.cleanslateinitiative.org.

Cleaves, Wallace and Charles Sepulveda. 2021. "Native Land Acknowledgments Are Not the Same as Land." *Bloomberg*, https://www.bloomberg.com/news/articles/2021-08-12/native-land-stewardship-needs-to-follow-acknowledgment.

Coady, C. A. J. 1992. *Testimony: A Philosophical Study*. Oxford: Clarendon Press.

Coalition for the International Criminal Court. n.d. "Dominic Ongwen." Accessed January 3, 2026, https://www.coalitionfortheicc.org/cases/dominic-ongwen.

Coates, Ta-Nehisi. 2016. "The Case for Reparations." *The Atlantic*, https://www.theatlantic.com/magazine/archive/2014/06/the-case-for-reparations/361631/.

Coetzee, Faan. n.d. "Have Employees Who Wish to Use Traditional Healer Certificates for Sick Leave Been Thrown a Bone?" Labour Guide South Africa. Accessed January 3, 2026, https://labourguide.co.za/general/have-employees-who-wish-to-use-traditional-healer-certificates-for-sick-leave-been-thrown-a-bone/.

Collins, Patricia Hill. 2000. *Black Feminist Thought: Knowledge, Consciousness, and the Politics of Empowerment*, Second Edition. New York, NY: Routledge.

Conee, Earl and Richard Feldman. 1985. "Evidentialism." *Philosophical Studies* 48: 15–34.

Cooley, Charles Horton. 1964 [1902]. *Human Nature and the Social Order*. New York, NY: Schocken Books.

Cooper, Kelly-Leigh. 2019. "Bianca Devins: The Teenager Whose Murder Was Exploited for Clicks." *BBC*, https://www.bbc.com/news/world-us-canada-49002486.

Cordova, Viola. 2007. *How It Is: The Native American Philosophy of V.F. Cordova*, edited by Kathleen Dean Moore, Kurt Peters, Tod Jojola, and Amber Lacy. Tucson, AZ: University of Arizona Press.

Corr, Charles A. 1999. "Enhancing the Concept of Disenfranchised Grief." *OMEGA—Journal of Death and Dying* 38: 1–20.

Council of Europe. n.d. *European Convention on Human Rights*. Article 8, "Right to Respect for Private and Family Life." November 4, 1950, as amended. https://www.echr.coe.int/documents/d/echr/convention_ENG.

Cover, Robert M. 1983. "The Supreme Court, 1982 Term—Foreword: *Nomos* and Narrative." *Harvard Law Review* 97: 4–68.

Cover, Robert M. 1985. "The Folktales of Justice: Tales of Jurisdiction." *Capital University Law Review* 14: 179–203.

Crawley, Elaine and Richard Sparks. 2013. "Older Men in Prison: Survival, Coping, and Identity," in Alison Liebling and Shadd Maruna (eds.), *The Effects of Imprisonment*. London: Routledge; 343–365.

Crenshaw, Kimberlé. 1989. "Demarginalizing the Intersection of Race and Sex: A Black Feminist Critique of Antidiscrimination Doctrine, Feminist Theory and Antiracist Politics." *University of Chicago Legal Forum* 1989: 139–167.

Crenshaw, Kimberlé. 1992. "Whose Story Is It Anyway? Feminist and Antiracist Appropriations of Anita Hill," in Toni Morrison (ed.), *Race-ing Justice, En-Gendering Power: Essays on Anita Hill, Clarence Thomas, and the Construction of Social Reality*. New York, NY: Pantheon Books; 402–440.

Cullen, Francis T., Gregory A. Clark, John B. Cullen, and Richard A. Mathers. 1985. "Attribution, Salience, and Attitudes Toward Criminal Sanctioning." *Criminal Justice and Behavior* 12: 305–331.

Da Silva, Sergio, Rashmi Gupta, and Dario Monzani. 2023. "Highlights in Psychology: Cognitive Bias." *Frontiers in Psychology* 14: 1–3.

Daughety, Andrew F. and Jennifer F. Reinganum. 2018. "Evidence Suppression by Prosecutors: Violations of the *Brady* Rule." *The Journal of Law, Economics, and Organization* 34: 475–510.

Davis, Emmalon. 2016. "Typecasts, Tokens, and Spokespersons: A Case for Credibility Excess as Testimonial Injustice." *Hypatia* 31: 485–501.

Davis, Emmalon. 2018. "On Epistemic Appropriation." *Ethics* 128: 702–727.

Daye, Russell. 2011. *Political Forgiveness: Lessons from South Africa.* Eugene, OR: Wipf and Stock Publishers.

de Beauvoir, Simone. 1988 [1949]. *The Second Sex.* London: Pan Books.

Deep Forgiveness. n.d. *Deep Forgiveness.* Accessed January 3, 2026, http://www.deepforgiveness.com.

de Greiff, Pablo. 2006. "Justice and Reparations," in Pablo de Greiff (ed.), *The Handbook of Reparations.* New York, NY: Oxford University Press; 451–477.

Department of Justice, South Africa. n.d. *Truth and Reconciliation Commission (TRC) - TRC Committee.* Accessed January 3, 2026, https://www.justice.gov.za/trc/trccom.html.

DeRose, Keith. 2002. "Assertion, Knowledge, and Context." *The Philosophical Review* 111: 167–203.

Dickinson, Connie and Thomas Givón. 1995. "Memory and Conversation: Toward an Experimental Paradigm," in Thomas Givón (ed.), *Conversation: Cognitive, Communicative, and Social Perspectives.* Amsterdam, the Netherlands: John Benjamins; 91–132.

Dixon, Travis L. 2017. "Good Guys Are Still Always in White? Positive Change and Continued Misrepresentation of Race and Crime on Local Television News." *Communication Research* 44: 775–792.

Doka, Kenneth J. 1989. *Disenfranchised Grief: Recognizing Hidden Sorrow.* Lexington, MA, England: Lexington Books/D. C. Heath and Com.

Doka, Kenneth J. 1999. "Disenfranchised Grief." *Bereavement Care* 18: 37–39.

Dooling, David J. and Robert E. Christiaansen. 1977. "Episodic and Semantic Aspects of Memory for Prose." *Journal of Experimental Psychology: Human Learning and Memory* 3: 428–436.

Dotson, Kristie. 2011. "Tracking Epistemic Violence, Tracking Practices of Silencing." *Hypatia* 26: 236–257.

Dotson, Kristie. 2014. "Conceptualizing Epistemic Oppression." *Social Epistemology* 28: 115–138.

Dotson, Kristie. 2017. "Theorizing Jane Crow, Theorizing Unknowability." *Social Epistemology* 31: 417–430.

Dotson, Kristie and Marita Gilbert. 2014. "Curious Disappearances: Affectability Imbalances and Process-Based Invisibility." *Hypatia* 29: 873–888.

Dovidio, John F., Marleen Ten Vergert, Tracie L. Stewart, Samuel L. Gaertner, James D. Johnson, Victoria M. Esses, Blake M. Riek, and Adam R. Pearson. 2004. "Perspective and Prejudice: Antecedents and Mediating Mechanisms." *Personality and Social Psychology Bulletin* 30: 1537–1549.

Drakulich, Kevin M. 2013. "Perceptions of the Local Danger Posed by Crime: Race, Disorder, Informal Control, and the Police." *Social Science Research* 42: 611–632.

Drizin, Steven. 2007. "Confessing to a Crime One Did Not Commit." *NBC News*, https://www.nbcnews.com/id/wbna18418460.

Drizin, Steven A. and Beth A. Colgan. 2004. "Tales from the Juvenile Confession Front: A Guide to How Standard Police Interrogation Tactics Can Produce Coerced and False Confessions from Juvenile Suspects," in G. Daniel Lassiter (ed.), *Interrogations, Confessions, and Entrapment* (*Perspectives in Law & Psychology* 20). New York, NY: Kluwer Academic/Plenum Publishers; 127–162.

Du Bois, W. E. B. 1989 [1903]. *The Souls of Black Folk.* New York, NY: Penguin Books.

Dular, Nicole. 2023. "Standpoint Moral Epistemology: The Epistemic Advantage Thesis." *Philosophical Studies* 181: 1813–1835.

Dworkin, Ronald. 2006. *Is Democracy Possible Here? Principles for a New Political Debate.* Princeton, NJ: Princeton University Press.

Ehlers, Anthony. 2024. "A Journey to Justice: Pondering 42 Years of Wrongful Incarceraton with James Soto." *Northwestern Prison Education Program Blog*, https://sites.northwestern.edu/npep/2024/01/10/a-journey-to-justice-pondering-42-years-in-prison-with-james-soto/.

Eisenberg, Avlana K. 2023. "Policing the Danger Narrative." *Journal of Criminal Law and Criminology* 113: 473–540.

Elgin, Catherine. 2006. "From Knowledge to Understanding," in Stephen Hetherington (ed.), *Epistemology Futures.* New York, NY: Oxford University Press; 199–215.

Ellison, Ralph. 1995 [1952]. *Invisible Man.* New York, NY: Vintage Books.

Emerick, Barrett. 2017. "Forgiveness and Reconciliation," in Kathryn J. Norlock (ed.), *The Moral Psychology of Forgiveness.* London: Rowman and Littlefield; 117–134.

Entman, Robert M. and Andrew Rojecki. 2000. *The Black Image in the White Mind: Media and Race in America.* Chicago, IL: The University of Chicago Press.

European Union. 2016. *Regulation (EU) 2016/679 of the European Parliament and of the Council of 27 April 2016 (General Data Protection Regulation)*, art. 17, "Right to Erasure ('Right to Be Forgotten')." *Official Journal of the European Union*, https://gdpr.eu/article-17-right-to-be-forgotten/.

Fader, Jamie J. 2019. "'The Game Ain't What It Used to Be': Drug Sellers' Perceptions of the Modern Day Underground and Legal Markets." *Journal of Drug Issues* 49: 57–73.

Fahmy, Nahla, Fiona G. Kouyoumdjian, Jonathan Berkowitz, Sharif Fahmy, Carlos Magno Neves, Stephen W. Hwang, and Ruth Elwood Martin. 2018. "Access to Primary Care for Persons Recently Released from Prison." *Annals of Family Medicine* 16: 549–551.

Fantl, Jeremy and Matthew McGrath. 2002. "Evidence, Pragmatics, and Justification." *Philosophical Review* 111: 67–94.

Feinberg, Joel. 1974. "The Rights of Animals and Unborn Generations," in William T. Blackstone (ed.), *Philosophy & Environmental Crisis.* Athens, GA: The University of Georgia Press; 43–68.

Feinberg, Joel. 1984. *Harm to Others: The Moral Limits of the Criminal Law.* New York, NY: Oxford University Press.

Fetterman, Adam, Carter Baker, and Brian Meier. 2023. "Crime in Your Area: Use of Neighborhood Apps Is Associated with Inaccurate Perceptions of Higher Local Crime Rates." *Psychology of Popular Media* 13. 10.1037/ppm0000466.

Findley, Keith A. and Michael S. Scott. 2006. "The Multiple Dimensions of Tunnel Vision in Criminal Cases." *Wisconsin Law Review* 2: 291–398.

Forman, Jr., James. 2017. *Locking Up Our Own: Crime and Punishment in Black America.* New York, NY: Farrar, Straus, and Giroux.

Forster, E. M. 1954. *Aspects of the Novel.* New York, NY: Harcourt, Brace.

Frank, Arthur W. 1995. *The Wounded Storyteller: Body, Illness, and Ethics*, Second Edition. Chicago, IL: The University of Chicago Press.

Frantz, Sue. n.d. "Availability Heuristic: A Nextdoor Example." *Macmillan Learning.* Accessed January 3, 2026, https://www.macmillanlearning.com/content-hub/highered/ref/psychology-blog/availability-heuristic-a-nextdoor-example/ba-p/6890.

Fraser, Rachel. 2021. "Narrative Testimony." *Philosophical Studies* 178: 4025–4052.

Freire, Paulo. 1990. *Pedagogy of the Oppressed*, trans. Myra Bergman Ramos. New York, NY: Continuum.

French, Peter A. 1982. "Forgiveness and Resentment." *Midwest Studies in Philosophy* 7: 503–516.

Fricker, Miranda. 2007. *Epistemic Injustice: Power & the Ethics of Knowing.* Oxford: Oxford University Press.

Friedman, Brandis. 2024. "'You Know You're Innocent, Yet Nobody's Hearing You.' Jimmy Soto Looks to Future After Serving 42 Years for Wrongful Conviction." *WTTW News*, https://

news.wttw.com/2024/01/18/you-know-you-re-innocent-yet-nobody-s-hearing-you-jimmy-soto-looks-future-after-serving.

Gajda, Amy. 2018. "Privacy, Press, and the Right to Be Forgotten in the United States." *Washington Law Review* 93: 201–264.

Galinsky, Adam D., Gillian Ku, and Cynthia S. Wang. 2005. "Perspective-Taking and Self-Other Overlap: Fostering Social Bonds and Facilitating Social Coordination." *Group Processes & Intergroup Relations* 8: 109–124.

Galinsky, Adam D. and Gordon B. Moskowitz. 2000. "Perspective-Taking: Decreasing Stereotype Expression, Stereotype Accessibility, and In-Group Favoritism." *Journal of Personality and Social Psychology* 78: 708–724.

General Services Administration. 2008. *Art in Architecture: Selected Artworks, 1997–2008*. U.S. General Services Administration, www.gsa.gov/system/files/GSA-AIA-Selected-Artwork-1997-2008.pdf.

Giannini, Mary Margaret. 2008. "Equal Rights for Equal Rites?: Victim Allocution, Defendant Allocution, and the Crime Victims' Rights Act." *Yale Law & Policy Review* 26: 431–484.

Gilbert, Daniel T. and Patrick S. Malone. 1995. "The Correspondence Bias." *Psychological Bulletin* 117: 21–38.

Gilbert, Keon L., Rashawn Ray, Arjumand Siddiqi, Shivan Shetty, Elizabeth A. Baker, Keith Elder, and Derek M. Griffith. 2016. "Visible and Invisible Trends in Black Men's Health: Pitfalls and Promises for Addressing Racial, Ethnic, and Gender Inequities in Health." *Annual Review of Public Health* 37: 295–311.

Global Strategy Group. 2021. *Innocent Until Proven Guilty? A Look at Media Coverage of Criminal Defendants in the U.S.* https://globalstrategygroup.com/wp-content/uploads/2012/07/GSG_Report_Innocent_Until_Proven_Guilty.pdf.

Goff, Phillip Atiba, Jennifer L. Eberhardt, Melissa J. Williams, and Matthew Christian Jackson. 2008. "Not Yet Human: Implicit Knowledge, Historical Dehumanization, and Contemporary Consequences." *Journal of Personality and Social Psychology* 94: 292–306.

Goldberg, Sanford. 2017. "Should Have Known." *Synthese* 194: 2863–2894.

Golding, Martin. 1984. "Forgiveness and Regret." *Philosophical Forum* 16: 121–137.

Goldman, Alvin I. 1967. "A Causal Theory of Knowing." *The Journal of Philosophy* 64: 357–372.

González, Thalia. 2015. "Reorienting Restorative Justice: Initiating a New Dialogue of Rights Consciousness, Community Empowerment and Politicization." *Cardozo Journal of Conflict Resolution* 16: 457–477.

Goodwin, Charles. 1981. *Conversational Organization: Interaction Between Speakers and Hearers*. New York, NY: Academic Press.

Google. n.d. *Requests to Delist Content under European Privacy Law. Google Transparency Report*. Accessed January 3, 2026, https://transparencyreport.google.com/eu-privacy/overview?delisted_urls=start:1401321600000;end:1519862399999&lu=delisted_urls&hl=en.

Gottlieb, Lisa. 2019. "How Changing Your Story Can Change Your Life." TED Video, https://www.youtube.com/watch?v=O_MQr4lHm0c.

Government of Canada. n.d. *Indian Residential Schools Settlement Agreement*. Crown-Indigenous Relations and Northern Affairs Canada. Accessed January 3, 2026, https://www.rcaanc-cirnac.gc.ca/eng/1100100015576/1571581687074#sect1.

Government of Canada. n.d. *Schedule N: Mandate of the Truth and Reconciliation Commission of Canada*. Accessed January 3, 2026, https://www.residentialschoolsettlement.ca/SCHEDULE_N.pdf.

Griffin, Lisa Kern. 2013. "Narrative, Truth, Trial." *Georgetown Law Journal* 101: 281–335.

Grimm, Stephen R. 2012. "The Value of Understanding." *Philosophy Compass* 7: 103–117.

Grimm, Stephen R. 2014. "Understanding as Knowledge of Causes," in Abrol Fairweather (ed.), *Virtue Epistemology Naturalized*. Cham: Springer International Publishing; 329–345.

Grimm, Stephen R. (ed.) 2017. *Making Sense of the World: New Essays on the Philosophy of Understanding*. Oxford: Oxford University Press.

Gross, James J. 1998. "The Emerging Field of Emotion Regulation: An Integrative Review." *Review of General Psychology* 2: 271–299.

Gross, Samuel R. 1998. "Make-Believe: The Rules Excluding Evidence of Character and Liability Insurance." *Hastings Law Journal* 49: 843–860.

Gross, Samuel R., Kristen Jacoby, Daniel J. Matheson, and Nicholas Montgomery. 2005. "Exonerations in the United States 1989 Through 2003." *Journal of Criminal Law & Criminology* 95: 523–560.

Grunwald, Ben and Jeffrey Fagan. 2019. "The End of Intuition-Based High-Crime Areas." *California Law Review* 107: 345–404.

Gudjonsson, Gisli H. 2003. *The Psychology of Interrogations and Confessions: A Handbook.* New York, NY: Wiley.

Haney, Craig. 2006. *Reforming Punishment: Psychological Limits to the Pains of Imprisonment.* Washington, DC: American Psychological Association.

Hardie-Bick, James. 2018. "Identity, Imprisonment, and Narrative Configuration." *New Criminal Law Review* 21: 567–591.

Harding, David J. 2003. "Jean Valjean's Dilemma: The Management of Ex-Convict Identity in the Search for Employment." *Deviant Behavior* 24: 571–595.

Hardy, Barbara. 1968. "Towards a Poetics of Fiction: An Approach through Narrative." *NOVEL: A Forum on Fiction* 2: 5–14.

Harris, Angela P. 1990. "Race and Essentialism in Feminist Legal Theory." *Stanford Law Review* 42: 581–616.

Harris-Perry, Melissa. 2011. *Sister Citizen: Shame, Stereotypes, and Black Women in America.* New Haven, CT: Yale University Press.

Hartman, Saidiya. 2008. "Venus in Two Acts." *Small Axe* 26: 1–14.

Hawkins, Orlando and Emmalon Davis. 2024. "The Future of Double Consciousness: Epistemic Virtue, Identity, and Structural Anti-Blackness." *Ergo* 11: 3. https://doi.org/10.3998/ergo.5708.

Hawthorne, John. 2004. *Knowledge and Lotteries.* Oxford: Oxford University Press.

Hawthorne, John and Jason Stanley. 2008. "Knowledge and Action." *The Journal of Philosophy* 105: 571–590.

Heart, Maria Yellow Horse Brave. 2003. "The Historical Trauma Response Among Natives and Its Relationship with Substance Abuse: A Lakota Illustration." *Journal of Psychoactive Drugs* 35: 7–13.

Herman, Judith. 1992. *Trauma and Recovery: The Aftermath of Violence—From Domestic Abuse to Political Terror.* New York, NY: Basic Books.

Hills, Alison. 2009. "Moral Testimony and Moral Epistemology." *Ethics* 120: 94–127.

Hirschfield, Paul J. and Alex R. Piquero. 2010. "Normalization and Legitimation: Modeling Stigmatizing Attitudes Toward Ex-Offenders." *Criminology* 48: 27–55.

Hoffman, Martin L. 2000. *Empathy and Moral Development: Implications for Caring and Justice.* Cambridge: Cambridge University Press.

Hope, Leah. 2024. "Protestors Hold Rally After Inmate Michael Broadway Dies at Stateville Correctional Center." *ABC7 News*, https://abc7chicago.com/post/protestors-rally-chicago-after-stateville-correction-center-inmate/15090690/.

Houston, Pam. 2003. "The Truest Eye." *O, The Oprah Magazine*, https://www.oprah.com/omagazine/toni-morrison-talks-love/4.

Hull, George. 2022. "Epistemic Redress." *Synthese* 200: 1–21.

Hurston, Zora Neale. 1950. "What White Publishers Won't Print." *Negro Digest* 8: 85–89.

Hurston, Zora Neale. 2010 [1942]. *Dust Tracks on a Road.* New York, NY: HarperCollins.

Hurston, Zora Neale. 2018. *Barracoon: The Story of the Last "Black Cargo."* New York, NY: HarperCollins.

Igneski, Violette. 2001. "Distance, Determinacy and the Duty to Aid: A Reply to Kamm." *Law and Philosophy* 20: 605–616.

Innocence Project in Print. 2015. "The Trials of Lewis Fogle." 11: 1–24. https://www.innocenceproject.org/wp-content/uploads/2017/05/IP-NewsletterDec2015_08-Final.pdf.

Itoi, Nikki Goth. 2023. "How Social Media Shapes Our Perceptions About Crime." *Stanford University Human-Centered Artificial Intelligence News*, https://hai.stanford.edu/news/how-social-media-shapes-our-perceptions-about-crime.

Jackson, Thomas W. and Pourya Farzaneh. 2012. "Theory-Based Model of Factors Affecting Information Overload." *International Journal of Information Management* 32: 523–532.

Jain, Neha. 2024. "Atrocity's Glass Booth." *Current Legal Problems* 77: 127–166.

James, Mike. 2018. "Parkland Killer in Video: 'I'm Going to Be the Next School Shooter.'" *News Center Maine, USA TODAY*, https://www.newscentermaine.com/article/news/nation-world/parkland-killer-in-video-im-going-to-be-the-next-school-shooter/507-560047424.

Johnson, Marcia K., Shahin Hashtroudi, S., and D. Stephen Lindsay. 1993. "Source Monitoring." *Psychological Bulletin* 114: 3–28.

Johnson, Mark. 1993. *Moral Imagination: Implications of Cognitive Science for Ethics*. Chicago, IL: The University of Chicago Press.

Jones, Edward E. and Victor A. Harris. 1967. "The Attribution of Attitudes." *Journal of Experimental Social Psychology* 3: 1–24.

Jones, Karen. 1999. "Second-Hand Moral Knowledge." *The Journal of Philosophy* 96: 55–78.

Joselow, Margaux. 2019. "Promise-Induced False Confessions: Lessons from Promises in Another Context." *Boston College Law Review* 60: 1641–1687.

Justice for Keith LaMar. n.d. *Freedom First*. Accessed January 3, 2026, https://www.keithlamar.org/product-page/pre-order-freedom-first-the-album-delivery-in-march.

Justice for Keith LaMar. n.d. *Justice for Keith LaMar*. Accessed January 3, 2026, https://www.keithlamar.org.

Justice for Keith LaMar. n.d. *Lyrics: LIVE from Death Row and Freedom First Songs*. Accessed January 3, 2026, https://www.keithlamar.org/lyrics.

Kahneman, Daniel, Paul Slovic, and Amos Tversky (eds.). 1982. *Judgment Under Uncertainty: Heuristics and Biases*. Cambridge: Cambridge University Press.

Kalla, Joshua L. and David E. Broockman. 2020. "Reducing Exclusionary Attitudes Through Interpersonal Conversation: Evidence from Three Field Experiments." *American Political Science Review* 114: 410–425.

Kalla, Joshua L. and David E. Broockman. 2023. "Which Narrative Strategies Durably Reduce Prejudice? Evidence from Field and Survey Experiments Supporting the Efficacy of Perspective-Getting." *American Journal of Political Science* 67: 185–204.

Kamm, F. M. 2004. "The New Problem of Distance in Morality," in Deen K. Chatterjee (ed.), *The Ethics of Assistance*. Cambridge: Cambridge University Press; 59–74.

Kärki, Kaisa and Visa Kurki. 2023. "Does a Person Have a Right to Attention? Depends on What She Is Doing." *Philosophy & Technology* 36: 1–16.

Kassin, Saul. 2018. "Why SCOTUS Should Examine the Case of 'Making a Murderer's' Brendan Dassey." *American Psychological Association*, https://www.apa.org/news/press/op-eds/scotus-brendan-dassey.

Kassin, Saul M. and Karlyn McNall. 1991. "Police Interrogations and Confessions: Communicating Promises and Threats by Pragmatic Implication." *Law and Human Behavior* 15: 233–251.

Kassin, Saul M., Steven A. Drizin, Thomas Grisso, Gisli H. Gudjonsson, Richard A. Leo, and Allison D. Redlich. 2010. "Police-Induced Confessions: Risk Factors and Recommendations." *Law and Human Behavior* 34: 3–38.

Kaupinnen, Antti. 2014. "Empathy, Emotion Regulation, and Moral Judgment," in Heidi Maibom (ed.), *Empathy and Morality*. Oxford: Oxford University Press; 97–121.

Kaupinnen, Antti. 2017. "Empathy and Moral Judgment," in Heidi Maibom (ed.), *The Routledge Handbook of the Philosophy of Empathy*. London: Taylor & Francis; 215–226.

Kaur, Harmeet. 2021. "Land Acknowledgments Are Often an Empty Gesture, Some Indigenous People Say." *CNN US*, https://www.cnn.com/2021/11/22/us/native-americans-land-acknowledgments-cec/index.html.

Kawall, Jason. 2002. "Other-Regarding Epistemic Virtues." *Ratio* 15: 257–275.

Keating, Caitlin. 2023. "How One Man Forgave His Brother's Killer—and Helped Him Be Released from Prison." *People*, https://people.com/darryl-green-deep-forgiveness-man-forgave-brothers-killer-exclusive-7506937.

Keegan, Rebecca. 2023. "Harvey Weinstein's 'Jane Doe 1' Victim Reveals Identity: 'I'm Tired of Hiding.'" *The Hollywood Reporter*, https://www.hollywoodreporter.com/feature/harvey-weinstein-jane-doe-victim-reveals-identity-1235333076/.

Kenrick, Andreana C., Stacey Sinclair, Jennifer Richeson, Sara C. Verosky, and Janetta Lun. 2015. "Moving While Black: Intergroup Attitudes Influence Judgments of Speed." *Journal of Experimental Psychology* 145: 147–154.

Kim, Jaegwon. 1994. "Explanatory Knowledge and Metaphysical Dependence." *Philosophical Issues* 5: 51–69.

Kim, Min-Young and Ian A. G. Wilkinson. 2019. "What Is Dialogic Teaching? Constructing, Deconstructing, and Reconstructing a Pedagogy of Classroom Talk." *Learning, Culture and Social Interaction* 21: 70–86.

Kissel, Ted B. 2020. "Bearing Witness." *USC Annenberg News*, https://annenberg.usc.edu/news/research-and-impact/bearing-witness.

Klaver, Jessica R., Zina Lee, and V. Gordon Rose. 2008. "Effects of Personality, Interrogation Techniques and Plausibility in an Experimental False Confession Paradigm." *Legal and Criminal Psychology* 13: 71–88.

Kreps, Daniel. 2021. "Monica Lewinsky Talks How Public Shaming Can Be 'Violence.'" *Rolling Stone*, https://www.rollingstone.com/tv-movies/tv-movie-news/monica-lewinsky-daily-show-cancel-culture-1238268/.

Krull, Douglas S. 2001. "On Partitioning the Fundamental Attribution Error: Dispositionalism and the Correspondence Bias," in Gordon B. Moskowitz (ed.), *Cognitive Social Psychology: The Princeton Symposium on the Legacy and Future of Social Cognition*. Mahwah, NJ: Lawrence Erlbaum Associates Publishers: 211–227.

Ku, Gillian, Cynthia S. Wang, and Adam D. Galinsky. 2015. "The Promise and Perversity of Perspective-Taking in Organizations." *Research in Organizational Behavior* 35: 79–102.

Kubota, Jennifer, Rachel Mojdehbakhsh, Candace Raio, Tobias Brosch, Jim S. Uleman, and Elizabeth A. Phelps. 2014. "Stressing the Person: Legal and Everyday Person Attributions Under Stress." *Biological Psychology* 103: 117–124.

Kurtz, Howard. 1985. "Meese Says Few Suspects Are Innocent of Crime." *The Washington Post*, https://www.washingtonpost.com/archive/politics/1985/10/11/meese-says-few-suspects-are-innocent-of-crime/272c4d16-f627-4ce4-896e-7faf8632a526/.

Kutz, Christopher. 2000. *Complicity: Ethics and Law for a Collective Age*. Cambridge: Cambridge University Press.

Kvanvig, Jonathan L. 2003. *The Value of Knowledge and the Pursuit of Understanding*. New York, NY: Cambridge University Press.

LaChance, Naomi. 2016. "Media Continues to Refer to Brock Turner as a 'Stanford Swimmer' Rather Than a Rapist." *The Intercept*, https://theintercept.com/2016/09/02/media-continues-to-refer-to-brock-turner-as-a-stanford-swimmer-rather-than-a-rapist/.

Lackey, Jennifer. 2008. *Learning from Words: Testimony as a Source of Knowledge*. Oxford: Oxford University Press.

Lackey, Jennifer. 2011. "Assertion and Isolated Secondhand Knowledge," in Jessica Brown and Herman Cappelen (eds.), *Assertion*. Oxford: Oxford University Press; 251–275.

Lackey, Jennifer. 2016. "Pitted Against Yourself: Credibility and False Confessions." *Blog of the American Philosophical Association*. https://blog.apaonline.org/2016/04/21/pitted-against-yourself-credibility-and-false-confessions/.

Lackey, Jennifer. 2018a. "Credibility and the Distribution of Epistemic Goods," in Kevin McCain (ed.), *Believing in Accordance with the Evidence: New Essays on Evidentialism.* Springer Publishing; 145–168.

Lackey, Jennifer. 2018b. "The Duty to Object." *Philosophy and Phenomenological Research* 101: 35–60.

Lackey, Jennifer. 2018c. "Group Assertion." *Erkenntnis* 83: 21–42.

Lackey, Jennifer. 2020a. "False Confessions and Testimonial Injustice." *Journal of Criminal Law & Criminology* 110: 43–68.

Lackey, Jennifer. 2020b. "Epistemic Duties Regarding Others," in Kevin McCain and Scott Stapleford (eds.), *Epistemic Duties: New Arguments, New Angles.* Routledge; 281–294.

Lackey, Jennifer. 2021a. "The Case for Epistemic Reparations." *Open for Debate.* https://blogs.cardiff.ac.uk/openfordebate/the-case-for-epistemic-reparations/.

Lackey, Jennifer. 2021b. *The Epistemology of Groups.* Oxford: Oxford University Press.

Lackey, Jennifer. 2022. "Epistemic Reparations and the Right to Be Known." *Proceedings and Addresses of the American Philosophical Association* 96: 54–89.

Lackey, Jennifer. 2023. *Criminal Testimonial Injustice.* Oxford: Oxford University Press.

Lambert, Michael C., Elisa J. Sobo, and Valerie L. Lambert. 2021. "Rethinking Land Acknowledgments." *Anthropology News,* December 20. https://anthropology.unc.edu/wp-content/uploads/sites/1302/2024/03/9-AN-Article-Rethinking-Land-Acknowledgments.pdf.

Lande, Nelson P. 1990. "Posthumous Rehabilitation and the Dust-Bin of History." *Public Affairs Quarterly* 4: 267–286.

Landler, Mark. 2004. "The All-Too Human Hitler, on Your Big Screen." *The New York Times,* https://www.nytimes.com/2004/09/15/world/europe/the-alltoohuman-hitler-on-your-big-screen.html.

Langton, Rae. 2000. "Feminism in Epistemology: Exclusion and Objectification," in Miranda Fricker and Jennifer Hornsby (eds.), *The Cambridge Companion to Feminism in Philosophy.* Cambridge: Cambridge University Press; 127–145.

Lavie, Nilli, Diane M. Beck, and Nikos Konstantinou. 2014. "Blinded by the Load: Attention, Awareness, and the Role of Perceptual Load." *Philosophical Transactions of the Royal Society of London. Series B, Biological Sciences* 369: 20130205.

Lawson, Brian. 2013. "Individual Complicity in Collective Wrongdoing." *Ethical Theory and Moral Practice* 16: 227–243.

Lazare, Aaron. 2008. "The Healing Forces of Apology in Medical Practice and Beyond." *DePaul Law Review* 57: 251–266.

Lazzaro, Jakob. 2021. "Elkhart Man Wrongfully Convicted of Murder Exonerated After 16 Years in Prison." *WVPE 88.1 Elkhart/South Bend,* https://www.wvpe.org/indiana-news/2021-07-21/elkhart-man-wrongfully-convicted-of-murder-exonerated-after-16-years-in-prison.

LeBel, Thomas P. 2008. "Perceptions of and Responses to Stigma." *Sociology Compass* 2: 409–432.

LeBel, Thomas P. 2011. "Invisible Stripes? Formerly Incarcerated Persons' Perceptions of Stigma." *Deviant Behavior* 33: 89–107.

Lebron, Chris. 2017. "An Open Letter to the Editors of the Journal of Political Philosophy; or How Black Scholarship Matters, Too." *Philosopher,* https://politicalphilosopher.net/2017/05/24/an-open-letter-to-the-editors-of-the-journal-of-political-philosophy-or-how-black-scholarship-matters-too/.

Leo, Richard A. 2009. "False Confessions: Causes, Consequences, and Implications." *The Journal of the American Academy of Psychiatry and the Law* 37: 332–343.

Leo, Richard A. and Richard J. Ofshe. 1997. "The Social Psychology of Police Interrogation: The Theory and Classification of True and False Confessions." *Studies in Law, Politics, and Society* 16: 189–251.

Lepore, Jill. 2020. "The Invention of the Police." *The New Yorker*. https://www.newyorker.com/magazine/2020/07/20/the-invention-of-the-police.

Levenbook, Barbara Baum. 1984. "Harming Someone After His Death." *Ethics* 94: 407–419.

Leydon-Hardy, Lauren. 2021. "Predatory Grooming and Epistemic Infringement," in Jennifer Lackey (ed.), *Applied Epistemology*. Oxford: Oxford University Press; 119–147.

Lewinsky, Monica. 2014. "Shame and Survival." *Vanity Fair*, https://www.vanityfair.com/style/society/2014/06/monica-lewinsky-humiliation-culture.

Lewinsky, Monica. 2015. "The Price of Shame." TED Video, https://www.youtube.com/watch?v=H_8y0WLm78U.

Lewinsky, Monica. 2019. "Monica Lewinsky on the Decade We Reclaimed Our Stories—and Ourselves." *Vanity Fair*, https://www.vanityfair.com/style/2019/12/monica-lewinsky-on-the-decade-we-reclaimed-our-stories?srsltid=AfmBOorFTddXBU8AwCfhWmDpmxrJv2iL76N12yCWj1piw0i0hReIB56h.

Li, Mengyao, Bernhard Leidner, and Silvia Fernandez-Campos. 2020. "Stepping into Perpetrators' Shoes: How Ingroup Transgressions and Victimization Shape Support for Retributive Justice Through Perspective-Taking with Perpetrators." *Personality and Social Psychology Bulletin* 46: 424–438.

Lindemann, Hilde. 2016. *Holding and Letting Go: The Social Practice of Personal Identities*. Oxford: Oxford University Press.

Lipton, Peter. 2004. *Inference to the Best Explanation*, Second Edition. New York, NY: Routledge.

List, Christian and Phillip Pettit. 2011. *Group Agency: The Possibility, Design, and Status of Corporate Agents*. Oxford: Oxford University Press.

Liu, Dixizi, Zhijie Sasha Dong, and Guo Qiu. 2022. "Exploring the Contagion Effect of Social Media on Mass Shootings." *Computers & Industrial Engineering* 172: 1–8.

Livanou, Maria, Kate Whittenbury, and Daniela Di Basilio. 2024. "Listening to Other People's Traumatic Experiences: What Makes It Hard and What Could Protect Professionals from Developing Related Distress? A Qualitative Investigation." *Stress and Health* 40: https://doi.org/10.1002/smi.3353.

Llewellyn, Jennifer. 2008. "Bridging the Gap Between Truth and Reconciliation: Restorative Justice and the Indian Residential School Truth and Reconciliation Commission," in Marlene Brant-Castellano, Linda Archibald, and Mike DeGagné (eds.), *From Truth to Reconciliation: Transforming the Legacy of Residential Schools*. Ottawa: Aboriginal Healing Foundation; 183–201.

Lodge, David. 1992. *The Art of Fiction: Illustrated from Classic and Modern Texts*. New York, NY: Penguin Books.

Loftus, Elizabeth F. and Jacqueline E. Pickrell. 1995. "The Formation of False Memories." *Psychiatric Annals* 25: 720–725.

Lopez, C. Todd. 2016. "Following Rape, 'Runner' Rather Than 'Victim' Defines Survivor's Identity." U.S. Army, https://www.army.mil/article/166506/following_rape_runner_rather_than_victim_def.

Lorde, Audre. 1984. *Sister Outsider: Essays and Speeches*. New York, NY: Crossing Press.

Lorde, Audre. 1990. "Foreword," in Joanne Braxton and Andree McLaughlin (eds.), *Wild Women in the Whirlwind: Afra-American Culture and the Contemporary Literary Renaissance*. New Brunswick, NJ: Rutgers University Press.

Luban, David. 2018. "The Enemy of All Humanity." *Netherlands Journal of Legal Philosophy* 47: 112–137.

Lucas, Brian J., Adam D. Galinksy, and Keith J. Murnighan. 2016. "An Intention-Based Account of Perspective-Taking: Why Perspective-Taking Can Both Decrease and Increase Moral Condemnation." *Personality and Social Psychology Bulletin* 42: 1480–1489.

Ludwig, Kirk. 2014. "Proxy Agency in Collective Action." *Noûs* 48: 75–105.

Macdonald, James S. P. and Nilli Lavie, N. 2008. "Load Induced Blindness." *Journal of Experimental Psychology. Human Perception and Performance* 34: 1078–1091.

Macdonald, James S. P. and Nilli Lavie, N. 2011. "Visual Perceptual Load Induces Inattentional Deafness." *Attention, Perception & Psychophysics* 73: 1780–1789.
Marcus, Paul. 2006. "It's Not Just About *Miranda*: Determining the Voluntariness of Confessions in Criminal Prosecutions." *Valparaiso University Law Review* 40: 601–644.
Marsy's Law. n.d. *Marsy's Law.* Accessed January 3, 2026, https://www.marsyslaw.us.
Martin, Dianne L. 2002. "Lessons About Justice from the Laboratory of Wrongful Convictions: Tunnel Vision, the Construction of Guilt and Informer Evidence." *UMKC Law Review* 70: 847–864.
Maruna, Shadd and Derek Ramsden. 2004. "Living to Tell the Tale: Redemption Narratives, Shame Management, and Offender Rehabilitation," in Amia Lieblich, Dan P. McAdams, and Ruthellen Josselson (eds.), *Healing Plots: The Narrative Basis of Psychotherapy.* Washington, DC: American Psychological Association Books; 129–151.
May, Vivian M. 2006. "Trauma in Paradise: Willful and Strategic Ignorance in *Cereus Blooms at Night*." *Hypatia* 21: 107–135.
Mayer-Schönberger, Viktor. 2009. *Delete: The Virtue of Forgetting in the Digital Age.* Princeton, NJ: Princeton University Press.
McAdams, Dan P. 1993. *The Stories We Live By: Personal Myths and the Making of the Self.* New York, NY: The Guilford Press.
McAdams, Dan P. 2019. "First We Invented Stories, Then They Changed Us: The Evolution of Narrative Identity." *Evolutionary Studies in Imaginative Culture* 3: 1–18.
McGary, Howard. 1989. "Forgiveness." *American Philosophical Quarterly* 26: 343–351.
McIntosh, Peggy. 1989. "White Privilege: Unpacking the Invisible Knapsack." *Peace and Freedom Magazine,* 10–12. https://med.umn.edu/sites/med.umn.edu/files/2022-12/White-Privilege_McIntosh-1989.pdf.
McMahon, Jeff. 2009. *Killing in War.* Oxford: Oxford University Press.
Medina, José. 2013. *The Epistemology of Resistance: Gender and Racial Oppression, Epistemic Injustice, and the Social Imagination.* Oxford: Oxford University Press.
Medina, José. Forthcoming. "Protest Movements and the Right to Make Oneself Known/Unknown." *Feminist Philosophical Quarterly.*
Methot, Suzanne. 2019. *Legacy: Trauma, Story, and Indigenous Healing*: Toronto: ECW Press.
Meyer, Philip N. 2014. *Storytelling for Lawyers.* New York, NY: Oxford University Press.
Miller, Arthur G. 1976. "Constraint and Target Effects in the Attribution of Attitudes." *Journal of Experimental Social Psychology* 12: 325–339.
Mills, Charles.1997. *The Racial Contract.* Ithaca, NY: Cornell University Press.
Mills, Charles. 2007. "White Ignorance," in Shannon Sullivan and Nancy Tuana (eds.), *Race and Epistemologies of Ignorance.* Albany, NY: SUNY Press; 11–38.
Mills, Charles. 2015. "Global White Ignorance," in Matthias Gross and Linsey McGoey (eds.), *Routledge International Handbook of Ignorance Studies.* London and New York, NY: Routledge; 217–227.
Minow, Martha. 1998. *Between Vengeance and Forgiveness: Facing History After Genocide and Mass Violence.* Boston, MA: Beacon Press.
Mitova, Veli. 2025a. "Decolonial Epistemic-Authority Reparations." *Episteme,* https://doi.org/10.1017/epi.2025.2.
Mitova, Veli. 2025b. "Hermeneutical Relationships." *Inquiry,* https://www.tandfonline.com/doi/full/10.1080/0020174X.2025.2539820.
*M.L. v. Slovakia.* Application no. 34159/17. European Court of Human Rights. Judgment of October 14, 2021 (final January 14, 2022). https://hudoc.echr.coe.int/fre#{%22itemid%22:[%22001-212150%22]}.
Mohamed, Saira. 2015. "Deviance, Aspiration, and the Stories We Tell: Reconciling Mass Atrocity and Criminal Law." *The Yale Law Journal* 124: 1628–1689.
Moody-Adams, Michele. 2022a. *Making Space for Justice: Social Movements, Collective Imagination, and Political Hope.* Columbia: Columbia University Press.
Moody-Adams, Michele. 2022b. "The Role of Narrative and Narrative Activism in Social Movements." *Columbia University Press Blog,* https://cupblog.org/2022/06/15/

the-role-of-narrative-and-narrative-activism-in-social-movements-michele-moody-adams/.

Morgan, Mary S. 2022. "Narrative: A General-Purpose Technology for Science," in Mary S. Morgan, Kim M. Hajek, and Dominic J. Berry (eds.), *Narrative Science: Reasoning, Representing and Knowing since 1800*. Cambridge: Cambridge University Press; 3–30.

Morgan, Michael and James Shanahan. 1997. "Two Decades of Cultivation Research: An Appraisal and Meta-Analysis." *Annals of the International Communication Association* 20: 1–45.

Moss, Sarah. 2015. "Time-Slice Epistemology and Action Under Indeterminacy." *Oxford Studies in Epistemology* 5: 172–194.

Msimang, Sisonke. 2016. "You May Free Apartheid Killers But You Can't Force Their Victims to Forgive." *The Guardian*, https://www.theguardian.com/world/2016/mar/11/chris-hani-apartheid-killers-cant-force-victims-to-forgive.

Muhammad, Ismail. 2018. "The Crushing Sorrow of Barracoon." *Slate*, https://slate.com/culture/2018/06/zora-neale-hurstons-barracoon-reviewed.html?pay=1767364003729&support_journalism=please.

Muhammad, Khalil Gibran. 2010. *The Condemnation of Blackness: Race, Crime, and the Making of Modern Urban America*. Cambridge, MA: Harvard University Press.

Munton, Jessie. 2023. "Prejudice as the Misattribution of Salience." *Analytic Philosophy* 64: 1–19.

Murphy, Gillian and Ciara M. Greene. 2016. "Perceptual Load Affects Eyewitness Accuracy and Susceptibility to Leading Questions." *Frontiers in Psychology* 7. https://doi.org/10.3389/fpsyg.2016.01322.

Murphy, Jeffrie G. 1988. "Forgiveness and Resentment," in *Forgiveness and Mercy*, by Jeffrie Murphy and Jean Hampton. Cambridge: Cambridge University Press; 14–34.

Murphy, Liam B. 1993. "The Demands of Beneficence." *Philosophy & Public Affairs* 22: 267–292.

Naef, Rahel. 2006. "Bearing Witness: A Moral Way of Engaging in the Nurse–Person Relationship." *Nursing Philosophy* 7: 146–156.

Natapoff, Alexandra. 2005. "Speechless: The Silencing of Criminal Defendants." *New York University Law Review* 80: 1449–1504.

National Centre for Truth and Reconciliation. 2020. "Lessons Learned: Survivor Perspectives on the Indian Residential Schools Settlement Agreement." https://nctr.ca/wp-content/uploads/2021/01/Lessons_learned_report_final_2020.pdf.

Ndebele, Njabulo. 1998. "Memory, Metaphor, and the Triumph of Narrative," in Sarah Nuttall and Carli Coetzee (eds.), *Negotiating the Past: The Making of Memory in Africa*. Cape Town: Oxford University Press; 19–28.

Ndlovu-Gatsheni, Sabelo J. 2018. *Epistemic Freedom in Africa: Deprovincialization and Decolonization*. London and New York, NY: Routledge.

Neimeyer, Robert A. and Finn Tschudi. 2003. "Community and Coherence: Narrative Contributions to the Psychology of Conflict and Loss," in Gary D. Fireman, Ted E. McVay, Jr., and Owen J. Flanagan (eds.), *Narrative and Consciousness: Literature, Psychology, and the Brain*. New York, NY: Oxford University Press; 166–191.

Nelson, Hilden Lindemann. 2001. *Damaged Identities, Narrative Repair*. Ithaca, NY: Cornell University Press.

Nelson, Mark. T. 2010. "We Have No Positive Epistemic Duties." *Mind* 119: 83–102.

Nesterak, Evan. 2014. "Coerced to Confess: The Psychology of False Confessions." *Behavioral Scientist*, https://behavioralscientist.org/coerced-to-confess-the-psychology-of-false-confessions/.

The New Yorker. 2020. "Kadir Nelson's 'Say Their Names.'" *The New Yorker*. https://www.newyorker.com/culture/cover-story/cover-story-2020-06-22.

New York State Association of Criminal Defense Lawyers. 2021. "The New York State Trial Penalty: The Constitutional Right to Trial Under Attack."

No Notoriety. n.d. *No Notoriety*. Accessed January 3, 2026, https://nonotoriety.com.

Nussbaum, Martha. 1990. *Love's Knowledge*. Oxford: Oxford University Press.

Nussbaum, Martha. 2006. *Hiding from Humanity: Disgust, Shame, and the Law*. Princeton, NJ: Princeton University Press.

Ofshe, Richard J. and Richard A. Leo. 1997a. "The Social Psychology of Police Interrogation: The Theory and Classification of True and False Confessions." *Studies in Law, Politics, and Society* 16: 189–251.

Ofshe, Richard J. and Richard A. Leo. 1997b. "The Decision to Confess Falsely: Rational Choice and Irrational Action." *Denver University Law Review* 74: 979–1122.

Oprah.com. n.d. "Wrongfully Accused." Accessed January 3, 2026, https://www.oprah.com/oprahshow/wrongfully-accused_1/all.

Orange, Tommy. 2024. *Wandering Stars*. New York, NY: Random House Large Print.

Orenstein, Aviva. 1998. "No Bad Men! A Feminist Analysis of Character Evidence in Rape Trials." *Hastings Law Journal* 49: 663–716.

Origgi, Gloria. 2012. "A Social Epistemology of Reputation." *Social Epistemology* 26: 399–418.

Origgi, Gloria. 2018. *Reputation: What It Is and Why It Matters*. Princeton, NJ: Princeton University Press.

Oxley, Julinna C. 2011. *The Moral Dimensions of Empathy: Limits and Applications in Ethical Theory and Practice*. Basingstoke: Palgrave Macmillan.

Paddock, Blair and Brandis Friedman. 2024. "Heat Stress 'Significant Contributing Condition' in Death of Michael Broadway, Who Died While Incarcerated at IDOC's Stateville." *WTTW News*, https://news.wttw.com/2024/09/13/heat-stress-significant-contributing-condition-death-michael-broadway-who-died-while.

Pager, Devah. 2007. *Marked: Race, Crime, and Finding Work in an Era of Mass Incarceration*. Chicago, IL: The University of Chicago Press.

Partridge, Ernest. 1981. "Posthumous Interests and Posthumous Respect." *Ethics* 91: 243–264.

Pasupathi, Monisha. 2001. "The Social Construction of the Personal Past and Its Implications for Adult Development." *Psychological Bulletin* 127: 651–672.

Pasupathi, Monisha, Lisa M. Stallworth, and Kyle Murdoch. 1998. "How What We Tell Becomes What We Know: Listener Effects on Speakers' Long-Term Memory for Events." *Discourse Processes* 26: 1–25.

Pasupathi, Monisha, Robyn Fivush, and Martha Hernandez-Martinez. 2016. "Talking About It: Stories as Paths to Healing After Violence." *Psychology of Violence* 6: 49–56.

Peeples Jr., William. 2020. "When You Know Better, You Do Better." *Northwestern Magazine*, https://magazine.northwestern.edu/features/prison-education-unlocks-potential/when-you-know-better-you-do-better.

Pennington, Nancy and Reid Hastie. 1993. "The Story Model for Juror Decision Making in Reid Hastie (ed.), *Inside the Juror: The Psychology of Juror Decision Making*. New York, NY: Cambridge University Press; 192–221.

Perlman, Marissa and Todd Feurer. 2024. "Longest-Serving Exonerated Man in Illinois Filing Lawsuit." *CBS News*, https://www.cbsnews.com/chicago/news/jimmy-soto-lawsuit-chicago/.

Petition for Executive Clemency of Brendan Ray Dassey. 2019. *Before the Wisconsin Pardon Advisory Board*, https://lavaforgood.com/documents/Brendan%20Dassey%20Petition%20for%20Executive%20Clemency.pdf.

Pettigrew, Jonathan. 2009. "Text Messaging and Connectedness Within Close Interpersonal Relationships." *Marriage & Family Review* 45: 697–716.

Philpott, Daniel. 2008. "Reconciliation: An Ethic for Responding to Evil in Global Politics," in Renée Jeffrey (ed.), *Ethical Responses to Problems of Moral Agency*. New York, NY: Palgrave MacMillan; 115–150.

Pickrel, Paul. 1988. "Flat and Round Characters Reconsidered." *The Journal of Narrative Technique* 18: 181–198.

Pranis, Kay. 2002. "Telling Our Stories and Changing Our Lives." *Connections: Victim and Offender Mediation Association* no. 10: 1–12.

Prescott, J. J. and Sonja Starr. 2020. "The Power of a Clean Slate." Cato Institute, https://www.cato.org/regulation/summer-2020/power-clean-slate.

Presser, Lois and Sveinung Sandberg (eds.). 2015. *Narrative Criminology: Understanding Stories of Crime*. New York, NY: New York University Press.

Price, Richard. 1974. *A Review of the Principal Questions in Morals*, Second Revised Edition. Oxford: Oxford University Press.

Prince, Gerald. 2003. *A Dictionary of Narratology*, Revised Edition. Lincoln, NE: University of Nebraska Press.

Raju, Dilpreet. 2024. "Communities, Commission Push Pritzker Admin for More Prison Plan Details." *Capitol News Illinois*, https://capitolnewsillinois.com/news/communities-commission-push-pritzker-admin-for-more-prison-plan-details/.

Rakoff, Jed S. 2014. "Why Innocent People Plead Guilty." *The New York Review*, November Issue. https://www.nybooks.com/articles/2014/11/20/why-innocent-people-plead-guilty/.

Ramos, Dino-Ray. 2019. "Michael B. Jordan, Jamie Foxx, Destin Daniel Cretton, And 'Just Mercy' Author Bryan Stevenson Talk Narrative Influence on Social Change, WB's Film Adaptation." *Deadline*, https://deadline.com/2019/06/bryan-stevenson-just-mercy-michael-b-jordan-jamie-foxx-destin-daniel-cretton-social-change-warner-brothers-1202637817/.

Raykov, Petar P., Dominika Varga, and Chris M. Bird. 2023. "False Memories for Ending of Events." *Journal of Experimental Psychology* 152: 3459–3475.

Reed, Baron. 2001. "Epistemic Agency and the Intellectual Virtues." *Southern Journal of Philosophy* 39: 507–526.

Reid, Fraser J. M. and Donna J. Reid. 2010. "The Expressive and Conversational Affordances of Mobile Messaging." *Behaviour & Information Technology* 29: 3–22.

Resnick, Brian. 2016. "These Scientists Can Prove It's Possible to Reduce Prejudice." *Vox*, https://www.vox.com/2016/4/7/11380974/reduce-prejudice-science-transge.

Resnick, Brian. 2020. "How to Talk Someone Out of Bigotry." *Vox*, https://www.vox.com/2020/1/29/21065620/broockman-kalla-deep-canvassing.

Resnick, Laura B, Christa S. C. Asterhan, and Sherice N. Clarke, S. with Faith Schantz. 2018. "Next Generation Research in Dialogic Learning," in Gene E. Hall, Linda F. Quinn, and Donna M. Gollnick (eds.) *The Wiley Handbook of Teaching and Learning*. Hoboken, NJ: Wiley Blackwell; 323–338.

Reynolds, Steven L. 2002. "Testimony, Knowledge, and Epistemic Goals." *Philosophical Studies* 110: 139–161.

Rideout, J. Christopher. 2008. "Storytelling, Narrative Rationality, and Legal Persuasion." *The Journal of the Legal Writing Institute* 14: 53–86.

Riggs, Wayne. 2003. "Understanding 'Virtue' and the Virtue of Understanding," in Michael DePaul and Linda Zagzebski (eds.), *Intellectual Virtue: Perspectives from Ethics and Epistemology*. New York, NY: Oxford University Press; 203–226.

Robertson, Katie. 2023. "*The New York Times* Passes 10 Million Subscribers." *The New York Times*, https://www.nytimes.com/2023/11/08/business/media/new-york-times-q3-earnings.html.

Robinson, Richard. 2019. "The Management Nexus of Imperfect Duty: Kantian Views of Virtuous Relations, Reasoned Discourse, and Due Diligence." *Journal of Business Ethics* 157: 119–136.

Roediger, David R., ed. 1998. *Black on White: Black Writers on What It Means to Be White*. New York, NY: Schocken Books.

Roht-Arriaza, Naomi. 2004. "Reparations in the Aftermath of Repression and Mass Violence," in Eric Stover and Harvey M. Weinstein (eds.), *My Neighbor, My Enemy: Justice and Community in the Aftermath of Mass Atrocity*. Cambridge: Cambridge University Press; 121–139.

Romphf, Jake. 2021. "Tsawout Residential School Survivor No Longer Afraid to Share Her Story." *Oak Bay News*, https://oakbaynews.com/2021/09/30/tsawout-residential-school-survivor-no-longer-afraid-to-share-her-story/.

Rondini, Ashley C. 2018. "White Supremacist Danger Narratives." *Contexts* 17: 60–62.

Rowan, Zachary R., Adam Fine, Laurence Steinberg, Paul J. Frick, and Elizabeth Cauffman. 2023. "Labeling Effects on Initial Juvenile Justice System Processing Decision on Youth Interpersonal Ties." *Criminology* 61: 731–757.

Rudinow, Joel. 1978. "Manipulation." *Ethics* 88: 338–347.

Russian, Ale. 2018. "Georgina Chapman Reveals What 'Initially' Attracted Her to Harvey Weinstein in First Interview." *People*, https://people.com/movies/georgina-chapman-harvey-weinstein-attraction/.

Salkin, Wendy. 2021. "The Conscription of Informal Political Representatives." *The Journal of Political Philosophy* 29: 429–455.

Salkin, Wendy. 2024. *Speaking for Others: The Ethics of Informal Political Representation*. Cambridge, MA: Harvard University Press.

Sanders, Tom. 2025. "Trump Posts Wild 'Villains, Rapists, Monsters' Rant from Stephen Miller." *Daily Beast*, https://www.thedailybeast.com/trump-posts-wild-villains-rapists-monsters-rant-from-stephen-miller.

Satz, Debra. 2012. "Countering the Wrongs of the Past: The Role of Compensation." *Nomos* 51: 129–150.

Saunders, Jessica. 2024. *Supervision Violations and Their Impact on Incarceration: A Technical Analysis of Prison Populations and Admissions from People Serving Community Supervision Terms*. The Council of State Governments Justice Center, https://projects.csgjusticecenter.org/supervision-violations-impact-on-incarceration/wp-content/uploads/sites/15/2024/01/Supervision-Violations-Impact-2024_508.pdf.

Scalf, Paige E., Ana Torralbo, Evelina Tapia, and Diane M. Beck. 2013. "Competition Explains Limited Attention and Perceptual Resources: Implications for Perceptual Load and Dilution Theories." *Frontiers in Psychology* 4. doi: 10.3389/fpsyg.2013.00243.

Scarre, Geoffrey. 2003. "Archaeology and Respect for the Dead." *Journal of Applied Philosophy* 20: 237–249.

Schacter, Daniel L. 1999. "The Seven Sins of Memory: Insights from Psychology and Cognitive Neuroscience." *American Psychologist* 54: 182–203.

Schacter, Daniel L. 2022. "The Seven Sins of Memory: An Update." *Memory* 30: 37–42.

Schacter, Daniel L., Donna Rose Addis, and Randy L. Buckner. 2007. "Remembering the Past to Imagine the Future: The Prospective Brain." *Nature Reviews Neuroscience* 8: 657–661.

Schank, Roger C. and Robert P. Abelson. 1977. *Scripts, Plans, Goals, and Understanding: An Inquiry into Human Knowledge Structures*, First Edition. Psychology Press.

Schechtman, Marya. 1996. *The Constitution of Selves*. Ithaca, NY: Cornell University Press.

Schmidt, Eric. n.d. "Every 2 Days We Create as Much Information as We Did up to 2003." *TechCrunch*. Accessed January 3, 2026, https://techcrunch.com/2010/08/04/schmidt-data/.

Schroeder, S. Andrew. 2013. "Imperfect Duties, Group Obligations, and Beneficence." *Journal of Moral Philosophy* 11: 557–584.

Sedova, Klara, Martin Sedlacek, Roman Svaricek, Martin Majcik, Jana Navratilova, Anna Drexlerova, Jakub Kychler, and Zuzana Salamounova. 2019. "Do Those Who Talk More Learn More? The Relationship Between Student Classroom Talk and Student Achievement." *Learning and Instruction* 63: 101217. https://doi.org/10.1016/j.learninstruc.2019.101217.

Senholzi, Keith B., Brendan E. Depue, Joshua Correll, Marie T. Banich, and Tiffany A. Ito. 2015. "Brain Activation Underlying Threat Detection to Targets of Different Races." *Social Neuroscience* 10: 651–662.

Shiller, Robert J. 2019. *Narrative Economics: How Stories Go Viral and Drive Major Economic Events*. Princeton, NJ: Princeton University Press.

Sills, John. 2002. "The Role of the United Nations in Forming Global Norms." *International Relations Studies and the United Nations Occasional Papers* 2. New Haven, CT: The Academic Council on the United Nations System.

Silvers, Anita. 1995. "Reconciling Equality to Difference: Caring (F)or Justice for People with Disabilities." *Hypatia: A Journal of Feminist Philosophy* 10: 30–55.

Singer, Peter. 1972. "Famine, Affluence, and Morality." *Philosophy and Public Affairs* 1: 229–243.

Singleton, Shaniqua. 2015. "Balancing a Right to be Forgotten with a Right to Freedom of Expression in the Wake of Google Spain v. AEPD." *Georgia Journal of International and Comparative Law* 44: 165–193.

Smiley, CalvinJohn and David Fakunle. 2016. "From 'Brute' to 'Thug': The Demonization and Criminalization of Unarmed Black Male Victims in America." *Journal of Human Behavior in the Social Environment* 26: 350–366.

Smith, David. 2021. "The Meaning of Hitler: Exploring Our Cultural Fascination with Nazism." *The Guardian*, https://www.theguardian.com/film/2021/aug/10/the-meaning-of-hitler-nazism-documentary-netflix.

Snell, Julia and Adam Lefstein. 2018. "'Low Ability,' Participation, and Identity in Dialogic Pedagogy." *American Educational Research Journal* 55: 40–78.

Snyder, Melvin and Edward E. Jones. 1974. "Attitude Attribution When Behavior Is Constrained." *Journal of Experimental Social Psychology* 10: 585–600.

Sommers Samuel R. and Phoebe C. Ellsworth. 2000. "Race in the Courtroom: Perceptions of Guilt and Dispositional Attributions." *Personality and Social Psychology Bulletin* 26: 1367–1379.

Song, Seunghyun. 2020. "Denial of Japan's Military Sexual Slavery and Responsibility for Epistemic Amends." *Social Epistemology* 35: 160–172.

Sosa, Ernest. 2021. *Epistemic Explanations: A Theory of Telic Normativity, and What It Explains*. Oxford: Oxford University Press.

South African Truth and Reconciliation Commission. n.d. *Report*. Volume 1, Chapter 5, Subsection 5. Accessed January 3, 2026, https://sabctrc.saha.org.za/reports/volume1/chapter5/subsection5.htm.

Srinivasan, Amia. 2018. "The Aptness of Anger." *Journal of Political Philosophy* 26: 123–144.

Stapleford, Scott. 2013. "Imperfect Epistemic Duties and the Justificational Fecundity of Evidence." *Synthese* 190: 4065–4075.

Stocker, Michael. 1967. "Acts, Perfect Duties, and Imperfect Duties." *Review of Metaphysics* 20: 507–517.

Staudt, Sarah. 2025. "The Myth of the 'Revolving Door:' Challenging Misconceptions About Recidivism." Prison Policy Initiative, https://www.prisonpolicy.org/trainings/recidivism.html.

Strauss, Gary. 2014. "No Jail for 'Affluenza' Teen in Fatal Crash Draws Outrage." *USA Today*, https://www.usatoday.com/story/news/nation/2014/02/05/no-jail-for-teen/5242173/.

Strawson, Galen. 2004. "Against Narrativity." *Ratio* 17: 428–452.

Strickland, Brent and Frank Keil. 2011. "Event Completion: Event Based Inferences Distort Memory in a Matter of Seconds." *Cognition* 121: 409–415.

Swann, Jr., William B. 1996. *Self-Traps: The Elusive Quest for Higher Self-Esteem*. New York, NY: Freeman.

Táíwò, Olúfẹ́mi O. 2022. *Reconsidering Reparations*. New York, NY: Oxford University Press.

Talbert, Bonnie M. 2015. "Knowing Other People: A Second-Person Framework." *Ratio* 28: 190–206.

Tarusarira, Joram. 2019. "The Anatomy of Apology and Forgiveness: Towards Transformative Apology and Forgiveness." *International Journal of Transitional Justice* 13: 206–224.

Taslitz, Andrew E. 1996. "Patriarchal Stories I: Cultural Rape Narratives in the Courtroom." *Southern California Review of Law and Women's Studies* 5: 387–500.

Taslitz, Andrew E. 2006. "Wrongly Accused: Is Race a Factor in Convicting the Innocent?" *Ohio State Journal of Criminal Law* 4: 121–133.

Taubman, Philip. 1988. "50 Years After His Execution, Soviet Panel Clears Bukharin." *The New York Times*, https://www.nytimes.com/1988/02/06/world/50-years-after-his-execution-soviet-panel-clears-bukharin.html.

Taylor, Shelley and Susan Fiske. 1975. "Point of View and Perceptions of Causality." *Journal of Personality and Social Psychology* 32: 439–445.

Thomas, Kimberly A. 2007. "Beyond Mitigation: Towards a Theory of Allocution." *Fordham Law Review* 75: 2641–2683.

Thompson, Janna. 2002. *Taking Responsibility for the Past: Reparation and Historical Justice.* Cambridge: Polity Press.

TikTok. 2023. "Celebrating Our Thriving Community of 150 Million Americans." *TikTok Newsroom*, https://newsroom.tiktok.com/150-m-us-users?lang=en.

Tirrell, Lynne. 2012. "Genocidal Language Games," in Ishani Maitra and Mary Kate McGowan (eds.), *Speech and Harm: Controversies Over Free Speech.* Oxford: Oxford University Press; 174–221.

Toole, Briana. 2023. "Standpoint Epistemology and Epistemic Peerhood: A Defense of Epistemic Privilege." *Journal of the American Philosophical Association* 10: 409–426.

Townsend, Leo and Dina Lupin Townsend. 2020. "Consultation, Consent, and the Silencing of Indigenous Communities." *Journal of Applied Philosophy* 37: 781–798.

Trudeau, Justin. 2017. "Remarks by Prime Minister Justin Trudeau to Apologize on Behalf of the Government of Canada to Former Students of the Newfoundland and Labrador Residential Schools." Government of Canada, https://www.pm.gc.ca/en/news/speeches/2017/11/24/remarks-prime-minister-justin-trudeau-apologize-behalf-government-canada.

Trump, Donald J. 2025. "Rebuild, and open Alcatraz! For too long, America has been plagued by vicious, violent, and repeat criminal offenders . . . " *Truth Social*, May 4, 2025 [@realDonaldTrump]. https://truthsocial.com/@realDonaldTrump/posts/114452025916969327.

Truth and Reconciliation Commission of Canada. 2015. "Honouring the Truth, Reconciling for the Future: Summary of the Final Report of the Truth and Reconciliation Commission of Canada." https://ehprnh2mwo3.exactdn.com/wp-content/uploads/2021/01/Executive_Summary_English_Web.pdf.

Truth and Reconciliation Commission of South Africa Report. Volume 1. 1998. https://www.justice.gov.za/trc/report/finalreport/volume%201.pdf.

Tsosie, Rebecca. 2007. "Acknowledging the Past to Heal the Future: The Role of Reparations for Native Nations," in Jon Miller and Rahul Kumar (eds.), *Reparations: Interdisciplinary Inquiries.* Oxford: Oxford University Press; 43–68.

Tutu, Desmond and Mpho Tutu. 2014. *The Book of Forgiving.* New York, NY: HarperOne.

Tversky, Amos and Daniel Kahneman. 1973. "Availability: A Heuristic for Judging Frequency and Probability." *Cognitive Psychology* 5: 207–232.

Tversky, Amos and Daniel Kahneman. 1974. "Judgment Under Uncertainty: Heuristics and Biases." *Science* 185: 1124–1131.

United Nations. 1997. "Question of the Impunity of Perpetrators of Human Rights Violations (Civil and Political), Revised Final Report Prepared by Mr. Joinet Pursuant to Sub-Commission Decision 1996/119." United Nations Document, E/CN.4/Sub.2/1997/20/Rev.1 (2 October).

United Nations. 2005. "Impunity: Report of the Independent Expert to Update the Set of Principles to Combat Impunity, Diane Orentlicher, Addendum, Updated Set of Principles for the Protection and Promotion of Human Rights Through Action to Combat Impunity." United Nations Document, E/CN.4/2005/102/Add. 1 (8 February).

United Nations General Assembly. n.d. "International Covenant on Civil and Political Rights." Adopted December 16, 1966, General Assembly Resolution 2200A (XXI), https://www.ohchr.org/en/instruments-mechanisms/instruments/international-covenant-civil-and-political-rights#article-9.

United Nations Human Rights Council. n.d. "Human Rights Council Complaint Procedure." United Nations Document, https://www.ohchr.org/sites/default/files/Documents/HRBodies/ComplaintProcedure/ComplaintProcedurebooklet_E.pdf.

United States Sentencing Commission. 2019. *Sourcebook of Federal Sentencing Statistics*. Washington, DC: United States Sentencing Commission, https://www.ussc.gov/research/sourcebook/archive/sourcebook-2019.

Vanden Bosch, Matthew D. 2020. "Rural Prison Siting: Problems and Promises." *The Mid-Southern Journal of Criminal Justice* 19. https://mds.marshall.edu/msjcj/vol19/iss1/5.

Velleman, J. David. 2003. "Narrative Explanation." *The Philosophical Review* 112: 1–25.

Velleman, J. David. 2005. "The Self as Narrator," in John Christman and Joel Anderson (eds.), *Autonomy and the Challenges to Liberalism: New Essays*. Cambridge: Cambridge University Press; 56–76.

Velleman, J. David. 2009. *How We Get Along*. Cambridge: Cambridge University Press.

Vescio, Theresa K., Gretchen B. Sechrist, and Matthew P. Paolucci. 2003. "Perspective Taking and Prejudice Reduction: The Mediational Role of Empathy Arousal and Situational Attributions." *European Journal of Social Psychology* 33: 455–472.

von Kleist, Heinrich. 1951. "On the Gradual Construction of Thoughts During Speech." *German Life and Letters* 5: 42–46.

Walker, Margaret Urban. 2006. "Restorative Justice and Reparations." *Journal of Social Philosophy* 37: 377–395.

Walker, Margaret Urban. 2010. "Truth Telling as Reparations." *Metaphilosophy* 41: 525–545.

Walsh, Savannah. 2025. "Monica Lewinsky Is *Reclaiming* Her Story With a New Podcast." *Vanity Fair*, https://www.vanityfair.com/hollywood/story/monica-lewinsky-reclaiming-podcast.

Wanzo, Rebecca. 2009. *The Suffering Will Not Be Televised: African American Women and Sentimental Political Storytelling*. Albany, NY: SUNY Press.

Ward, Bryan H. 2006. "Sentencing Without Remorse." *Loyola University Chicago Law Journal* 38: 131–168.

Watkins, Jeremy. 2015. "Unilateral Forgiveness and the Task of Reconciliation." *Res Publica* 21: 19–42.

Watson, Lani. 2022. *The Right to Know: Epistemic Rights, and Why We Need Them*. London: Routledge.

Watzl, Sebastian. 2017. *Structuring Mind: The Nature of Attention and How It Shapes Consciousness*. Oxford: Oxford University Press.

Webb, Lindsey. 2021. "True Crime and Danger Narratives: Reflections on Stories of Violence, Race, and (In)justice." *Journal of Gender, Race & Jus*tice 24: 131–170.

Weigand, Heather. 2009. "Rebuilding a Life: The Wrongfully Convicted and Exonerated." *Public Interest Law Journal* 18: 427–437.

Weisman, Richard. 1999. "Detecting Remorse and Its Absence in the Criminal Justice System." *Studies in Law, Politics, and Society* 19: 121–138.

Welsch, Kathleen A. 1998. "History as Complex Storytelling." *College Composition and Communication* 50: 116–122.

White, James Boyd. 1985. *Heracles Bow: Essays on the Rhetoric and Poetics of the Law*. Madison, WI: University of Wisconsin Press.

Whiteley, Ella. 2022. "Harmful Salience Perspectives," in Sophie Archer (ed.), *Salience: A Philosophical Inquiry*. New York, NY: Routledge; 193–212.

Wiesel, Elie. 1993. "Remarks at the Dedication Ceremonies for the United States Holocaust Memorial Museum." United States Holocaust Memorial Museum, https://www.ushmm.org/information/about-the-museum/mission-and-history/wiesel.

Wilkinson T. M. 2002. "Last Rights: The Ethics of Research on the Dead." *Journal of Applied Philosophy* 19: 31–41.

Williams, Bernard. 1995. *Making Sense of Humanity*. Cambridge: Cambridge University Press.

Williams, Fannie Barrier. 1905. "The Colored Girl." The Voice of the Negro 2: 400–403.

Wilson, John Paul, Kurt Hugenberg, and Nicholas O. Rule. 2017. "Racial Bias in Judgments of Physical Size and Formidability: From Size to Threat." *Journal of Personality and Social Psychology* 113: 59–80.

Winter, Stephen. 2010. "Against Posthumous Rights." *Journal of Applied Philosophy* 27: 186–199.

Wolff, Robert Paul. 1970. *In Defense of Anarchism*. New York, NY: Harper.

Wood, Allen. 2014. "Coercion, Manipulation, Exploitation," in Christian Coons and Michael Weber (eds.), *Manipulation: Theory and Practice*. Oxford: Oxford University Press; 17–50.

Wood, Graeme. 2021. "'Land Acknowledgments' Are Just Moral Exhibitionism." *The Atlantic*, https://www.theatlantic.com/ideas/archive/2021/11/against-land-acknowledgements-native-american/620820/.

Woods, Jordan Blair. 2019. "Policing, Danger Narratives, and Routine Traffic Stops." *Michigan Law Review* 117: 635–712.

Woodson, Carter Godwin. 1933. *The Mis-Education of the Negro*. New York, NY: AMS Press.

Worth, Sarah E. 2008. "Storytelling and Narrative Knowing: An Examination of the Epistemic Benefits of Well-Told Stories." *The Journal of Aesthetic Education* 42: 42–56.

Wrenn, Chase B. 2007. "Why There Are No Epistemic Duties." *Dialogue* 46: 115–136.

Wright, Sarah. 2025. "The Keystone Loop, Self-Trust, and Epistemic Reparations to Oneself," in Mylan Engel Jr. and Joseph Campbell (eds.), *The Philosophy of Keith Lehrer: Essays on Knowledge, Consciousness, and Freedom*. Synthese Library, vol. 503. Cham: Springer.

Wyles, Paul, Patrick O'Leary, and Menka Tsantefski. 2023. "Bearing Witness as a Process for Responding to Trauma Survivors: A Review." *Trauma, Violence, & Abuse* 24: 3078–3093.

Yahr, Natalie. 2019. "When Coverage Is What They Want: Covering Mass Shootings Without Perpetuating Them." Center for Journalism Ethics, https://ethics.sjmc.wisc.edu/2019/12/12/when-coverage-is-what-they-want/.

Yazzie, Robert. 1996. "'Hozho Nahasdlii'—We Are Now in Good Relations: Navajo Restorative Justice." *St. Thomas Law Review* 9: 117–124.

Young, Iris Marion. 1997. "Asymmetrical Reciprocity: On Moral Respect, Wonder, and Enlarged Thought." *Constellations* 3: 340–363.

Zagzebski, Linda. 2001. "Recovering Understanding," in Matthias Steup (ed.), *Knowledge, Truth, and Duty: Essays on Epistemic Justification, Responsibility, and Virtue*. New York, NY: Oxford University Press; 235–256.

Zornosa, Laura. 2022. "Jazz Freed Keith LaMar's Soul. Can It Help Him Get Off Death Row?" *The New York Times*, https://www.nytimes.com/2022/02/11/arts/music/keith-lamar-death-row-freedom-first.html.

# Index

## D

**F**

## O



## P

## S

## T